BUSINESSMAN

in the

STATEHOUSE

BUSINESSMAN
in the
STATEHOUSE

*Six Years as Governor
of North Carolina*

by LUTHER H. HODGES

Chapel Hill

THE UNIVERSITY OF NORTH CAROLINA PRESS

This book is gratefully dedicated to my wife

MARTHA BLAKENEY HODGES

Foreword

THIS book was begun with some reluctance on my part, but now that it is finished I am glad to have written it.

A year or more before I left the office of governor of North Carolina, I received a request from Mr. Lambert Davis of the University Press at Chapel Hill to write a book on developments in the state during my six years as governor. Mr. Davis was extremely helpful in the planning and development of the book.

I owe thanks to many people for their assistance and advice. Chief among these is Charles Dunn of the *Durham Morning Herald,* who has helped tremendously in the research and in the preparation of the final manuscript. He gave invaluable aid in the preparation of the chapter on North Carolina's reaction to the United States Supreme Court's May, 1954, decision affecting public school segregation, a subject on which he had written a master's thesis.

Miss Harriet Herring, a long-time friend and associate from Chapel Hill, was of great help, particularly in her insistence on the anecdotes and other human interest touches that help to give life to the book. Ed L. Rankin, Jr., my private secretary during most of my term as governor, assisted greatly in checking my accounts of the experiences we shared and in improving the felicity of my phrases throughout.

Two other former associates in the governor's office, Paul Johnston and Robert Giles, gave advice and assistance, especially on the subjects of budget making and the Henderson strike.

The cartoons used in the book were drawn during my administration by Hugh Haynie and William Sanders of the *Greensboro Daily News* and John Sink of the *Durham Morning Herald,* and are used here with their permissions.

This book is written from my own experiences and recollections of certain highlights in an exciting and challenging period in North Carolina's history. It was a great privilege to serve the state during these years.

LUTHER H. HODGES

Chapel Hill, North Carolina

Contents

BUSINESSMAN

in the

STATEHOUSE

CHAPTER I

In the Middle
of the Stream

I WAS reading a newspaper at my home in Leaksville, North Carolina, before dressing for church that first Sunday morning in November, 1954. As lieutenant governor of North Carolina, I had presided over one session of the State Senate, in 1953, and was looking ahead with much enthusiasm to the 1955 session, some two months away. Fiscal problems, always of primary interest to me in light of my previous business career, and reaction to the United States Supreme Court's May 17 decision on public school segregation already loomed as key issues to come before the members of the General Assembly, and I was eagerly reading all I could find on the subjects.

The telephone rang and I answered it and recognized the voice of Ed Rankin, private secretary to Governor William B. Umstead. "Governor Hodges," Rankin said in a calm, controlled voice, "Governor Umstead died a little after nine o'clock this morning." Governor Umstead had been sick practically from the beginning of his administration in January, 1953. But knowing his fierce determination to complete his term of office, I could not immediately bring myself to believe the governor was dead.

I hung up the telephone receiver and sat back in my chair, stunned. My mind went back to the time when I was campaigning

for lieutenant governor. I had on many occasions told North Carolinians that they should be very careful about selecting a lieutenant governor because someday a governor might die in office.
Slowly I began to realize that that day had come and as of
November 7, 1954, I was governor of North Carolina. The thought
had occasionally flashed across my mind during Governor Umstead's prolonged illness. However, the idea had never dwelled in
my mind and I had made no plans, no decisions, and had no
practical reaction.

For a while I prayed there in that chair. Presently, I got up,
finished dressing and, with my wife Martha, went to church as I
had planned to do before I was notified of Governor Umstead's
death.

That afternoon I met with newsmen and photographers and
discussed with various state officials the steps that had to be taken.
We had decided already that I would not be sworn in as governor
immediately as it did not seem to show proper respect for Governor Umstead. However, I called up Secretary of State Thad
Eure in Raleigh and asked him about it. Since the Civil War,
North Carolina had had only one instance in which a governor
had died in office, and in the secretary's mind there was some
question about succession. He not only thought it quite all right to
wait to be sworn in, but made the point during our conversation
that I would not really be governor. According to Secretary Eure,
I would be only an "acting governor."

I did not take what the secretary said too seriously. As a matter
of common sense it did not seem practical for the state to have
only an acting governor. However, to be certain, I called Maurice
Victor Barnhill, chief justice of the North Carolina Supreme
Court, and discussed the matter with him. He told me that I
would be governor, and that in his opinion it was essential that
I be sworn in. He added that he thought it also proper to wait
until after Governor Umstead's funeral before taking the oath of
office.

At four o'clock on Tuesday afternoon, November 9, a few hours after the last rites were held for Governor Umstead in Durham, I formally took the oath of office as governor of North Carolina before Chief Justice Barnhill in a brief and solemn ceremony in the Capitol's Hall of the House of Representatives.

The oath ceremony was, as it should have been, a sober one. Among those attending were many of Governor Umstead's friends, both personal and political. As I was relatively new to the North Carolina political scene and totally uncommitted to any group, I felt that many present at the ceremony were wondering what "this new fellow" was going to do and probably a few thought, "This guy doesn't deserve it."

I determined at that moment that I would, as far as humanly possible, honor all of Governor Umstead's commitments or implied commitments. I would not change people that he had appointed to state positions, boards, or agencies, and would try to carry out any promises that he had made and would attempt to follow through with the program that I thought he had set for the state and himself. And for the remainder of the term for which Governor Umstead was elected this was done.

Foremost, as I took the oath of office of governor, I determined, with God's help, to serve North Carolina and its people to the best of my ability.

That night, my first as governor, Mrs. Hodges and I stayed in a hotel in downtown Raleigh. We had sent word to Mrs. Umstead, whom we had known since she and Governor Umstead were courting, for her and her daughter not to hurry about leaving the Governor's Mansion. Mrs. Hodges and I were quite comfortable at the hotel and I thought Mrs. Umstead should take her time in vacating the Mansion. We had known Merle Umstead long before she married William Umstead. She was a friend of great friends of ours in Durham—Gene and Annie Laurie Newsom. We visited Durham quite often and saw Merle at the Newsoms frequently. She was then and has always been very sweet and thoughtful and understanding. Her daughter, also named Merle and now quite a young lady, was always very close to her father and meant much to him.

The next morning, Wednesday, November 10, 1954, I went to my office at the Capitol for the first time. As soon as I was settled I called Ed Rankin. He had been private secretary to Governor Umstead during his twenty-two months as governor and when he was United States senator. I told Ed that I had no political friends to pay off and although I knew that new governors usually brought in their own private secretaries as well as personal secretaries, I had no desire to make a change. "I want to see things carried on in as normal a way as possible," I told him, "and as much like Mr. Umstead had wanted it as can possibly be."

Ed pointed out the contrast in my attitude to that when Governor Umstead succeeded Governor Kerr Scott. He told me that when he and Governor Umstead arrived at the office after the inauguration, there was not a single soul left in the front office. This was not unusual, he added. Despite the usual, however, Ed agreed to try it my way. He continued to have the responsibility of the office, including press relations, through most of my administration.

After Ed had left I noticed a row of buttons on my desk. I began to punch them to see what would happen and just who might come in my office. I said "hello" to the various people who responded to my button pushing, asked them in turn what they did and how they were getting along, and told them to carry on.

Hardly had the push-button staff introductions ended when a secretary slipped into my office through a back door and laid a paper in front of me. "Governor," she said, "please sign this." This was my first hour in office and already there was something for me to sign. Probably showing a little impatience, I asked, "Sign what?" And probably showing just as much impatience, she added, "Sign this paper." I wanted to know what it said, and finally, with some exasperation, she said, "Your signature on this paper will simply indicate that you are on the payroll as governor and that your money will be sent to you at the end of the month."

"This is not the army! I'm not going to sign any payroll. They have a record of when I came. I see no reason for my signing it," I told the secretary. She asked, with faint disgust, "You won't sign it?" I answered flatly, "No. Not until I get a good reason for signing it." She walked out of the back office, through the hall to the front office and presented her problem to Ed, who in turn called the attorney general for an opinion. The attorney general replied, "No, he does not have to sign. Now that someone is questioning it, I can say this practice has been going on for scores of years and is completely unnecessary."

This was a small matter but it lent credit to a pet theory of mine that the sound principles of good business could and should apply to government. I had done this kind of thing and made this type of approach when I worked with a large corporation and later when I worked for the federal government. This small incident over the pay voucher, however, was my first effort to make North Carolina state government more efficient and more economical. It was not my last.

Those first few hours as governor were extremely busy ones but I did have time to look back at my youth and my thirty or more years in the textile business and to assess the value of my background in business administration and government work. Despite my newness to state government I had had considerable experience with various agencies of the federal government. And, too, my campaign for lieutenant governor and the twenty-two months I served in that position had been invaluable training.

I was born on March 9, 1898, near the village of Cascade in Pittsylvania County, Virginia, the next to the youngest of nine children of James and Lovicia Gammon Hodges. My father was a tenant farmer when I was born but around the turn of the century the price of tobacco fell to five cents a pound and he moved the family to the textile town of Spray, just about eight miles from the farm, but in North Carolina. He went to work in the textile mills, as did eight of his children at one time or another, and later he operated a small grocery store.

At the age of twelve I was working for the textile company as an office boy, and received five cents an hour for a ten-hour day. My workweek was sixty hours and I received a total of $3.00 a week. I received no raise in the seventeen months that I worked at that job. During that time the plant was bought by Marshall Field and Company of Chicago.

I did not have to work those seventeen months even though our family was poor. From the time I was six years of age, my schooling had been in a company-operated school housed in one of the mill tenements. The building probably cost some $750 when it was built about 1900 and was painted red. It is still there. By the time I had reached the sixth grade, the school had deteriorated and the professor or supervising principal left much to be desired. My father accepted my plea to let me go to work and agreed I would probably learn as much as an office boy as at that particular school.

There was not a single public school in Spray or Leaksville when I became office boy at the mill. Seventeen months later, the first public school opened in Leaksville, headed by the Reverend P. H. Gwynn, a great scholar and administrator. I entered at the opening of school.

In 1915 I had finished about two and one-half years in the Leaksville High School. That fall, with "conditions" on three subjects and with a total of $62.50 saved from summer employment as a mill hand, I entered the University of North Carolina at Chapel Hill. I stayed there four years and had the opportunity of working my way through with a debt of only about $200 at the end of my time there. While at Carolina I was active in as many extra-curricular activities as my studies and work would allow and was at one time president of the Student Council and was president of my senior class.

At the University I specialized in economics, but by the end of my senior year I had made no decision as to a vocation. Finally I turned down a $3,000-a-year offer as secretary of the Young Men's Christian Association of one of the southern states, and accepted in 1919 a $1,000-a-year job as secretary to the general manager of the Marshall Field and Company mills in the Leaksville-Spray area. I felt that in the long run I could do better in industry and I also wanted to prove to certain skeptics that I could make good in my home town.

In 1920 I became personnel manager of the mills in the Leaksville-Spray area. Seven years later they named me manager of the blanket mill and then in 1934 production manager for all the company's mills in the Leaksville area. In 1938 I was named general manager, in charge of sales as well as production, of all twenty-nine Marshall Field mills in the United States and foreign countries. This promotion resulted in my moving to New York in 1940, where I lived until returning to Leaksville in 1947. I was made vice president of Marshall Field and Company in 1943.

During this time I was interested in many community and civic affairs. Having served briefly with the army during the latter part of World War I, I became active in the American Legion, worked with the Boy Scouts, the YMCA, and participated in fund drives for various worthwhile charities. I belonged to the Rotary Club in Leaksville and later in New York City and in 1948 was chairman of the Rotary International Convention at Rio de Janeiro. I also represented Rotary International as consultant and observer at the organization of the United Nations in San Francisco in 1945 and later before the Security Council of the United Nations.

In Spray in 1932 I got my first taste of politics. I was elected Democratic chairman of my precinct, which, under the influence of the Morehead and Patterson families, had been going Republican for many years. I did a lot of organizational work and had a fair amount of success at fund raising. The precinct did go Democratic that fall and for a while I thought I had had something to do with it. Later, I realized that Franklin D. Roosevelt had probably been responsible for the change. I was asked later by Leroy Shuping of Greensboro to do the same type of work in some state campaigns.

On the state level during the 1930's I served as a member of the North Carolina State Board of Education under Governor O. Max Gardner and on the State Highway and Public Works Commission under Governor J. C. B. Ehringhaus. From time to time during this period I worked with candidates for state offices and for the United States Congress. I recall working for Frank Hancock of Oxford in one of his bids for re-election from the old Imperial Fifth District. I had given him my pledge of support only to be embarrassed when Mrs. B. Frank Mebane of my home town announced for the office. Although I did not feel right about not supporting Mrs. Mebane, I was not politician enough to know how to get out of my earlier commitment.

In 1944, while living in New York, I volunteered to be of any service to the federal government and asked for a tough assignment. They gave me one: price administrator of the textile division of OPA. Chester Bowles was the administrator of OPA at that time. My division had about $4 billion worth of sales or production subject to price control. The job was exasperating, not only because of difficulties I had with the professional bureaucrats, but because of equal difficulties with some of the mill owners and sales managers who came to get price relief for changes in regulations. From certain experiences in this job, I learned a lot about government.

One day after I had completed my OPA war job, a telephone call came from Clinton Anderson, then Secretary of Agriculture, who is now United States senator from New Mexico. He wanted me to be assistant secretary of agriculture, and, like too many businessmen, I declined. Finally I agreed to work with him as a consultant and to investigate the sprawling Commodity Credit Corporation, which was annually lending huge sums of money. My job was to find the inventory and verify the accounts, and after a six-months' study, the secretary was good enough to say this was well done.

I did a thirty-day stint of duty as a textile consultant for the United States Army in Germany in 1948. General Lucius Clay, who was then in charge of United States Forces and Administration in Germany, had begun to set up the West German government. At his request, I made an intensive but short survey of the textile situation in the country and recommended that the whole control section affecting textiles be liquidated. After that, I returned to the United States to give full time to my duties with Marshall Field and Company.

After thirty-two years with the company, I retired from the textile business on April 1, 1950. Being only fifty-two, I was not planning to retire to the rocking chair. During the several periods I had worked for the government I had been impressed by the tremendous amounts of money handled and had seen some of the complicated administrative problems a government runs up against. Feeling that what government needed was more businessmen, and, as I had said in a statement on retiring from Marshall Field and Company, that I wished to give the rest of my life to public service, I decided to quit private industry. I had no idea what that public service would be.

My new career was not long in getting started. Very soon I was asked by the late Robert M. Hanes, then mission chief to Germany, to be chief of the industry division of the Economic Cooperation Administration in West Germany. I accepted and for the next year worked in various West German cities, including Frankfurt, Munich, Stuttgart, and Berlin. My job was to protect the allied powers from any build-up of military or strategic items but to see that the rest of the economy was turned over to the Germans as fast as possible. A second major part of the job was to see that the Marshall Plan money being given the West German government was spent wisely.

As I was finishing up this job in the latter part of 1951, I was called upon by the State Department to serve as a consultant on the International Management Conference. I helped organize the conference and then invited about a hundred European industrialists and businessmen to visit the United States to see the latest techniques in management and manufacturing. Meetings were held in Washington and New York and the industrialists toured the country. It was called a top-level technical assistance program and meant a great deal to some of Europe's leading corporations.

After that assignment was completed I returned to my home in Leaksville and began to catch up on personal business matters. These included the organization of several corporations, among them some Howard Johnson restaurants. It was at this time that the idea of seeking elective office in North Carolina was planted. A friend telephoned me early in 1952 and suggested that I run for lieutenant governor of North Carolina. My reaction was instantaneous. "Not me," I said. He then mentioned my theory about businessmen in government and said something about "Practice what you preach," and in the end I agreed to think it over for a few days.

For the next two weeks I talked with friends, friends-politicians, and politicians. In most cases they said I should run. Some reserved judgment and others said, "I'll let you know," and never did. One friend took me to see what he termed a political power in the state, a man very active in Alcoholic Beverage Control work. I was shocked when the man said with a condescending air, "I don't know yet whom I am going to bring out for lieutenant governor." He wanted someone he could be pretty sure of and I was fresh to the scene. I could tell at a glance I was wasting my time, so I got up and left, mumbling my thanks for his seeing me.

In the end, I decided to make the plunge, and announced my candidacy for the Democratic nomination for lieutenant governor of North Carolina just before the party's annual Jefferson-Jackson Day dinner in 1952.

The campaign for the Democratic nomination for lieutenant governor was an interesting and rewarding experience. I soon realized that I was in a new line of business, and one I did not really understand. Considering my age and experience, I was probably more naive about politics than I should have been. Once I was in the race some of my original optimism faded. Most of the politicians did not take me seriously, the political experts did not give me any hope, and some of my close friends doubted I could defeat my chief opponent, veteran legislator Roy Rowe of Pender County.

It did not take me too long to realize the job before me. Mrs. Hodges and I attended the Jefferson-Jackson Day dinner in Raleigh and were treated royally by scores of people before and after the dinner. Many left the impression that they would support me; but, in looking back, I realized that I had received firm commitments from only a handful, including Congressman Herbert Bonner of the First District, Jack Spain, and the late Lee Gravely of Rocky Mount. However, at the time I was in good spirits over the nice things people were saying about my candidacy. Mrs. Hodges was more cautious and told me, "I don't think most of them mean what they say."

Much to my sorrow I found out during the next few days that she was certainly right. I talked with party leaders in various parts of the state and they introduced me to many of their friends. All were extremely fine people and I appreciated their courtesy. But I was careful to note that I received very few commitments. The morning after a dinner meeting at the Goldsboro Country Club, I made up my mind that I was not going to get elected by the active support of the leaders I had met. I decided that if I wanted to be lieutenant governor I had to do it myself and in my own way, which would be very simple and very direct to the people.

I had had some cards printed soon after I had decided to run but up to that time had not given out any. I went downstairs at the hotel in Goldsboro for breakfast and toyed with one of the cards a long time. I started to give one to the waiter but for the first time in my life I found my hand sweaty. I was nervous. The waiter did not get one of the cards, but after paying my check I did hand one to the cashier. I said quickly, "I'm Luther Hodges. I am running for lieutenant governor. I have never been in office before and I would like for you to vote for me," and started toward the door. "I'm for you," she called after me. I went back and talked with her.

That started one of the most interesting experiences of my whole life. I started out to cover the one hundred counties in North Carolina, driving a large Buick which ate up gas only too rapidly. I bought one gallon of gas at a time. At filling stations I would hand out my card to the attendant and others who were around, and tell them that I would appreciate their votes. I traveled from Monday morning until Friday night, to town after town and to county after county. On week ends I dictated into a dictaphone machine letters to people I had met during the week and had a part-time secretary come in to write them.

In traveling about the state I quickly learned two important lessons from the people. The cashier in Goldsboro pointed out one when she told me "a lot of people" wanted to see new faces or someone other than politicians in public offices in Raleigh and Washington. The other came at a country store in northeastern North Carolina one cold, rainy day. I handed my card to a couple of tobacco-chewing men with the comment, "I hope you will vote for me." One said to the other, "I don't know why we shouldn't be for him. Ain't nobody else been around." The people wanted to see the candidates.

I stuck to my plan of covering all one hundred counties. I never had public meetings or made public speeches in this campaign, but made personal contacts in every county. In Pender County, the home county of my chief opponent, I only went to the court-house. In Avery, one of the western counties, I was busy going around the courthouse seeing officials and asking them for support. Finally one of the elected officials there could stand it no longer. "Mister, you don't know much about this business, do you?" he asked. "This is a Republican county."

My campaign efforts were rounded out with a brochure, written by W. C. "Mutt" Burton of Reidsville and describing my background, several thousand posters that were put up on trees and posts around the state, and a few large billboards. The total campaign expense was around $6,000. I paid for about half of this and several friends volunteered the balance. During the weeks of campaign, I traveled eleven thousand miles and shook hands with thousands of people.

As I crisscrossed North Carolina visiting all of its counties, many of them more than once, I saw my pictures with a start—the smaller posters on trees and the larger ones on the big bill-boards on the highways. I did not want to have the smaller posters of my picture put on the telephone poles and trees and in store windows throughout the state, but I was told that everybody else did it and that I would have to do it. I reluctantly agreed, and I think they did some good. I never could quite get over the shock of seeing my picture and others, and I felt that they were littering up the countryside.

So when the campaign was over I did, according to some of the newsmen, an unusual thing. I had the signs taken down. I paid some people to ride around the state and take them down, and I wrote to the volunteers in other parts of the state and asked them, when they had put them up or had them put up at their expense, to please see that they were taken down. It was effectively done and I felt better.

In the several western counties the other side of Buncombe, most of my contacts, including the people who had put up the posters, were handled by my friend, Bill Shope, mayor of Weaverville. I got in touch with him one day and told him I would like to come up the following week and spend several days in the counties west of Buncombe to meet the various people who could be of some help to us. Naturally we would want to meet the political leaders and at least get the lay of the land and, where we could, try to get their support.

Even when I was campaigning, I guess I was in too much of a hurry because Bill, who is an extremely friendly sort of fellow and likes people immensely, wanted to stop and "set" and talk. I would spend only a few minutes at a place, thank the man, and move on. In the many cases where we simply dropped in on a lawyer or some other person and the secretary said, "Mr. So-and-So is quite busy, but he'll see you when he gets to it—why don't you just have a seat and wait," I never accepted the invitation because I never knew how long it would take. I thought I would rather come back later if I were making a trip through there, or drop him a letter. I knew I had to cover territory and cover it fast, and in many cases several times. Bill Shope could never understand. He chalked it up to impatience, and it could have been true, but I was trying to be effective by covering territory and seeing as many people as possible.

I am sure my friend Percy Ferebee, of Andrews, will not mind my telling the story of what happened in his home town. Bill and I went by to see him and he was sitting there in a dignified way, as the president of a bank should sit, and we introduced ourselves and asked him about the lieutenant governor's race. Percy, in a benign fashion and with some curiosity about the amateur standing before him, said, "We're all for Rowe up here and we will elect him." "Well," I said, "is there any use of my spending my time in the town of Andrews?" and he said, "None whatsoever." We told Percy good-bye and went out into the street. As we drove away going toward Murphy, I said to Bill, "I just don't believe there's anybody that good. I couldn't be and I don't think you could be and I don't think Mr. Ferebee can be. Why don't we stop at this filling station?"

I spoke to the man who was running the filling station, introduced myself and told him about our experience at Mr. Ferebee's bank. I told him Mr. Ferebee said that there was no use of my fooling around there, everybody was going to be for Rowe, and I said, "What do you think?" He said, "That's not true. Mr. Ferebee is not speaking for all of us." I said, "Who is the man for me to see to get some help in trying to get a good vote for me as lieutenant governor?" He said, "Chunk Love." I said, "Where do you find Chunk Love?" He pointed toward a house where a man was standing on a roof fixing shingles and said, "That's Chunk."

Bill and I went over and asked Mr. Love if he would mind coming down and talking with us. Chunk was a short, pleasant, intelligent person, and was friendly from the start. We told him our story and asked for his help. Chunk said, "I'll be glad to do whatever I can." Chunk did quite a lot and we came out all right in Andrews.

With no reflection on Percy Ferebee, I felt then and I have felt increasingly since that time that no man or any small group of men can control an election or elect a man. Organization helps, but you have to reach the people and they make up their own minds in a more independent fashion than they formerly did. I would not have had a chance if that had not been true.

Despite my efforts, as the May primary approached, neither my opponents for the nomination nor the press took me seriously. Even as I was ahead the night of the primary, Lynn Nisbet, the dean of the Raleigh press corps, and radio commentator Carl Goerch could not understand how a new man with no background of political campaigning and no real support from any so-called political machine could lead the field. I listened to the radio as they gave possible reasons for the vote. At that point I did not care what reason they ascribed for my being in the lead as long as I was in the lead.

The results of the May, 1952, Democratic primary showed that I had received 226,167 votes. Roy Rowe of Pender County was second with 151,067 votes, while Marshall C. Kurfees of Winston-Salem received 55,055 and Ben J. McDonald of Wilmington received 52,916 votes. I did not have the necessary majority and there was a good possibility that Rowe would call for a runoff.

A few days after the primary I went to the beach for some much-needed rest. I soon received a telephone call from a prominent lawyer-politician of Raleigh who said he was speaking for several groups, including the liquor interests. He said his clients had asked him to say to me that if I was willing to sit down and come to an understanding with them they would try to persuade Roy Rowe not to ask for a second primary. Although I was not as shocked at this as I would have been at the start of the campaign, the "offer" perturbed me and made me somewhat angry. I told the caller flatly that I did not care to sit down with anyone to try to reach an understanding as to how I would operate as lieutenant governor and that I felt my majority would be even greater in a runoff primary.

I never felt, then or later, that Roy Rowe was a party to this. Indeed, Roy and I established a friendship which has lasted through the years and I later had the honor to appoint him to a distinguished committee.

There was no second primary and naturally I was happy about it. During the next months I campaigned about the state but not at the torrid pace I set for myself before the primary. In the November general election Democrats turned out in fine fashion and I was elected lieutenant governor over Republican Warren H. Pritchett of Spruce Pine, by a vote of 783,792 to 374,530.

The first Thursday in January, 1953, I was sworn in as lieutenant governor during the inauguration ceremonies of Governor Umstead. The proceedings were somewhat barbaric. They started with the inaugural ceremony at the Memorial Auditorium in Raleigh, where Governor Umstead gave a speech on statecraft. Following this, Governor Umstead, looking wan and unhappy in his morning attire, led the way for all of us to the automobiles for the parade. Then we stood for what seemed to be endless hours on the platform on Fayetteville Street, watching floats and marching groups go by.

Later the governor gave a luncheon for a tremendous crowd of people. Then there was a dinner, followed by a reception at the Mansion to which the public was invited. All day long there had been the shaking of hands without a moment's rest, and the reception only prolonged the process. Probably four thousand people came and all came through the line to shake hands. Sometime during the evening, about the time the 2,500th person crushed down on Governor Umstead's hand and then mine, he turned to me and said with a grimace, "My right leg is hurting me," I was not surprised, but neither was I aware of what it might mean.

After the reception at the Mansion, we went our separate ways back to the Memorial Auditorium for the Governor's Ball, another tradition. Although it is not run by the state, the governor and his wife are expected to be there to lead the dance and stay as long as their weary bodies will allow them. During the ball, Governor Umstead was called upon to play the mouth harp. He demurred, but finally did it. The crowd enjoyed it, but I could tell Governor Umstead was tired and that he was in no mood for even being up, much less playing the harmonica. He was then a sick man.

During my months as lieutenant governor nominee and lieutenant governor, I learned a great many of the "dos" and more of the "don'ts" of politics. I was such a newcomer to active politics in North Carolina and so completely outside the ranks of the official group that I was not even selected as a delegate or alternate to the National Democratic Convention in Chicago in August of 1952. By tradition, Governor Kerr Scott should have been elected chair-

man of the North Carolina delegation. But there were such bitter
feelings between factions of the party that supporters of William
Umstead, then Democratic nominee for governor, denied Governor Scott the chairmanship.

I was asked to go to the convention and given the badge which
allowed me on the convention floor with one of my friends,
Everett Jordan, who had helped me in my campaign for the lieutenant governor nomination. I enjoyed the convention and worked
hard for the selection of Governor Adlai Stevenson of Illinois as
the Democratic nominee for President of the United States.

Frankly, I was never taken into the confidence of Governor
Umstead. He clearly impressed this upon me after a casual conversation between me and the late Tom Wolfe, a strong Umstead
man, in Albemarle after my nomination as lieutenant governor.
I said to Wolfe that I was working right along with Mr. Umstead
in the campaign pointing to the November election and added
that I felt pretty sure we agreed on many things. I had not
checked with Mr. Umstead on this and he had never volunteered
anything to me, but I thought my statement was fair and truthful.
Within a few days Mr. Umstead telephoned and made it quite
clear that he did not want me to use his name in connection with
my campaign because, as he emphasized, we were "not running
together." I apologized and did not use his name again in connection with my campaign.

Between the November election and our inauguration in January, 1953, Governor Umstead called me in to only one meeting to
discuss a program for the state. On the first Thursday in January
we went through the exhausting inauguration day program I have
described, starting early in the morning and ending late at night.
The next day, after the State Senate session had ended, I went to
his office and offered to help in any way I could to get his program
enacted by the General Assembly. He thanked me and said he
would have his budget message ready the following week. He was

stricken the following night in Durham and taken to a hospital there.

Governor Umstead was in and out of the hospital during the remainder of his life. After the first few days of his illness, however, he kept the reins of government in his hands and called the shots during the tough 1953 legislative session. He practically never confided in me or asked me to do anything and did not once do me, as lieutenant governor, the courtesy of asking for suggestions as to legislation or how to get it through the Senate. Governor Umstead carried this feeling so far that, although he was in the hospital, he insisted that the state not be represented at the inauguration of President Dwight D. Eisenhower, rather than have the lieutenant governor go. He was, however, dissuaded by State Chairman Jordan, and I did attend the inauguration.

I was extremely sorry that Governor Umstead had such a feeling toward me and could not determine the reason, unless he had held a grudge against me for not supporting him when he ran for the United States Senate. At the time, however, it never occurred to me that anyone in his position would hold that against me when we found ourselves on the same team.

From the time of my nomination for lieutenant governor by the Democratic party until the start of the 1953 session of the General Assembly, I spent my time getting prepared for the job of presiding over the State Senate, as well, of course, as running a campaign against my Republican opponent. Although he did not have to do it, Governor Scott invited me to sit in and observe the activities of the Advisory Budget Commission and to listen to the presentations of the various state institutions and agencies. From these hearings the budget presented to the 1953 General Assembly was formed.

I also traveled throughout the state again, meeting each of the fifty senators, including a freshman named Terry Sanford, and asking them what they thought would be the problems facing us during the 1953 session. At that time most of them were non-committal. One man was frank enough to say that he was only interested in getting good committee assignments but had no suggestions about how to better serve the state. I was somewhat impressed with what he had to say about committee assignments and did not give him very important ones. He never forgave me.

A day or so before the General Assembly convened I was in the Sir Walter Hotel when a lobbyist with some twenty years experience came up to me. I hardly knew him, but he said boldly and without apology, "Let's you and I take a bottle of Scotch and go up to my room and set up your Senate committees." I asked him to repeat his statement. He did and added that he had done it before. I told him flatly, "Well, this is where it stops. No one is going to appoint my committees but me."

Without any criticism of any past procedures, I simply felt that to come in with a fresh point of view we ought to use fresh methods. I did and still do feel we should not appoint a legislator to a committee because of the influence of people who have a personal or corporate interest in it. In naming senators to committees, I studied their interests, their biographies, their geography, their previous committee assignments. I learned as much about them as I could. No one, besides myself, knew of the committee appointments before the Senate convened. I distributed the list of appointments simultaneously to the senators and to the press, and it was necessary to make only two or three changes in the days following.

For the public good and for the sake of economy, I recommended to the senators that the thirty-seven or more committees be reduced by at least a dozen and that the clerical force be reduced. Some of the senators did not like the recommendations, but a majority did and they were approved.

The 1953 session of the General Assembly was an interesting and informative one for me. I presided over the Senate as impartially as possible and reserved my ideas and opinions until some member of the Raleigh press corps asked for them. The lieutenant governor is the presiding officer and can vote only when there is a tie, and I got to vote only once during the session. It came on a bill to require the withdrawal of a driver's license if he were caught speeding over seventy miles an hour. I unhesitatingly cast my vote for the law.

It was during this session of the General Assembly that I started wearing a white carnation. It became a tradition with me and my badge as governor. On my first day as presiding officer of the Senate, I walked up from the Sir Walter Hotel by myself and on impulse went into a florist shop and bought a white carnation. I needed it for my spirits. For the next eight years, as lieutenant governor and governor, I was never without a carnation, unless by chance I lost one by having it brushed off. I never wore the carnation after I left the governorship.

With this background in business and government I settled down to my new duties as governor. I determined that every decision I made as governor would be made without regard to future consequences. My primary interest was to do a conscientious job. From the beginning, my thirty years' training in a large corporation that practiced and demanded efficiency helped me greatly. I had learned through experience, when a problem presented itself, inquire into it, size it up, and then make a definite decision. Decisions were made on the basis of the best solution to the problem, not because of politics.

Another part of my business training that came in handy was the delegation of responsibility. I created a lot of curious interest and excitement around the office those first few days by never hesitating to ask people to take responsibility for certain duties. And, at the same time, I never hesitated to hold these same people responsible after the duties had been delegated to them.

At the same time, I began looking ahead and asking people what their plans were for the future of their departments or agencies.

For example, I soon sent out a memo to the leading departments and agencies, including the Department of Revenue, the Budget Bureau, the Department of Education, and others, and asked them what would be their needs and programs in 1964—ten years in the future. Many of them must have thought the request was crazy, but they came through with reports. These reports gave us some idea of how things might grow and what might be needed.

More pressing, however, were the immediate policy matters which confronted me when I became governor. In less than two months the General Assembly would be in session upstairs and I, as governor, would have to present a program. Despite being the only governor in the United States who does not have the veto power, the governor of North Carolina has a very heavy responsibility to lead the General Assembly and work with it in preparing a program for the state.

When I was catapulted into the office of governor, the members of the Advisory Budget Commission had been working for months to reach conclusions on the budget. They were just about ready to "tie up the package" when I was sworn in. As lieutenant governor, I had spent some time on my own listening in at the sessions of the Advisory Budget Commission, although, as mentioned, I had not been invited by Governor Umstead. After taking office as governor it was my responsibility and privilege to meet again with the members of this group and to get their advice on a program to present to the General Assembly.

Times had not been too good and money was not too plentiful. But, as always, there was the usual heavy demand for state services—education, highways, mental institutions, welfare, agriculture, conservation and development, and many special demands. They exceeded by far the estimated revenue for the coming biennium. The Advisory Budget Commission and I saw that under the existing tax system the appropriations needed would exceed the estimated revenues by approximately $52 million for the bien-

"Desist, knave—unhand yon damsel!"

nium. This meant that the new governor had to go before the 1955 General Assembly and recommend an imposition of new taxes to the tune of $52 million.

The legislators came to Raleigh early in January, 1955, and, at their invitation, I went before a joint session of the Senate and the House of Representatives on January 6 with my "State of the State" or biennial message. In it I recognized that many deserving requests for appropriation increases had been denied but pointed out that I felt the state could not, at the time, do more than had been recommended by the Advisory Budget Commission. By just following the spending recommendations of the Advisory Budget Commission, in fact, there would be a need for new revenue of approximately $26 million for each year of the biennium. This meant, of course, that new taxes were needed. There had been no material tax increase or change in the revenue structure since 1939.

Coupled with the normal growth of state services, the state was confronted with the fact that during the 1953-55 biennium general fund expenditures exceeded general fund revenue collections by approximately $30 million. It did not mean that North Carolina was operating under an unbalanced budget, which it cannot do by law. It did mean, however, that North Carolina no longer had the surplus of some $32 million which it had had on June 30, 1953. With this as background, I concluded to the legislature: "With no surplus of revenues and with growing requirements for state services—reflected most emphatically in our public schools—it is apparent that we must either cut the services our state has been rendering or raise additional revenues."

For the needed funds, we had exhaustively explored many new sources of revenue and did recommend to the General Assembly the use of some of these sources to obtain the increase. We did not feel, however, that it would be economically sound to recommend an increase in individual or corporate tax rates at the time.

The first potential source, then, was the sales tax. Our law then contained thirty-two exemptions and a limitation of liability on a single article. Many of the exemptions, especially food, we considered essential because of the relatively low per capita income in our state and the effect on the family budget. We did propose that the single-article limitation be removed, which would produce an estimated $7,250,000 annually, and the fleet owners' exemption be repealed, which would produce an estimated $450,000 annually. Another $1,170,000 could be raised annually, we proposed, by taxing domestic insurance companies at the same rate as foreign companies. And $172,195 could be raised annually by increasing the prices of licenses of insurance agents.

The major part of the revenue we proposed to raise by taxing tobacco products, soft drinks, and spiritous liquors. As I declared in the biennial message:

In our situation there is the choice, as suggested, between greatly broadening the base of our sales tax by taxing food, prescription drugs, most building materials, production materials and fuel, and seed, feed, and fertilizer, or excise taxes on other consumer goods. We have recommended a low rate excise tax on tobacco products, which will annually produce an estimated $8,945,000. We are not unmindful of the importance of our tobacco growing and manufacturing industries in this state; however, information obtained from reliable sources discloses that other states which have in recent years imposed excise taxes on tobacco products have not experienced any appreciable decline in the consumption of such products. . . .

We recommend an excise tax on soft drinks which would likewise be borne at the consumer level. It is estimated that this will annually produce $7,125,000. . . . We also recommend an increase of 1.5% in the rate of tax on the sale of spiritous liquors. This would produce annually approximately $900,000. It is thought that the state should derive from this source a reasonable tax yield which would not tend to drive the consumer to the bootleggers. The retail price would still compare very favorably with that in other states.

The proposals to tax tobacco products and soft drinks in my biennial message started the session off with a bang. It was not too long before the fur began to fly. I was under severe criticism for having recommended the tobacco tax. Finally, I went before the people in a statewide broadcast to defend the tobacco tax and point out that it would not hurt the farmer.

This was a very important broadcast. There was great interest in it because there was such a difference of opinion among the General Assembly as well as among the public. The broadcast originated at the television studio at State College. Several senators were there, including Ralph Scott of Alamance and Carl Hicks of Greene County. Although Carl and I were good personal friends, he resented very bitterly my broadcast that night and did not hesitate to tell me so. He was rough but not discourteous. His main point to me was that he did not blame me for mentioning the tax or recommending it, but he did not think I ought to go to the public and argue for it. I suppose Carl thought, and he was correct, that he and others could beat it in the Senate, but he did not want me to try to sell it to the people in order to bring pressure on the General Assembly, especially the Senate. Carl got over his anger and we became friends again and I hope still are.

I agreed then and I agree now that it was psychologically bad to have a tobacco tax in North Carolina. My reason for this is that we produce about two-thirds of all the bright leaf tobacco grown in the United States and we manufacture more than 50% of all the cigarettes and smoking tobacco in the country. We are afraid that something will happen to us if we make changes.

Opponents to my proposed tax for tobacco products felt that if North Carolina, the prime tobacco state, put a tax on the product, then other states would do likewise. This argument did not hold water, but it was hard to even deny it. At that time, forty-one of the forty-eight states and the District of Columbia imposed consumer taxes on tobacco products. Other states have since levied taxes on tobacco products, but North Carolina has not.

It would take a separate book to describe the tugging and pulling of the next few weeks. Legislators tugged and pulled at appropriations and ways to finance them, and lobbyists of all sorts tugged and pulled at the legislators. Members of the Joint Finance Committee, which had to raise the money, were particular targets. Pressure groups, lobbyists, interested agents, and all kinds of people made protests to them, and many of these were effective protests. The Finance Committee would come to a tentative agreement late in the week. Over the weekend, the legislators would go home where they would be bombarded anew with views and ideas. Back in Raleigh, they would cancel out the previous week's agreement and start all over again.

The Honorable Nelson Woodson was chairman of the Senate Finance Committee at this time and the Honorable William Rodman was chairman of the Finance Committee in the House. These were two good men. They were fair-minded and they would listen to any presentation made to them. But as the weeks passed, their nerves were worn. I never saw William Rodman tense or showing a deep concern except in the last few weeks of this General Assembly. He was worried, he was irritated, and for a time he felt the situation was hopeless. But he and Nelson got together and decided they would work something out—and they did.

As the weeks passed, many proposals for balancing the budget were made, studied, heard, and discarded. Almost every possible answer to the problem was thoroughly explored in the hope that the need for new taxes could be avoided or greatly reduced. When the chairmen of the Finance Committees came out with a "package" that omitted both the excise tax on soft drinks and on manufactured tobacco products, I stated publicly that if they could raise the money without these controversial items, it would be smart. There was apparently no such thing as a non-controversial tax, and the pressures and tensions continued to grow.

Luckily, the revenue outlook got somewhat better as the session wore on. Revised revenue estimates made in March reduced the original estimate of needs from about $52 million for the biennium to an estimated $37 million. By May, as I was able to report to the General Assembly in a special message, revenues looked better still, and we then estimated that only around $20 million would be needed from new taxes. These factors, reducing the original estimates of needed revenue by $32 million, were improved economic conditions causing increases in our estimates, savings by the administration, and greater effectiveness in the collections of income and sales taxes.

The improved estimates were good news, of course, but it only made the task of the General Assembly more difficult. With a smaller amount to raise, those who were opposed to various kinds of taxes felt that the items they were against should be dropped. There was quite a bit of talk of the General Assembly's closing up and going home without balancing the budget, which it was required to do under the Executive Budget Act. I took this talk seriously and took steps to counter it. I knew that good business principles and sound fiscal management, which have characterized North Carolina government, demanded that the budget be balanced before the legislators went home.

In a special message to the General Assembly in May, I told the legislators that I was confident they had the courage to solve the fiscal problems and balance the budget. The people of the state were expecting them to do that. "A balanced budget," I told the General Assembly, "is necessary for the orderly development of our state. To fail in this responsibility would blacken our financial reputation, seriously damage our credit, and be a backward step." I added that until the budget was balanced their mission was not fulfilled and declared it would be "unthinkable for you to abdicate your responsibility."

The General Assembly stayed on in session and worked hard to find ways to meet the state's needs for increased revenue. Finally, they passed the necessary taxes, primarily on beer and wine, and adopted a budget of around $640 million. It was the largest budget in the history of the state up to that time.

CHAPTER II

The Bread and
Butter Problem

I WAS shocked in the early days of my administration to receive a report from the United States Department of Commerce that listed North Carolina as forty-fourth among the then forty-eight states in per capita income. At first I frankly did not believe the report. Being a part of North Carolina and knowing how much progress we had made, I was certain our state was better off than many other states around us and throughout the country. Despite the elaborate study of the Department of Commerce concerning wages, salaries, income from profits, dividends, rents, sales of crops, government payments, births, migration, deaths, and other data, I thought the rank of North Carolina had been misstated. North Carolina's per capita income just could not be as low as that.

North Carolina's rank, however, had not been misstated. My early disbelief had been so strong that I had the report double-checked through Gordon Gray, who was then president of the consolidated University of North Carolina. After I could not disprove the figure, I had to accept it. All through the 1955 General Assembly's hassle over revenues and expenditures, it became increasingly apparent to me that low per capita income was North Carolina's major problem—a bread-and-butter problem that affected everyone in the state and every aspect of its future. Our low economic state was an unhappy fact, and I determined to do what I could to improve it. My continuous efforts to do this, largely through industrialization, caused me to be labeled an "industry hunter." My administration was considered by many to be "industry hungry." It was!

My concern was that despite all the progress North Carolina had made in the preceding two decades it had been just standing still. Since the turn of the century, in fact, North Carolina had experienced a slowly rising economy. Except during the depression, our per capita income had steadily increased. However, despite this trend, we found ourselves in no better *relative* position than we had been in three decades before. For example, in 1929 the per capita income in North Carolina was $309 and we ranked forty-fourth in the nation. In 1953 our per capita income was $1,097 and we still ranked forty-fourth in the country.

During none of these years had the per capita income in North Carolina equalled the average income for the southeastern region, which was $344 in 1929 and $1,159 in 1953. When we took into consideration that the southeastern average was the lowest in the nation, the reason for our forty-fourth position was more easily understood. In 1953 our per capita income average of $1,097 was just about two-thirds of the national average of $1,709.

Looking into the problem further, it was found that North Carolina had a total state income of between $6 and $7 billion—the highest in the Southeast—and a population of nearly 4.5 million—also the largest in the Southeast. North Carolina, furthermore, had more than the average percentage of young people and older people. Much of our industrial income came from low-skill industries that normally paid comparatively low wages. These included furniture, tobacco, and textiles, including garment manufacturing. North Carolina was dependent upon and satisfied with these industries, but other industries that paid higher wages were needed.

Agriculture, the bedrock of the state's economy, was far too demanding of North Carolina's resources, particularly its human resource, for the return it gave. About one-third of our people lived and worked in rural farm areas, and North Carolina had about two and one-half times the national average of people on the farms. Over 19 million of the state's 31.5 million acres of land were in farms, and of this 19 million almost 8 million acres were in cropland. North Carolina had more farms than any state in the union except Texas, and the average size of farm families was among the largest. But the average size of farms in North Carolina was the smallest in the nation. Per capita income for farmers was roughly $500 annually, compared with roughly $1,600 for Tar Heels not dependent on agriculture.

The crux of the problem was emphasized by figures published about that time which compared Trenton, New Jersey, and Greensboro, North Carolina, on per capita income. Trenton's per capita income was $1,672; Greensboro's was $1,685. On the other hand, New Jersey's was $1,731, while North Carolina's was $1,091. The difference was in the rural income of the two states. Ocean County, New Jersey, for example, had a per capita income of $912; while Franklin County, North Carolina, had a per capita income of only $580.

North Carolina, on the other hand, received a higher percentage of its income from manufacturing payrolls than was the average for the states in the southeastern district. The figures were 24.8% for North Carolina and 17.5% for the southeastern district. North Carolina's percentage of income was lower than the southeastern average in government income, trade and service income, and all other. Manufacturing was North Carolina's bright spot—the state ranked fifteenth among all the then forty-eight states in its per capita income from manufacturing—and it was the unprecedented business of our factories during the preceding ten years that had enabled us even to hold our place of forty-fourth among the states.

Even in its manufacturing industry, North Carolina had a peculiar condition. This was in the distribution of the plants. Just ten of the one hundred counties * had 50.3% of the employment and 53.9% of the payroll in the state. Eight of these were in the Piedmont section of the state and, outside of the tobacco and furniture industries, were primarily engaged in the textile business. Thus, the remaining 49.7% of the employment was scattered throughout the remaining ninety counties of the state.

It was easy to reach the conclusion that what was badly needed in North Carolina was more industry in the other ninety counties, and particularly those counties east of Raleigh. It was the best way to increase the per capita income of the state as a whole.

Industrialization, then, with all of its advantages to the people and to the state, became the number one goal of my administration. I began at once the long and intensive campaign to acquaint the people of the state with the actual situation of North Carolina and its relation to the other forty-seven states and to point out that we had to raise the per capita income if we were to raise the standard of living of our people. One of the best means of achieving this was, of course, more local industries, more small factories, and more processing plants for converting the state's raw materials into greater income-yielding products. This would also give work and wages to our under-employed. It would give opportunity for our trained specialists and a broad base for taxation from which we could get revenue to carry on the needed services for our people.

It was strange and disappointing not to find anyone around me in state government who was really seriously concerned about this situation. We were still teaching farmers how to raise more of what they were already raising and also how to diversify their crops. The State Department of Agriculture was doing a good job as far as we could tell in regulation and inspection, but we did not

---

* These ten counties were Mecklenburg, Guilford, Forsyth, Gaston, Cabarrus, Durham, Wake, Buncombe, Alamance, and Catawba.

find people going down to bedrock and finding the problems that were creating difficulty. The Department of Conservation and Development had an industry division that was primarily responsible for securing new industry. It had done a reasonably good job, but nothing outstanding.

I am sure there were many people in Raleigh and about the state who knew where we were and who had some idea about what we should do about it. However, with the exception of State Treasurer Edwin Gill and his predecessor, Brandon Hodges, I did not get much encouragement from talking to the members of the Council of State and others around me. Both Gill and Hodges, with whom I worked very closely, made the point to me early and continually that we needed to look at our tax structure if we were going to do a real job in building up the state industrially.

The work began immediately. It included a rejuvenation of the Department of Conservation and Development plus a number of government-backed but privately financed enterprises, such as the governor's Small Industries Plan, the Business Development Corporation, and the Research Triangle.

Looking to the Department of Conservation and Development and the Board of Conservation and Development, both of which boasted many high-grade men, I did not find the active leadership needed to correct the problems that confronted the state. It appeared then that the leadership had to come from the working head of the Department of Conservation and Development or from the governor, who also serves as chairman of the Board of Conservation and Development.

About this time Conservation and Development Director Ben Douglas resigned to go back to his personal business in Charlotte. With Governor Umstead, he had promoted a series of meetings throughout the state during the preceding year in an attempt to interest communities in industrial development. As lieutenant governor, I had attended one of these meetings at the Capitol and a

"You've gotta do something besides smoking and chewing the rag"

luncheon that followed at the Mansion. Brandon Hodges, mentioned above, was guest of honor at that meeting. Such meetings lead me to believe that had Governor Umstead lived and kept his health he would have done a good job in the area of industrialization.

We began to look for someone to head the Department of Conservation and Development. William P. Saunders, a friend of mine since our days at the University of North Carolina whom I had known through the years in the textile business, had recently retired to Southern Pines. He had contacts all over the country, knew how to run a large organization, and knew a lot about administration and people. I telephoned him and said, "Bill, are you tired of fishing and resting?" He answered that he was. I then told him that we wanted him to come up and head the Department of Conservation and Development and to help us put the state in the forefront of industry. I told him I was going to spend a lot of time working personally with him and that as a team I thought we could do a job.

Bill accepted the challenge and in November of 1955 he became director of the Department of Conservation and Development. He stayed with me through the next five years and we built up the organization gradually and effectively. One of the first things we did was to look at our Commerce and Industry Division. It was not too well staffed from the standpoint of leadership. There were some good men in the division who had worked long and hard, but it needed a more imaginative, objective, and independent leadership. Changes were made in the leadership of the Industry Division for the next two or three years, until William Henderson, then State Purchasing Officer, moved over to head the important division. He did and continued to do an outstanding job throughout my administration.

The Department of Conservation and Development and its industry division wasted no time in getting to work, especially with local and regional groups, to show what industries needed and must have to persuade them to move to North Carolina. The communities wanted new industry and several were willing to do anything within reason to attract reputable industries who wanted to settle down and pay their fair share of the cost of government and governmental services.

The Department of Conservation and Development had to be strengthened to be able to push development, but we also had to do things more fundamental. The mid-fifties were at hand, and we had to pull ourselves up by our bootstraps with small industries. And the success of any movement to build up small industries in the state depended largely on the inspiration of every ambitious young citizen to look about him and consider what commodity or service he could make in his community that could have a profitable market. So certain was I of the necessity of the small industries project that I started at once looking for ways to spread this needed inspiration.

With this in mind, I telephoned Smith Richardson, Sr., chairman of the board of Vick Chemical Industries which had its beginnings near Selma, North Carolina, and discussed the problem with him. I told him I wanted to find out the real situation in North Carolina and just how we could set up a program that would help us build our per capita income and that particularly would help us get more jobs for people who were being displaced from farms in increasingly large numbers. Mr. Richardson, looking as always to the future, said he was interested and would be glad to help in any way he could.

The two of us decided that it would be a good idea to have a study made of our whole situation in North Carolina with particular reference to the small or local industries. If we could get hundreds and thousands of people throughout our state interested in the program, we felt it would do more good than just looking for large industries. The idea of local industry appealed particularly to Mr. Richardson, who began as an itinerant drug salesman and later built his company into a great international enterprise. We also had in mind other large family businesses in North Carolina such as those of the Cannons, the Cones, the Chathams, the Broyhills, which also had begun in a small way. We decided to try to find out just what our situation was at the local level. I told Mr. Richardson we would need about $25,000 for such a study. He made one requirement: "Get a good man to run it."

I had such a man in mind—the Honorable Capus Waynick, who was then living in semi-retirement at his home just outside High Point. He had just completed a brilliant tour of duty as United States ambassador to Nicaragua and Colombia. He had also had the rare experience of being the first administrator of Harry Truman's famous Point Four program. When called upon to serve his state by developing a small industries plan, Mr. Waynick went to work with great enthusiasm. He grasped the problem quickly, did a far-reaching survey under the guidance of the governor's Small Industry Committee, and came in with a report.

One of the chief recommendations of the Waynick report had to do with long-term credit. The study found plenty of young men in North Carolina with ideas and ambition. However, these young men usually lacked the necessary money to go into business. The report pointed out that with today's high costs and extreme competitive risks, it was not as easy as it had been in the old days to initiate and carry through local projects. Early entrepreneurs generally had fewer problems and could operate with limited capital. Things had changed. Even the banks, the report pointed out, now were generally not in a position to lend money for long periods of time.

Out of the report, then, came a strong recommendation that we form a credit or development corporation that would furnish long-term capital for individuals and groups to start small businesses or to expand existing businesses. It was decided on the basis of the Waynick report that we should try to get through the

1955 legislature a bill that would enable us to form a corporation
to raise and lend money under certain conditions.

I proposed to the 1955 General Assembly the formation of a
development credit corporation as a facility for the promotion of
small industry in North Carolina. The corporation was fashioned
on the same lines as those specified in enabling statutes already
adopted in some of the New England states. These states were
witnessing the dwindling of some industry in the face of competition from the South and elsewhere, and had resorted to this device
to encourage the creation of new industries. The General Assembly enacted the legislation and we had an organization and an
opportunity on paper. But we had no money. It was set up as a
private corporation, without state aid, and there was no pledging
of state money or credit.

The North Carolina Business Development Corporation was to
operate on a strictly business basis, and that meant shares of stock
had to be sold before the corporation could get on its feet. Although this was one of my chief interests, I naturally had many
other things to do and could not devote to it the time that it should
have had. Waynick had to carry the ball pretty much in our early
efforts to promote and develop the corporation. By then he had
recruited Warren Williams of Sanford, a good friend of mine who
was willing to give his time on a voluntary basis because he believed in what we were doing.

They recommended that we raise $100,000 by selling stock in
the North Carolina Business Development Corporation at $10 a
share. Although the statute authorized the corporation to have a
maximum of $1 million in stock, we thought that $100,000 was
all North Carolina could raise. After all, Massachusetts with all
its wealth had been able to raise only $300,000 for a similar cor-
poration. Waynick and Williams, it was decided, would try to
sell the stock and they started with me.

"Governor," Waynick said to me, "I think you should buy the

first shares. I would like to sell you a thousand dollars' worth. We may never pay a dividend, you may never get it back, but we believe it is a sound investment in North Carolina and it may help us start on the upward road to greater industrialization, higher per capita income, and a better standard of living for our people." How could anybody resist a pitch like that! I did not resist. I gave him the thousand and the campaign was underway.

Waynick had discussed the corporation with Bill Henderson of Reidsville, when he was president of the North Carolina Junior Chamber of Commerce. The program had received the whole-hearted endorsement of the Jaycees, and those young men did a magnificent job of pushing the sale of stock. Waynick and Williams stayed busy, too. But selling stock at $10 a share did not add up very fast.

Even before we had reached the original $100,000 goal, however, we came to the conclusion that we ourselves had not shown enough faith in the project and that we should go out and raise a larger amount. We appreciated the small subscriptions, not only for the money, but because of the widespread participation. As Waynick noted, "We will work ourselves to death trying to sell stock at $10 a share to individuals." After discussing the need, we decided to go as far as we could toward raising the full $1 million authorized by the legislative act. As a start, Waynick sold me another $4,000 worth of stock.

Waynick then told me that only the governor of the state could reach some of the larger groups and get the large amounts of money needed and stated that I was going to have to get more into the business of selling the stock. Knowing that this was one of the many things that could not be done by proclamation or by appointment or anything besides hard work, I accepted the challenge and entered the stock-selling campaign with great enthusiasm. I felt that various groups such as bus lines, motor trucks, railroads, and utilities ought to be in the middle of the campaign since they would benefit quickly. Still it was a tremendous selling job. No state, not even Massachusetts, had thought in terms of a million dollars.

Selling stock in the North Carolina Business Development Corporation was a wonderful experience. Never have I seen such interest, patriotism, and downright loyalty to an idea, to an administration, or to a state as was evidenced by people throughout North Carolina. Hundreds bought small amounts of stock and they continually talked up the campaign.

To get a large purchase of stock to serve as an example for other firms, I went in person to the power companies, starting with the largest—Duke Power Company. Norman Cocke was head of Duke Power at the time and, although friendly, he was conservative and cautious about my proposal. I made my sales talk and then he wanted to know how much I wanted Duke Power to contribute. I told him I did not want a contribution. I was selling stock in a great venture that sooner or later would pay dividends and I wanted him to buy $100,000 worth of the stock. He said no and I told him we could not get proper amounts from other companies unless Duke Power did its part. He turned me down, but I did not reduce my request or accept his decision as final.

Shortly after that, I was in New York on a visit and I went by to see George Allen, the dominant figure in all the Duke enterprises. Mr. Allen, then in his eighties, was a grand old man. Originally from Warrenton, North Carolina, he had been connected with Duke interests for more than a half century. Mr. Allen and I had shared on many visits our love for North Carolina and he immediately realized my request was in the best interest of the state and also of Duke Power. I pointed out that the Duke family and the Duke interests had in many ways served the state. And I added that Duke Power would itself receive benefits in extra customers if the program was realized.

Later Mr. Cocke and other Duke Power officials from North Carolina told Mr. Allen about that "crazy Luther Hodges" asking them for $100,000. Mr. Allen then told Mr. Cocke he thought the plan was sound and should be invested in. Duke Power Company subscribed for $100,000 worth of stock, and we were on our way. Utilities and other business groups fell in line and made their pledges for stock. There were some business groups with which we had some difficulty, but they all finally came through in fine fashion. And before too long the $1 million worth of stock in the North Carolina Business Development Corporation was a reality.

The law which allowed us to sell stock in the corporation also authorized us to canvass banks and insurance companies and allowed them to make money available on call to the Development Corporation based on a certain percentage of the capital and reserves. After getting the $1 million in stock sold, we turned our attention to these financial institutions. We had to get them into the picture if the Development Corporation was to succeed. A million dollars could not do very much in total and it was felt that we ought to have the million as base capital. This was a strong point in our campaigns with the banks.

We were able to get a few contributions fairly quickly and were encouraged. One large bank, however, wanted to know who was going to run the program and how it was going to be handled, and said it would not contribute until it knew. We answered that it was a job for the board of directors to determine and that the board had not been set up yet. We kept talking, mentioned a few names of prospects, and our banker friends decided that the program would be handled soundly. It came in for a large participation. Insurance companies, led by Jefferson Standard Life Insurance Company, came in for their part. Building and loan associations were a little slow because of legal requirements, but the law was amended and finally most of them came in.

After we had sold the $1 million in stock and had the participation of the banks and insurance companies, which gave us between $4 million and $5 million to lend, we went to work immediately to set up an organization so the North Carolina Business

Development Corporation could begin operations. There was considerable interest throughout the state and inquiries had begun to come in even before the board of directors was organized. A board of eighteen outstanding citizens, including a number of bankers, was formed. All served without compensation and gave the corporation great leadership and conservative direction.

The $1 million raised from stock sales was soon gone, and the corporation began making calls on the financial institutions for their participation in the development program. One of the most important results, however, was the spirit of the people who had decided that we in North Carolina could pull ourselves up by our bootstraps. All over North Carolina there began to rise up small companies, partnerships, individuals with ideas who could now get capital to put to work. It was wonderful to watch.

Later, at one of the meetings of the North Carolina Business Development Corporation, I asked the board of directors why they did not pay a small dividend. I did this, not because I thought the stockholders needed the money, but because I thought it would show that the corporation was being run on a businesslike basis if it could make a profit and still perform the great service for which it was intended. The corporation made a little money from the very first year and within a few years it was paying dividends.

The North Carolina Business Development Corporation was successful as far as it went. Some of the firms that have received their start with funds borrowed from the Development Corporation will in twenty to thirty years be large corporations. It has happened here in North Carolina before.

We continued to work on this local initiative basis throughout my administration. Industrial development organizations were formed in towns, counties, and regions. They did wonders. All of these things, however, were not enough to pull North Carolina's per capita income up as rapidly as it should. We found early that to do this we would have to set up a more imaginative and stronger program for larger, skilled industries. So we began working for larger industries while we were pushing small ones.

At the very outset we found a serious problem that had to be licked. This had to do with state taxes on multi-state corporations. North Carolina was then taxing some of its corporations inequitably. For example, a company like Cone Mills, which did business in other states as well as North Carolina, was being taxed unduly and harshly by this state for the business it did in other states. This state's tax law was, in other words, a barrier, not only to out-of-state firms looking for sites for expansion, but to the expansion of firms already in the state. Something needed to be done and the sooner the better.

The 1955 General Assembly authorized me to appoint a commission to study and make recommendations for the revision and the recodification of the Revenue Act. It was to report to the 1957 legislature. The resolution noted that there had been no major revision or basic change in the state's tax structure since 1932 and that it was "proper and desirable" that North Carolina and its tax structure be encouraging to businessmen and business enterprises from other states.

One of the duties set for this commission by the legislature was "to recommend changes in the basic tax structure of the State and in the rates of taxation, together with predicted revenue effects thereof, together with proposed alternate sources of revenue, to the end that our revenue system may be stable and equitable, and yet so fair when compared with the tax structures of other states, that business enterprises and persons would be encouraged by the economic impact of the North Carolina Revenue Laws to move themselves and their business enterprises into the State of North Carolina."

It was a big order for the commission, and far-sighted men were needed to find the answer. Selected to head the commission * was Brandon Hodges who had been state treasurer for some years and was then associated with the Champion Paper and Fibre Company of Canton. During the months of the commission's study, its members worked with Commissioner of Revenue Eugene G. Shaw as well as numerous professors at the University of North Carolina at Chapel Hill and State College in Raleigh. The commission's tax study report was one of the major legislative packages presented to the 1957 legislature.

The commission's report concluded: "It is not always true that the total tax package in North Carolina is as reasonable as that of the other Southeastern States." Elaborating on this point, it added: "We find that concerns with large capital investments here which have a reasonably satisfactory profit margin pay quite a high tax bill. The corporate executives making plant location decisions may well find the present North Carolina tax situation a considerable deterrent. It has proved to be a considerable problem to some concerns which have recently located here."

The important recommendations in the tax study report had to do with a change in the allocation formula by which North Carolina taxed the income of domestic and foreign corporations doing business in more than one state. The major change recommended was that the income tax of 6% be levied only on the portion of a company's income which is reasonably attributable to the operations performed or property owned in North Carolina. At that time corporations in North Carolina were being taxed upon their entire net income, whether it was earned in this state or others. The old formula thus resulted in the taxing of a greater portion of the net income of corporations operating in interstate business than was reasonably attributable to North Carolina from

---

* The eight other capable men named to serve on the commission were C. Gordon Maddrey, Frank Daniels, Howard Holderness, J. Y. Jordan, Jr., W. P. Kemp, Sr., E. M. O'Herron, Jr., James M. Poyner, and R. Grady Rankin.

"It's a pretty picture—I hope it works"

any practical business viewpoint. The commission thus recommended the changes that would give North Carolina a direct,
businesslike approach to the taxing of corporations.

Despite the fairness of the bill introduced in the General Assembly on the basis of the commission's report and the need for
changes in our system of taxation, some newspapers and some
legislators complained that we were giving tax concessions to
large corporations and that this should not be done. More cause
for opposition was the report that the changes would result in a
loss of revenue of an estimated $7 million in the 1957-58 fiscal
year, or a total of $14 million for the biennium. Fortunately, this
proved to be an overestimate.

North Carolina's need for a fairer tax for multi-state corporations was urgent. Even though North Carolina was a so-called
rural state with a so-called rural legislature, the legislators wanted
to see their state develop. They saw the equity of what we were
talking about and they had no hesitation in passing the recommended changes in the tax laws. Of the 170 legislators, only about
a dozen voted against the tax changes. This was a remarkable action from a good General Assembly. Their action opened up a
new door for development in North Carolina.

The changes in the formula placed North Carolina in a more
competitive position among her sister states for new industry. It
encouraged local corporations not to move home offices, sales offices, or accounting offices outside of the state as a means of
reducing their income taxes. It demonstrated to corporations
throughout the United States that North Carolina, its legislature,
and its tax laws took account of modern business's needs and that
in this state we were willing to give not concessions but equal
treatment to all business.

The tax changes were soon receiving publicity all over the coun-
try. On June 20, a full-page advertisement in the *Wall Street
Journal* told of the changes in the corporate tax system in North
Carolina. The same night State Treasurer Edwin Gill was speak-

ing in New York on the changes in North Carolina's tax structure. During his speech Mr. Gill received this telegram from me:

HAVE JUST ANNOUNCED MY PRESS CONFERENCE R. J. REYNOLDS TOBACCO COMPANY ADDING THIRTY-FIVE MILLION DOLLAR MANUFACTURING FACILITY THIS STATE BECAUSE OF NEW ALLOCATION FORMULA.

It was certainly a good beginning for the changes in the state's tax laws. Businesses began to consider North Carolina for their new homes and as sites for expansion. In the coming years industrialists would listen to the advantages that North Carolina had to offer. And the expected revenue loss for the state of around $14 million because of the change in the tax law failed to materialize. The uniformity of treatment adjusted the tax bills of some firms upward instead of downward, and revenue from corporate income tax during that biennium was down less than $5 million.

In a report from Commissioner of Revenue James Currie in November, 1958, it was stated: "In general, corporations manufacturing in this state and selling on the national market have on the whole benefited from the change which eliminated discrimination against multi-state manufacturers. And, in general, corporations manufacturing elsewhere and selling in North Carolina experienced a tax increase.... The net result has been to produce a more equitable measure of the amount of income earned in North Carolina by multi-state companies regardless of place of charter."

It was a good beginning.

Even as the North Carolina Business Development Corporation was being put on its feet and the state's tax structure was being oriented to a more equitable base, people from the Department of Conservation and Development and I were continually working with local communities to get them interested in seeking industry themselves.

However, in those early days of my administration the general

attitude was to "let the governor" bring industry to the communities in the state. That feeling came to the surface down in the
eastern part of the state one day when I was there for a bridge
dedication. A rather ambitious mayor said before over two thousand of his constituents: "I want to say to Governor Hodges who
is here today that I want him to bring us an industry."

In my response I told the mayor and his constituents that the
governor would not bring them an industry. Further, the governor
could not bring them an industry. My goal was to get certain
state taxes and state attitudes changed so that the many wonderful communities in North Carolina could organize and prepare
themselves for industry. These localities—with the leadership of
their mayors, their councilmen, their county commissioners, and
their businessmen—could then form organizations dedicated to
their communities' progress to go throughout America selling their
communities to prospective industry. The state and its governor
can, and should, furnish leadership in industrial development,
but the "point of sale" for each industrial prospect remains in
the local community.

This philosophy took hold. Backed by the fair corporate tax
law, a capable Department of Conservation and Development
Department, and countless communities with a desire for industry, North Carolina began an industry-hunt unparalleled in its
history.

As a part of its program of encouragement to industry, my administration was vitally concerned with the State Ports Authority,
which directs the operations of the state docks at Wilmington and
Morehead City. These ports are of great importance to the further
development of North Carolina, but when I became governor they
were not doing the business that they should have been doing.
The reason for this, I found after studying the situation, was
largely that the SPA had absorbed too much of the rivalry between Wilmington and Morehead City. The economic rivalry be-

tween the port cities was healthy. But when it was carried over to the activities of a governmental body like the SPA it was most unhealthy for the ports in particular and the state in general.

Our State Ports Authority had been created by an act of the General Assembly in 1945 to allow the state to engage in promoting, developing, constructing, equipping, maintaining, and operating the harbors or seaports within the jurisdiction of the state. The SPA was created through the efforts of many people who believed in the future of these two ports and in the future of North Carolina as an agricultural, industrial, and business leader in the Southeast. The facilities at the ports were dedicated in 1952 and for the next few years they grew, but not at the pace at which they should have grown.

That they progressed and grew in spite of many handicaps reflected the potential of the ports and the hard work of a few people. Morehead City and Wilmington both had representatives on the SPA, and the rivalry of the cities carried over to the authority. The fact that the headquarters of the SPA was located in one of the port cities did not help the situation. In addition, the ports did not have the public relations set-up they needed to really grow. There was, too, a definite need for an executive director who would operate above the jealousies of the two ports, and the organization needed to have a statewide point of view. It was, in short, time for a fresh start.

The 1957 General Assembly agreed. It changed the law to allow the governor to appoint the seven-member State Ports Authority from the state at large. I named a completely new authority.* The seven men appointed in the fall of 1957 faced a difficult task.

* It included John Mercer Reeves of Pinehurst, a businessman; William Grimes Clark, Jr., of Tarboro, a business man; Collier Cobb, Jr., of Chapel Hill, a businessman; Earl Norfleet Phillips of High Point, a manufacturer; Kirkwood Floyd Adams of Roanoke Rapids, a paper company executive; Robert L. Eichelberger of Biltmore Forest, a retired army general; and Charles Dowd Gray, Jr., of Gastonia, a businessman. Two years later, the membership of the board was increased by two and I appointed Tom Evins of Durham, a tobaccoman, and Harvey Hines of Kinston, a businessman.

But they came on the job fresh and without prejudice and without any connections with either of the ports. These things were tremendously important. In announcing the appointment of the new State Ports Authority, I said, in part:

It is not easy to change completely the membership of an important state agency such as the State Ports Authority. Such changes have to be made, however, when conditions and circumstances—many times beyond the control of any individual involved—make it necessary. Above all, it is my responsibility as governor to seek always what is best for the state as a whole in the operation of these two deep-water port facilities. After months of study and consideration, I reluctantly came to the conclusion that serious problems in public relations and morale required a complete change in the authority.

I should like to make it clear that this decision was entirely mine, and that it is not meant to cast reflection on any member of the old authority because they are my friends and men with outstanding records in their individual fields of endeavor. It is always difficult to please two different port cities and their citizens, but it is more difficult when the executive director of the ports lives in one of these cities. I shall recommend to the new Ports Authority that the new director be located in Raleigh.

The next week the new Ports Authority was sworn in and I suggested to its members that the ports needed their constructive, objective, and far-sighted leadership. First, we needed a better public understanding of the goals and objectives of our port operations. Next, we needed the support of each port city in the operations of its own state port and also in the total program. Next, we needed business from North Carolina organizations, both private and governmental, who imported or exported. Finally, I challenged the new Ports Authority to develop a port program that was modern and up-to-date in every detail and that could compete with comparable ports in other states.

The SPA set out to meet my challenge and to make a lasting contribution to the economic progress of our state. John Mercer Reeves was elected chairman, and soon after the Ports Authority selected D. Leon Williams as executive director. He had served in a similar capacity with the Georgia Ports Authority and knew his business. He said he welcomed the challenge and set as his aims the operation of the ports on firm business lines, the development of commerce through the ports, and the aiding in the economic development of the state. In the spring of 1958, the SPA executive offices were moved from Wilmington to Raleigh.

The new SPA and its new director greatly aided the development at the ports. The set-up placed the direction of the two ports' facilities above the competition of the two cities. Several members of the new authority were from the Piedmont and the western part of the state, and this helped to make these sections more conscious of the importance of the ports. The members were dedicated to the job they were doing and it was noticeable in the results they produced. The business at the ports had been increasing by between 10% and 15% annually. Under the new SPA, increases jumped to between 40% and 50% annually in revenues.

The total gross revenue at the ports for the year ending June 31, 1955, was $471,000. The revenue climbed yearly from $533,000 to $587,000 to $633,000 in the fiscal year 1957-58. The following year it jumped to $733,000. Then in the fiscal year 1959-60 it totaled $1,090,000; and in the next fiscal year it climbed to $1,150,000. The net profit increase at the ports was even more impressive. It totaled $43,000 in the fiscal year 1954-55; then jumped to $128,000 in the fiscal year 1957-58; and to $482,000 in the fiscal year 1960-61. In tonnage figures as well, the imports and exports through the state facilities at Wilmington and Morehead City continued to grow by leaps and bounds.

The changes in the SPA, ridding it of the rivalry between the two port cities and causing all North Carolina to become aware of the importance of the ports, opened up a period of healthy growth of the state facilities. The ports contributed much to the state during my administration and their future development is practically unlimited. The state ports at Wilmington and Morehead City have a significant role in the state's industrial program.

I have never had much patience with those people who think that there is some necessary opposition between conservation and development, and especially that industrial development in the state can take place only with the waste or sacrifice of irreplaceable natural resources. Of course they are the two sides of the same coin, and I always knew that any program for expanding industry would depend in the long run on following the soundest principles of conservation.

Water resources are a fine case in point. A large paper mill may use fifty million gallons of water a day—more than the total domestic water use of five of the larger cities of North Carolina. Manufacturing a pound of cotton goods requires eight to forty gallons of water; a pound of rayon, ninety to two hundred gallons. A steam generating plant needs about two hundred thousand gallons for each ton of coal used. Add this industrial use of water to the enormous use of water for agriculture, and to the domestic, health, and recreation needs of a growing population, and it can be seen that the water-supply problem for an expanding economy can be a serious one, even in a state with such an abundant supply as North Carolina.

Public attention in North Carolina was focused on the seriousness of the water problem in the early 1950's. We then had several extremely dry summers which stunned many of our people who were accustomed to taking the water supply for granted. There were great dollar losses in agriculture. A number of our towns and cities were faced, for the first time in many years, with serious water shortages. At one time, we had as many as six municipalities desperately scrambling to pump water into their storage reservoirs from auxiliary supplies. In one unusual case, a community found that its water supply, which came from a large creek, had actually vanished overnight. The governor's office had to call for federal assistance to provide drinking water for the people of that community until they could provide themselves with another source of water.

In the fall of 1953 Governor Umstead appointed a Water Resources Advisory Committee to consider this problem and to advise what steps could be taken to deal with it. This committee worked diligently and reported to me in the early part of 1955. Earlier that year, in my "State of the State" message to the General Assembly, I had pointed to the gravity of the water supply problem and urged the legislators to give the report serious consideration. The assembly realized that something had to be done, and a complete water law, patterned somewhat after water laws in the semiarid western states, was introduced; but after much study and discussion it was abandoned as being too extreme at that time. But the legislature did create a Board of Water Commissioners, with powers to co-ordinate our efforts in conservation of water resources and to prepare and disseminate information gathered from research on our water problems. The commission was also given emergency powers which could be invoked during periods of drastic water shortages. This was a forward step in the solution of a long-term problem.

Later that year, 1955, I spoke on this subject at the Southern Governors' Conference in session at Point Clear, Alabama. I pointed with pride to our early recognition of the importance of water resources and to the close attention we were giving to the subject. I told my fellow governors that the problems involved in water conservation and development fell into two categories, administrative and legal. The most outstanding need, I added, was for co-ordination of the work done by the many governmental agencies—city, county, state, and federal—that were concerned with water resources.

In North Carolina, we had already started working toward coordinating the efforts of the various state agencies concerned with water resources. The Commission on Reorganization of State Government, headed by David Clark of Lincoln County, had found that there were five such agencies. They were the recently formed Board of Water Commissioners and two agencies each in the State Board of Health and the Department of Conservation and Development. The Commission on Reorganization of State Government found that "The administration of North Carolina's water resources is now in a state of confusion. The confusion exists because of (1) the uncertainty as to the state's future role in the water resources area, and (2) the duplication of responsibilities in the water resources area."

The commission made four recommendations for reducing the duplication and overlapping of state water resource agencies, all of which were enacted by the 1957 General Assembly. They helped but did not really solve the problems. One of the recommended proposals was that the Board of Water Commissioners continue to study the problem and recommend to me and the General Assembly laws, policies, and administrative organization necessary for a more profitable use of our water resources.

I thought the best interests of the state would be served if all the agencies dealing with water resources were put together in one department and I asked the Board of Water Commissioners to study this proposal. After study, the board so recommended, and later the Board of Conservation and Development and the Commission on Reorganization of State Government joined in this recommendation.

In its report to me before the 1959 meeting of the General Assembly, the Commission on Reorganization recommended "the creation of a Department of Water Resources, to which would be transferred the existing functions of the State Board of Water Resources, Inlets and Coastal Waterways, and the ground water research functions of the division of mineral resources of the Department of Conservation and Development." It also recom-

mended that the State Stream Sanitation Committee be transferred to the Department of Water Resources with jurisdiction
over the classification of streams and the issuing of special orders
and that the Department of Water Resources be designated to act
as the administrative agent of the State Stream Sanitation Committee.

These recommendations were introduced in the 1959 General
Assembly and were enacted into law. The act noted that its purpose was "to create a state agency to co-ordinate the state's water
resource activities; to devise plans and policies and to perform
the research and administrative functions necessary for a more
beneficial use of the water resources of the state, in order to insure
improvements in the methods of conserving, developing and using
those resources."

I was directed by the law to appoint a Board of Water Resources * to govern the new Department of Water Resources.
General James R. Townsend was designated to serve as chairman
of the board, and Colonel Harry E. Brown, who had done much
on hurricane work for the state, was named director of the department.

Colonel Brown proposed that the department be organized in
five units. The division of stream sanitation and hydrology and the
division of navigable waterways were required by the Water
Resources Act. Other units proposed were the office of the director, the division of ground water, and the division of staff
services. The plan was approved. The Department of Water Resources began its work on September 1, 1959, with two divisions.
The other three were functioning before the end of the year.

Although the course had been long, we had finally achieved
a new beginning for the water resources program. There could

---

* I named to the board James R. Townsend of Greensboro, Dan K. Moore
of Canton, Glenn M. Tucker of Carolina Beach, C. H. Pruden, Jr., of Wind-
sor, P. D. Davis of Durham, S. Vernon Stevens, Jr., of Broadway, and Ben R.
Lewis of Goldsboro.

now be a co-ordinated effort to conserve and develop the state's water. Colonel Brown immediately began a new study on the ground water. It will be a tremendous asset in the future planning by communities and the state. Records are being kept of the flow of surface water, and studies are being made of municipal water supplies and waste disposal. Work is being done with the federal government in planning on ways and means to rehabilitate shorelines, on flood control, on river basins, and on other aspects of water conservation.

The Department of Water Resources is, in brief, seeing that the state's water resources are developed and utilized to their fullest. Its fine work is already benefiting Tar Heels through health and recreation, as well as providing methods to supply North Carolina with enough water for the ever-growing needs of agriculture, industry, and domestic consumption. As well as solving water problems now, the Department of Water Resources is working to insure a good quantity and quality of water for North Carolina's future.

North Carolina's bread-and-butter problem—the need for a higher per capita income—will not be solved easily or quickly or permanently. I have described some of the ways we went about trying to deal with it: by stimulating small industry through privately-subscribed credit corporations; by fair tax legislation for industry; by an improved state authority for ports and shipping; by long-range planning for the best use of water resources.

CHAPTER III

Industry Hunting
at Home and Abroad

NORTH CAROLINA had the product—numerous good locations for new and expanded industries—but it still had to be sold to most industrialists outside the state and the South. "The North Carolina Story" had to be told and no one could tell it better than Tar Heels themselves. Since aggressive salesmen take their message directly to the prospects, we decided that our administration would use this technique. With this idea in mind, the Conservation and Development Department organized a trip to New York City in the fall of 1957. In answer to a call for volunteer salesmen nearly seventy-five representatives of communities throughout the state joined up for the industry hunt. And they all paid their own expenses.

These leaders were to sell the state as a whole and under no conditions were they to discuss their communities when they talked with prospects on the trip. The same rule applied in the later industry hunts. Plans were made so that the Tar Heels would go out in pairs and call on prospects whose names were given them by the Department of Conservation and Development to discuss North Carolina as one of the great states of the Union and its potential for industrial growth. They were to point out the advantages the state had from the standpoint of business climate, of attitude, of research and education, of equitable taxes, of its forward look in education, health, highways, recreation, and general state welfare.

North Carolina was not trying to steal industry from other states. The industry hunters did not urge industrialists to move a plant from its present location. Our story was simple and direct: "if you are thinking of expanding your manufacturing activities or of finding a new location in order to serve your markets better, especially in the Southeast, you certainly should consider North Carolina. There are no tax gimmicks or anything free offered. North Carolina is on the move and offers those things that a progressive corporation would like to have, namely an opportunity to live in a good community in a good state and make a profit."

Everything about the trip to New York and those that followed was well organized and was worked out in great and careful detail. We worked hard to improve every procedure. Breakfasts, luncheons, and dinners were sponsored by business firms in the name of the state so we could reach and entertain industrial prospects in the city where we were working. During the week of October 14-19, 1957, the Tar Heel industry hunters combed New York City, talking with industrialists interested in chemicals, electronics, metal working, and the like. The group in that week was able to make personal visits to about 250 prospects in industry, business, and food distribution fields.

I made a point of explaining the purpose of our visit to the mayor or other local officials so there would be no misunderstanding. In general, they were very cooperative and very complimentary. During that first trip to New York, I delivered three major addresses, including one advertising North Carolina's special advantages to food processing. During the week I addressed or greeted more than six hundred persons at five luncheons and four receptions. In addition, I made appearances in behalf of the group and North Carolina on twelve television and radio shows. We did

"North and South they knew our fame, grey ghost is what they called me, Luther is my name—"

not miss any opportunity to speak for North Carolina and the opportunities it offered.

One might wonder how a group of people coming into a city like New York could get on national TV and radio shows to advertise their state. The answer with us from North Carolina was a unique group of people called Honorary Tar Heels. These people—mostly writers, photographers, commentators, and other specialists in the communications field—were of great help to us wherever we went. Bill Sharpe, who helped organize the Honorary Tar Heels under Governor Gregg Cherry's administration, and Hugh Morton, who helped Bill keep things going in the intervening years, simply made contacts with one or more of our HTH friends, told them that the governor and his party would be there, and asked them to arrange some news coverage and broadcasts. It was just that simple and we owe them a great deal for their help.

The opportunities offered in North Carolina were, of course, many, as could be demonstrated by our already developing industrial potential. They were evidenced by the faith in the future that many forward-looking companies—including banks, trucking companies, power companies, other utilities companies, and other firms—had exhibited by sending their people on the industry hunt. They were willing to share with new industries, but wanted it made clear that special inducements, tax exemptions, public financing of industry, or other so-called give-aways were not offered by North Carolina.

I would testify from my own experience as a manufacturer that there was in North Carolina genuine interest on the part of communities and employees in new firms and the jobs they had to offer. The people of North Carolina, we told the industrialists, appreciate the opportunity to work. They prove it to the hilt day after day by furnishing a full day's work for a fair day's wage. This, plus the fact that in North Carolina an industry would find itself surrounded by people intensely interested in its success and welfare, was different from the attitude of people and communities in some other areas.

As an illustration of our statement to prospects throughout the country that North Carolinians are anxious to work and are interested in their jobs, I told of an experience I had in the town of Weaverville, N.C. While traveling across the state on appointments of various kinds, I liked to drop by a new industrial plant whenever I could. It was always helpful to see how these companies were getting along and what the management people thought of North Carolina and particularly what they thought of their workers. I was paying such a visit to a new plant of a firm that had been founded in Ohio and had expanded its operations into Weaverville to make fine sweaters.

I asked the president of the company, who happened to be there on a visit from Cleveland, "How are these folks getting along?" He answered, "Wonderful, Governor, I'd like to tell you a story of something that happened to me the other day, which gave me such a pleasant surprise. These sweaters of ours are extremely delicate and costly and I wanted to see some of them laid out as samples on a table, and with my rough and awkward hands, I didn't want to lay them out myself.

"So I went to a woman at one of our sewing machines and said to her, 'Would you mind coming over here and helping me lay out some samples?'" He added dryly, "I know what a worker in our Cleveland plant would have told me had I asked her to do such a thing, but this woman said in a friendly voice but with the proud manner of a good mountain woman, 'No, sir, I don't mind. I'll be glad to.'" She expertly helped the president and then started back to her machine when she turned toward him and said, "How are we getting along here? Are we making any money?"

The president said he had never had such a shock or pleasant surprise in his life to find a production worker so much interested in her employer that she wanted to know whether or not the company was making money. He said, "This is an intangible thing but priceless." And he added, "We like North Carolina."

In telling the story of the state on the industry hunts, we explained that geographically North Carolina ranged from the ocean to the mountains, which included the highest peaks east of the Mississippi. The state was sixth in the nation in the production of hydroelectric power, a fact that clearly indicates our abundance of water. Our population of nearly 4.5 million was 99.4% native born and was 66% rural or small town. Since the turn of the century North Carolina had not hesitated to invest in schools, roads, port terminals, health centers, hospitals, mental institutions, and colleges. These were all selling points for North Carolina.

Good government was another strong point for the state. North Carolina was widely known for its sound and progressive government. Through strong executive leadership and the devoted service of the members of the General Assembly during the years, government in the Tar Heel state had kept step with the times and the needs of the people. A conservative-progressive state, North Carolina operated squarely in the middle of the fiscal road. A balanced budget, containing plans for the future, had always been the cornerstone of North Carolina's financial policy.

That is the story we told during that week in New York to a number of prominent and influential people. The majority of them was greatly impressed. Other industrial missions followed during my administration. In the latter part of April, 1958, Conservation and Development officials and another group of North Carolina businessmen, some sixty strong, spent a week hunting industry in the Chicago area. The same pattern was followed—volunteer salesmen, special luncheons and dinners, addresses, personal contacts, special state ads, and reports in all the news media. This time, however, we could tell more of North Carolina's expansion, progress, and growth.

In November of 1958, 122 Tar Heels joined an industry-hunting caravan to Philadelphia. There I called on the governor and city officials and assured them we were in Philadelphia on a good will mission and had no intention of raiding their city or of taking any of its existing industries away. The success of the earlier industry hunts was repeated. And it was always a thrill to sell North Carolina because it was such a good product.

In a speech in Philadelphia, I stressed that "one of the most exciting things about development work generally—whether industrial, agricultural, educational, or cultural—is the unlimited opportunity that stretches before us. Within past decades we have witnessed tremendous advances on all fronts of science and technology which truly stagger the imagination of man. Even the most cynical observer hesitates today to predict the final results of anything in this material universe." And then I noted that in North Carolina we liked industries that are research-minded. As evidence of that fact, I pointed to North Carolina's then great new venture, the Research Triangle.

"The North Carolina Story" was continually told throughout my administration. Other industry hunts were made by groups of citizens in 1960. In May of that year, one hundred Tar Heels went back to New York, and, in October, eighty Tar Heels paid their own way for a second visit to Chicago to help tell "The North Carolina Story." In addition, on all of my travels across America, I tried to do a selling job on North Carolina's potential. The story of North Carolina's many hopes and aspirations went from coast to coast. The results—first inquiries about sites, and later new industries and new jobs for North Carolina citizens— were well worth the effort.

The early successes of our industry-hunting caravans to cities in the North and Midwest caused us in early 1959 to ask: "What should be our next target?" Voit Gilmore of Southern Pines, a member of the Conservation and Development Board, had a ready answer—go over and tell "The North Carolina Story" to in-

"What d'you mean, did I get th' turkey or th' bird?"

dustrialists in western Europe. At first it seemed a little fanciful. After further study and after discussing it with the Conservation and Development Board and others, however, it was concluded that it was worthwhile and should be done.

Representatives of the commerce and industry division of the Conservation and Development Department went to Washington and talked over the proposed trip with the Department of Commerce people there. In Washington, they received a lot of data plus a great deal of encouragement, and were aided greatly in working out an itinerary and a program. John Harden of Greensboro, who was to be director of the tour, made a quick planning trip to Europe, along with a Conservation and Development staff member. They visited each country and city that we proposed to visit on the tour and set up local arrangements for our hard-hitting trip to follow.

Back home we announced through the press a North Carolina Trade and Industry Mission to Europe and, as we had done for the trips to cities in the United States, said that volunteers would be welcome. Each of the volunteers, including me, was to pay his own expenses as on the earlier trips to American cities. It was first thought that perhaps fifty people might want to go. Then the applications began to pour in and before they stopped we had nearly a hundred volunteering. The list had to be limited to sixty-eight because of plane space requirements and the need to move quickly on a tight schedule in Europe. To achieve maximum results, the sixty-eight men were divided into three working groups.

The European mission was co-sponsored by the State Board of Conservation and Development and the State Ports Authority. The purposes were threefold: (1) to develop stronger trade with Europe through North Carolina state ports at Wilmington and Morehead City and to express appreciation to European companies already doing business with these ports; (2) to seek added industrial development for North Carolina through European-

financed plants, through European-controlled franchise agreements, and through assembly or re-packing operations in the state;
and (3) to create a better understanding and good will between
the United States and the nations in western Europe.

The sixty-eight members of the North Carolina Trade and Industry Mission to Europe left the Raleigh-Durham Airport on
Saturday, October 31, 1959. Their schedule for the next two weeks
included visiting business leaders in ten major cities in England,
the Netherlands, Germany, Switzerland, France, and Belgium. All
travel was by air. The plan for this unique tour was for Group I
and Group II to alternate on the cities and to spend approximately
two and one-half days in each discussing North Carolina with
industrialists. I headed Group III, accompanied by the tour director, Ed Rankin of my staff, and four North Carolina newsmen.
Our assignment was to visit all ten cities in the six countries.

The mission arrived in London, on a foggy Sunday morning,
November 1, and was greeted by a statement from the British
Board of Trade, through its president, Reginald Maudling. The
next morning, my first official gesture was to lay a wreath at the
statue of Sir Walter Raleigh, for whom the North Carolina capital
city was named. After that I made a brief courtesy call on United
States Ambassador John Hay Whitney at the United States Embassy. A briefing for the entire North Carolina delegation was
held before noon in Grosvenor House in preparation for the luncheon and the work to be accomplished in London. It was at the
North Carolina luncheon that many of the Tar Heels were first
pleasantly surprised by the customs of old England.

Guests arriving were greeted by John Mills, a professional
major-domo, who was dressed in a red uniform and white stockings. He pretty much ran the show, announcing the name of each
visitor in a loud clear voice, and moving the group—including
eight lords and eighteen knights—quickly to the tables after a brief
reception. Mills presided over the luncheon and gained attention
by banging a large gavel much like the speaker of the House of

Representatives back home. Then Mills added, "My lords and gentlemen, PRAY silence. . . ."

The British guests warmly received my luncheon speech. Several times they cried "hear, hear" and hand-thumped the table tops as I outlined what North Carolina was doing to raise its own standard of living and to offer the best possible economic opportunity to its people and to those who settle there. Lord William Rootes, chairman of Britain's Export Council and a well-known automobile manufacturer, gave the response and assured us that our mission would achieve "positive results."

Group III, plus the members of the State Ports Authority, went to Hamburg, Tuesday, November 3, and attended a luncheon for fifty-eight German guests who represented many of the leading shipping, import-export, trade, and manufacturing firms in that city. Emphasis here was more upon ports, and I thanked them for the shipping business they were already giving us. Hamburg Mayor Max Brauer welcomed the group to his city. Later, the members of the Ports Authority toured the harbor while I held a press conference. I did not speak German and most of the reporters did not speak English. It was a long news conference, but interesting.

It was after this luncheon in Hamburg that one of the German businessmen, Herr Pleuger, commented to a Tar Heel that he was "impressed" with North Carolina. He said he would soon send a representative to visit our state. This chance conversation resulted in the first concrete benefits of the trade mission to Europe, as will be explained later.

That night we joined Group II in Amsterdam. The next day, Wednesday, November 4, we were greeted by Amsterdam Burgomaster Gijsbert Van Hall and his wife. Later at the Krasnapolsky Hotel, 153 Dutch business and industrial leaders gathered for a luncheon that featured smoked eel. The Dutch, as others, were impressed with the explanation of our nickname, Tar Heel. Another press conference and we were off for Rotterdam to visit the American Farm Bureau foreign trade office there. George Dietz, director of the trade office and our host at a reception and buffet dinner Wednesday night, impressed us with his grasp of America's problems in selling its farm products in Europe.

Group I greeted members of Group III when we arrived in Stuttgart, very early on Thursday, November 5. Some of the busiest hours of the mission followed, under the leadership of Consul General Allen B. Moreland. We made courtesy calls to Baden-Württemberg Minister President Kurt-Georg Kiesinger and to the Lord Mayor of Stuttgart, Dr. Arnulf Klett. The largest number of guests for any single event on the trip—251—turned out for a reception and luncheon held at the Liederhalle in Stuttgart. Some, who had called late for reservations, had to be turned away.

This turned out to be an outstanding luncheon for both Germans and Tar Heels. In addition to Minister President Kiesinger, many distinguished Germans attended. One was the recently retired President of the West German Republic, Dr. Theodore Heuss. As a part of the program, in addition to my usual speech, I presented President Heuss an electric blanket made, of course, in North Carolina. It had earlier been my pleasure to serve in West Germany in 1951 as chief of the industry division of our Economic Cooperation Administration, and I was well aware of the great contribution President Heuss had made to his country and the world.

That afternoon, many of the industry hunters held prearranged interviews and consultations with some forty German businessmen and industrialists at the Stuttgart Chamber of Commerce. I held another of those long press conferences, this time with about forty people, including representatives of the Armed Forces Network. In the evening, we were guests of Minister President Kiesinger at his official residence in Stuttgart. It was a brilliant dinner and it enabled our industry hunters and top Stuttgart business leaders to discuss common problems and goals.

"Auf Wiedersehn, *you-all* . . ."

While the work continued in Stuttgart, Group III, plus representatives of Groups I and II, flew to Frankfurt on Friday, November 6, for lunch with five top German industrialists. The informal affair had been suggested and arranged through Dr. Henri A. Abt of the German-American Chamber of Commerce in New York City. Dr. Hans C. Boden, chairman of the foreign trade committee of the Federation of German Industries and chairman of the board of Allgemeine Electric Company, introduced the other Germans there. Dr. Boden's first question was, "How did you know to come now?" Our answer was equally brief: "In North Carolina we try to keep informed." A three-hour discussion followed and we received many suggestions from the

German leaders about how to make the best approach to many German industries.

Dr. Boden, whose job would be equal to that of president of General Electric here in the United States, was very curious about why and how the governor and representatives of a practically unknown state should come to Germany to tell prominent German industrialists the story of North Carolina and its industrial opportunities.

"Governor, I wanted to do my homework last night because I confess I knew nothing whatever about North Carolina," he said. "I did not even know where it was located. In the only encyclopedia where I could find any reference to North Carolina, I found just two items, namely, the area in square miles and the percentage of Negroes in the state." He added, "I wasn't very well prepared to hear this wonderful story." I replied, "Doctor, I hope you'll come to North Carolina and learn more about our great state, especially since I have tried to learn about your wonderful country of West Germany."

Group III flew from Frankfurt to Munich on Friday night, where it was joined by Group II from Amsterdam. The next afternoon Group I arrived by bus from Stuttgart. This was the first time all three groups had been together since we arrived in London. And no groups of traveling salesmen had ever been more in need of rest—a well-deserved rest. Another busy week was still before us.

In Munich that Saturday several of us made a tour of Voice of America and Radio Free Europe and I taped programs there for later use by their stations. I spoke about my then recent experiences while visiting the Soviet Union and related the growing threat of Soviet economic competition to the free world and especially to western Europe. The next day, Sunday, was a free day and many of us went traveling, some through the Bavarian Alps to Garmisch, others to Vienna; and a few to Berlin. Some of us visited art museums.

Monday, November 9, was another work day. After an early morning briefing, the hunt was on again. It started with another press conference for me, followed by observing the one hundredth anniversary of the discovery of oil with some fifty Germans gathered at the Amerika Haus. A reception and a luncheon was attended by two hundred German guests, and we Tar Heels found a lively interest among the Bavarian businessmen in the possibilities offered by North Carolina. That evening the Baye-rische Vereinsbank, one of Munich's leading banks, gave an informal party for the North Carolinians and there we met and talked with some fifty top German businessmen for two hours.

Groups I and III flew through the rain and mist to land at the Zurich airport on Tuesday, November 10. Wednesday morning I again met the press, and as at most of the European press conferences, the newsmen did not ask many questions but ex-pected the person being interviewed to make a substantial state-ment and have copies in writing. For a luncheon at the beautiful Zünfthaus zur Meisen, there were 105 Swiss business and indus-trial leaders present. Heinrich Wagner, a Swiss businessman and president of the Swiss Friends of the United States of America, served as master of ceremonies.

Tables for the luncheon had been organized by Mr. Wagner to group together Tar Heels interested in textiles, furniture, tobacco, etc., and our Swiss guests selected the tables in which they were most interested. It was a wonderful system and we soon found we were dealing with sharp, shrewd businessmen and traders who knew their fields.

When it came time to make my brief talk on North Carolina to these Swiss businessmen, I said, "I have met many of you before and some of our people have told of their visits with you individually. From your reputation, you're intelligent and good traders. This is not news to North Carolina because the capital of your country, Bern, means a great deal to us in our state. Baron de Graffenried settled some two centuries or more ago the town of New Bern, North Carolina. But before he would go through the formal ceremonies of actually 'founding a city' he required a certain number of gold pieces to pay him for his service." I added, "From what I see and hear today in Zurich I don't think that you Swiss have changed very much." This brought a roar of laughter from our Swiss guests.

After an afternoon of personal interviews, the North Carolina industry hunters were the guests at dinner of the Champion Paper and Fibre Company of Canton, North Carolina, through the courtesy of Percy Paetz, European manager. There were no other guests present.

Group III left Group I at work in Zurich, Thursday, November 12, and headed for Paris to join Group II which had gone there the day before. We were guests at the American Club of Paris for lunch. At the head table was the Honorable Henry J. Taylor, United States Ambassador to Switzerland, who was in Paris at the time. Some 125 club members attended the luncheon. During the afternoon Group II made business contacts, while I toured the city for the press and held another news conference.

Following a brief reception that evening, the North Carolina dinner began in the Grand Hotel with 140 French guests attending. At each place was a free sample of French perfume provided by a French perfume manufacturer. The Honorable Amory Houghton, the United States Ambassador to France, introduced me to the French audience, and the response to my remarks was given by a representative of the French Economic Minister.

Group I arrived from Zurich, Friday morning, November 13, and proceeded directly to the NATO Embassy for a joint briefing on NATO with the remainder of the party. After that the rest of the day was spent on calls to industrial prospects and in last-minute shopping in preparation for the return trip to North Carolina.

Meanwhile that Friday, several of us flew to Brussels for a brief visit. A luncheon was given at the Plaza Hotel in my honor by Jean Souweine, a young Belgian businessman who is the son-in-law of G. E. Hutchins of High Point, a member of the North Carolina mission. Mrs. Souweine also attended the luncheon, along with fifty Belgium businessmen and industrialists, and the Honorable William A. M. Burden, the United States Ambassador to Belgium. Following a local custom, I spoke to the group at the pre-luncheon reception while all the guests stood. It was a short speech!

The Belgians indicated warm interest in the North Carolina mission's goals in Europe. And since the European Common Market headquarters is located in Brussels, there was even greater emphasis here on the need for increased trade among the European nations and the world market. In this matter North Carolina was ahead of the nation. It was not until the Kennedy Administration that the United States became interested in significant trade arrangements with the Common Market. At the conclusion of the luncheon in Brussels, there was a brief ceremony and I was officially appointed an honorary member of the European Common Market.

That afternoon we returned to Paris where the other members of the mission were getting ready for the trip home. I joined them after taping an interview for the Columbia Broadcasting System. The interview was used on a CBS coast-to-coast broadcast in the United States on Sunday. While in Paris, we Tar Heels voluntarily refrained from wearing our usual neckties bearing Tar Heel imprints and Tar Heel emblems on our coat lapels. This was done because of the possibility that they might be misinterpreted as symbols representing "black feet," a controversial term for European settlers in Algeria. We put the pins and ties back on as we were leaving.

On the way home the mission was delayed seventeen hours in Iceland after our plane developed landing-gear trouble. Shortly after the plane took off from Keflavik on the way home, the pilot announced that the nose landing gear was stuck and would not retract. The incident was handled beautifully by the flight personnel and was somewhat exciting. The crew was extremely careful in dumping ten thousand gallons of jet fuel over the ocean before returning to the ice-covered runway at Keflavik, where we waited for the arrival of another plane before continuing to New York.

The North Carolina Trade and Industry Mission to Europe finally got back to the Raleigh-Durham Airport on Sunday, November 16, and was greeted by about 250 persons, most of whom were relatives of the industry hunters. All sixty-eight of us were tired out after the two-week tour of western Europe but all of us were happy at the work we had done. In the two-week period the group carried "The North Carolina Story" directly to some one thousand, six hundred business leaders in ten cities in England, the Netherlands, Germany, Switzerland, France, and Belgium.

I have given the schedule of our European trip in some detail, primarily to show how the organizational work was done to a fine detail and to indicate what a thorough and complete job can be done in a few days if a group works hard at it.

I recall writing to the sixty-eight people who had planned to go to Europe with us. My letter reached them several weeks before we were to fly to Europe. "This is going to be an extremely hard trip," I wrote. "It's going to be all business. You may have a night or part of a day in Paris at the end of the trip, but in between you'll be expected to work all day, be on time, and be serious about your undertaking. If you can't live up to this, then I suggest you not go." Only one man backed out and he said that his doctor told him that he was foolish to try to keep up with Luther Hodges anyhow—it would not be good for his health. Be that as it may, I have nothing but highest praise for people like Norman Cocke, Louis Sutton, and other older men who took this terrific pace and who made a great contribution.

The visit of the sixty-eight North Carolinians and their rigorous, businesslike schedule made a great impression all over Europe.

The United Press International manager there told me that our visit in those few days was the biggest piece of news that he had his correspondents cover.

Although the basic purpose of the mission was long-range development for North Carolina, it was gratifying that at least 276 of the Europeans we talked with indicated an immediate interest in North Carolina during the tour. A total of seventy-nine people showed definite interest in our ports, twelve in the Research Triangle, twenty-six in possible manufacturing operations, forty-one in sales outlets or similar arrangements, seven in licensing agreements, and eighty-three indicated a general interest in North Carolina. Additional inquiries kept coming to the State Department of Conservation and Development and the State Ports Authority as more European businessmen looked to America for increased trade, more production facilities, and investment opportunities. We received many letters from Europeans who had noticed the accounts of our visit in their local newspapers and wanted more information about what North Carolina had to offer.

The State Department of Conservation and Development, the State Ports Authority, and other state agencies almost immediately began a follow-up program. Personal letters over my signature were sent to the 276 contacts as well as all of our European friends who attended North Carolina luncheons or dinners.

The first western European manufacturing plant to be located in North Carolina as a result of the trade and industry mission was announced in June of 1960. Then Pleuger Submersible Pump Company of Hamburg announced that its first plant in the United States would be located in Statesville. The plant was to cost over $200,000 and would eventually provide employment for more than five hundred persons, if business conditions justified it.

Beyond all of this, the reputation achieved by the State of North Carolina for its forward-looking work and what the state meant had tremendous effect. One of the chief benefits derived from the trip to Europe was that it was widely publicized throughout the United States. In the weeks and months that followed, North Carolina received inquiries from many domestic concerns. These people figured that if North Carolina had that much ingenuity and had as much to offer as we did, they had better look into it. Many liked what they found so much that they decided to come to North Carolina and stay.

The drive for industry continued throughout my administration as governor of North Carolina. I am, very naturally, proud of the part that the various agencies of the state's government played in this. The major portion of the credit, however, must go to the people of North Carolina. Nothing could have been accomplished without their full cooperation at every level. The energetic, capable and dedicated people were the ones who, in the final analysis, got the job done. These were the people who banded together in the more than two hundred industrial development organizations and many chambers of commerce that worked and continue to work enthusiastically and effectively to build better communities for a better North Carolina.

And there was local pride among these groups, as I found out when I stated during a speech that in North Carolina we faced many challenges "especially in eastern North Carolina." I created some animosity among a few people in the east by saying that not everything was being done that could be done to take full advantage of that area's abundant resources. For the most part the people of the eastern counties realized that my statements were prompted, not by a desire to criticize, but by a very genuine and long-standing interest in the section and a very sincere desire to do everything possible to help.

I did not, as some people contended, say that nothing was being done in the east. I did say that not enough was being done. Many people in the eastern counties accepted the challenge I made to them and did exert greater effort. There was a marked increase in activity and cooperative endeavor in eastern communities and counties, and Conservation and Development officials told me that never before had there been as much activity in eastern North Carolina. The effort began to pay dividends to the people who became concerned. It was very gratifying to me.

It proved again that a vital key in the great effort of North Carolina is the attitude and leadership of citizens at the community and regional level. I do not wish, however, to take any credit away from the magnificent work done by the State Department of Conservation and Development people. It was this agency that showed the individual citizen where he fitted into the picture, how he could and why he had to participate in the local, county, and regional programs for promoting progress. New records for new and expanded industry became the expected, and each year's report was dramatic evidence of the continued progress in North Carolina.

At the first Southern Governors' Conference I attended—at Point Clear, Alabama, in October, 1955—I suggested to my fellow governors that North Carolina would be glad to join with their states in a common advertising and promotion campaign to attract industry to the South. My offer was not accepted by any of the governors. It was just as well. Later events proved that it was better that North Carolina went it alone. After all, each state had its own industrial development program.

For the following years during my administration, from 1955 through 1960, we made steady additions to the number of new industries brought to North Carolina and expansions of existing industries. Generally speaking, the investments in capital expenditures and the number of employees and amount of payrolls increased each year, although there were variations in these categories because of differences in types of industries that came in during individual years and also because of changes in general business conditions in the United States during this period.

For the six full years of my administration 1,053 new industries came to North Carolina and expansions were made by 1,405 of the industries here. New industries during these six years represented a total capital investment of $509,016,000; jobs for 79,588; and a payroll of $248,461,000. Expansions represented a capital investment of $605,934,000; new jobs for 60,645; and a payroll of $189,092,000. Totals for the six-year period were a capital investment of $1,114,950,000; jobs for 140,233; and a payroll of $437,553,000.

And with the end of my administration in early 1961 the industrial development program did not slow down. Governor Terry Sanford named Hargrove Bowles, Jr., of Greensboro, director of the State Department of Conservation and Development when William Saunders resigned to go back into retirement. William Henderson remained administrator of the commerce and industry division of the department for a while, and his people continued the fine work they had been doing. Industries continued to come to North Carolina and those already here continued to grow.

I am proud of the industrial progress we made in North Carolina during the six years I was governor and I am proud of the progress being made under the administration of my successor. But my pride is tempered by the knowledge of the vast potential we have yet to develop in North Carolina.

CHAPTER IV

The Court's Decision
and the Public Schools

IN May of 1954, while I was still lieutenant governor, I was attending a meeting at Lake Placid, New York, before boarding a special Rotary train to go to the International Rotary Convention in Seattle, Washington. While at Lake Placid, I first heard of the United States Supreme Court's May 17, 1954, decision declaring that "in the field of public education the doctrine of separate but equal has no place." The decision, in a word, meant that it was unlawful for a public school to deny admission of a child solely because of race. It affected immediately only a handful of cases, including ones from Virginia and South Carolina, then before the Supreme Court.

North Carolina was not a party in any of these cases, but my state—as well as sixteen other southern and border states—was affected by the principle of the Supreme Court's ruling. I immediately cancelled my plans to go to Seattle, hurried back to North Carolina, and called a meeting of the State Board of Education, of which I was an *ex officio* member and which had elected me its chairman. In light of the Supreme Court's decision I felt that the board and its work could be seriously affected.

I then went to see Governor Umstead to tell him of my calling the board meeting and to ask him his view of the court's decision.

He was obviously concerned over the court's action but he had very little to say to me other than that he was thinking about the subject. I told him that my idea in calling the State Board of Education together was to get the board to appoint a committee to study the court's decision from the board's point of view. He did not encourage me to have such a committee, but he did not say "no."

The State Board of Education did appoint a committee, which looked at the various problems the State Board of Education might have to face. But this committee was not to bear the major burden.

At my meeting with Governor Umstead he indicated that he, as governor, would need to appoint a special statewide committee to study the court's decision and its possible effects on the North Carolina school system. He did so on August 4, 1954. The Honorable Thomas J. Pearsall of Rocky Mount, a former speaker of the State House of Representatives who had served the state with distinction in a number of capacities, was named by Governor Umstead to be chairman of the Governor's Special Advisory Committee on Education. The nineteen-member committee, including three Negroes, was charged with the job of making recommendations in light of the Supreme Court's decision. It began at once to study the problem confronting the state.

After becoming governor at Governor Umstead's death, I asked the committee to continue its work. It did, and on December 30, 1954, submitted its report, which I in turn presented to the General Assembly on January 6, 1955, in my State of the State message. In the report was the recommendation that "complete authority over the enrollment and assignment of children in public schools and on school buses" be transferred from the State Board of Education to the county and city boards of education throughout the state. This was the Pupil Assignment Plan, which for all practical purposes became the basis for North Carolina's approach to the problem created by the Supreme Court's decision.

I read the report of the Governor's Special Advisory Committee on Education to the members of the General Assembly. Its objectives were the preservation of public education and the preservation of the peace throughout North Carolina. The committee's conclusions were: first, the mixing of the races forthwith in the public schools could not be accomplished and should not be attempted; second, attempts should be made to meet the requirements of the Supreme Court's ruling without materially altering or abandoning the existing school system; third, another committee should be appointed to give further study to problems arising from the court's decision.

This report, with its recommendation of the Pupil Assignment Plan, was a unanimous document of great significance and it gave the 1955 General Assembly and all of North Carolina a starting point from which the state could move toward a solution of the problem. Shortly after my State of the State message was completed, Senator Paul H. Jones of Pitt, Representative George Uzzell of Rowan, and others introduced bills in both houses to give county and city school boards full authority to rule on what school a child should attend. The bills also provided that parents not satisfied with decisions on the assignment of their children could appeal to the courts.

There was soon opposition to these administration bills; and other bills, aimed at preserving segregation but going far beyond the committee's recommendations, were introduced. One proposed that state funds be cut off for any school that might proceed to integrate white and Negro pupils, and another proposed a constitutional amendment that would have the effect of authorizing the spending of state funds to support private schools.

The "local option" bills came out of committee in mid-March. The House bill met with some opposition on the floor, notably from Representative Byrd Satterfield of Person County, but when the vote was called the Pupil Assignment Plan was passed in both houses with a large majority. There were only a few "no's" heard in the voice vote. The plan, in effect, removed the State Board of Education as a party in litigation on the segregation issue by providing for the right to appeal the decisions of local boards on assignment and enrollment directly to the courts.

The Pupil Assignment Act was North Carolina's first major step relating to the May 17, 1954, decision of the Supreme Court. It did not conflict with the court's anti-segregation decision; it did not promise the people there would be no integration; and it did not threaten to close all the schools if the color barrier was broken in one. It was just the first of several steps North Carolina was to take in seeking a solution to a very difficult problem.

The 1955 General Assembly realized this. After adopting one resolution stating that the mixing of the races in the public schools could not be accomplished and if attempted would seriously endanger the operation of schools throughout the state, the lawmakers approved the recommendation of the Governor's Special Advisory Committee on Education that an advisory committee be set up to work continually on the problem. The duties of the new committee were to study the problems "which exist and may arise in this state directly or indirectly" from the May 17 decision of the Supreme Court. It was to report to me its findings and recommendations.

Speaking at a law school conference at Duke University in Durham on June 21, 1955, I announced the appointment of Mr. Pearsall to head the seven-man committee the General Assembly had authorized. He had, of course, headed the earlier nineteen-member committee. Others appointed to the new committee were William T. Joyner of Raleigh, R. O. Huffman of Morganton, State Senator Lunsford Crew of Roanoke Rapids, State Senator William Medford of Waynesville, State Representative Edward F. Yarborough of Louisburg, and State Representative H. Cloyd Philpott of Lexington, who was to be elected lieutenant governor in the 1960 elections.

Three of the members—Pearsall, Crew, and Yarborough—were from eastern counties and three—Medford, Huffman, and Philpott —were from the western part of the state. Joyner was from Raleigh. They reflected effective political thinking throughout the state, and all had previous experience in state government and were well acquainted with legislative affairs and the legislative process. They had open minds and were thoroughly in support of public schools and public education. At the same time, they recognized in a realistic manner the attitudes of the average citizen in North Carolina toward the racial problem.

Governor Umstead's original committee had had a membership of nineteen including three Negroes. Unfortunately, these particular Negro representatives were on the state payroll and were "suspect" by the state's Negro citizenship. They were high-grade, honest representatives on this difficult committee, but they were in a tough situation. The average person, white and Negro, had not really studied the court order, but believed that the court had ordered integration, which it had not. These Negro committee members were under great pressure from their fellow-Negroes, many of whom felt strongly that there should be immediate integration.

Mr. Pearsall, others, and I discussed carefully and prayerfully the problem of the racial composition of the new, smaller committee of seven. We finally decided that we would not include a Negro because a Negro member of such a small group would have to work under almost impossible conditions because of outside pressure.

As I told an audience at Duke University, I considered the selection of the members of this committee one of the most important tasks I was to face during my administration. Two days later the committee and Attorney General Harry McMullen met with me at the Executive Mansion in Raleigh. I requested at the time that the committee study carefully and with objectivity the

decision of the Supreme Court and its probable effect on North
Carolina and its schools. And I charged the committee to come
up with a program for our state that would recognize that the
court decision was the law of the land even though we disagreed
with the decision.

The committee went straight to work. Headquarters were set
up in the Agriculture Building in Raleigh. W. W. Taylor of
Warren County was engaged to serve as executive secretary and
chief council of the committee. Later Thomas Ellis was engaged
as an assistant to Taylor. The committee met periodically, often
twice a week, to study the problems of other southern states as
well as what was happening in North Carolina. The committee's
study continued for nearly a year.

During this time the mood of North Carolina was one of deep
concern. It was not one of hate or extreme bigotry. Our citizens,
who on previous tense occasions had shown tolerance and understanding, were faced with a most critical problem. There was no
essential difference between our citizens and those of fellow-
southerners in Virginia or South Carolina, but ours responded
to moderate leadership. Further, they were willing to get facts
before they "blew off" to the detriment of their schools and their
state.

During the year following the United States Supreme Court's
decision emotions built up in members of both races. Talk of
immediate integration of the public schools was counterbalanced
by talk of abolition of the public schools and their replacement
to a most uncertain extent by private ones. This verbal battle
of the extremes was exemplified in the incident that developed
over a speech Dr. I. Beverly Lake, then an assistant attorney
general, made in Asheboro in the summer of 1955. The speech
caused the National Association for the Advancement of Colored
People to demand that Dr. Lake be fired. He was not.

Dr. Lake, as an assistant attorney general to the late Attorney

General Harry McMullen, had carried much of the state's legal burden in matters growing out of the Supreme Court's decision. In behalf of the ailing attorney general, he had presented an *amicus curiae* brief for North Carolina before the United States Supreme Court in the spring of 1955. In the brief it was stated that "an attempt to compel the intermixture of the races in the public schools of North Carolina would result in such violent opposition as to endanger the continued existence of the schools."

Lake's brief added, however, "It is impossible at this time to foresee what the final results would be even if the court should recognize the divergent conditions existing in the state and allow sufficient time and ample discretion in the district judges to frame final decrees after full hearings to meet these conditions. This, however, would seem to be the only way, if any way can be found, which might possibly have the result which the decision of this court contemplates."

In light of this background, Dr. Lake, speaking as a private citizen or at least attempting to do so at an Asheboro meeting, advised communities to close their schools rather than submit to the Supreme Court's decision. This speech was made before the Supreme Court's 1955 decision implementing its 1954 decision and before the state had any official policy other than the Pupil Assignment Act. That act, of course, did not provide any means for the closing of any schools.

The National Association for the Advancement of Colored People issued a resolution to the press requesting me as governor to use my official position to remove Dr. Lake from office. I was away from Raleigh for the weekend when the NAACP resolution was first published in the press, but my staff immediately attempted to contact me. A State Highway Patrol car finally found me on one of my occasional trips of relaxation knee-deep in a mountain stream in a western county, fishing for trout. Via the patrol car radio I learned of the NAACP resolution.

I immediately answered the request that I fire a state official for expressing his own views as a private citizen. In a statement I said, "I am amazed that this private organization, whose policies are determined in its national office in New York and are obviously designed to split North Carolina citizens into racial camps, and which I am convinced does not actually represent any substantial portion of our Negro citizens, should have the effrontery to make such a request. Of course I will not attempt to influence the attorney general, for whom Dr. Lake works, to remove Dr. Lake from office. On the contrary, it is my intention to use every means at my command to retain for the state the services of this distinguished lawyer."

Two days later, on July 19, 1955, I said in an address at Lincolnton that as long as I was governor of North Carolina I did not propose to be forced by pressure groups. "Such authority as is vested in the chief executive shall be independently exercised by me in the light of what I believe to be right and just, and with the benefit of the best advice and counsel I can obtain," I declared. "I will probably make mistakes, but these mistakes will be honest mistakes and my own; they will not be errors into which I have been pushed by extremists."

Turning to Dr. Lake's statement on the closing of the schools in the event of integration, I noted that although other southern states had considered the possibility of operating schools through private corporations leasing state-owned buildings, it had not been previously suggested for North Carolina. Proposals of that kind assumed the abandonment of our public school system and even if they had legal validity I did not believe we were yet at a point where we should seriously consider them. The abandonment of our public schools was and is a course of action which is always available as a last resort if it should be decided a proper step to take.

North Carolina, of course, never did need that last resort. Dr. Lake, of course, was not fired. Later that year, however, he resigned as assistant attorney general and began a private law practice in Raleigh. And the NAACP continued its opposition to any program other than total integration of the public schools.

Meanwhile the beginning of another school year was approaching. The official policy of North Carolina was against integration of the races in the public schools, but it had no means of preventing integration other than the Pupil Assignment Act. A crisis could have developed in North Carolina that fall as occurred in other southern states.

I discussed this possibility many, many times with Pearsall and his committee, Attorney General William Rodman, Assistant Attorney General Robert Giles, and many citizens, both in North Carolina and outside. Naturally Paul Johnston and Ed Rankin, both stalwarts on my staff, and I discussed it several times a day. We tried always to maintain an objective point of view, but it was difficult.

I was besieged from both sides. I knew that our schools must be kept open. They were more important than all else and they could easily be put in danger! Foreseeing the dangers to the public school system of the state, as well as to the long-standing good race relations between North Carolinians, I went before the people on August 8, 1955, with a practical approach to the problem of segregation in the public schools. It was carried live by sixty radio and ten television stations and received extensive coverage in the daily press. In it I proposed a plan of voluntary separation of the races.

"North Carolina now stands at the crossroads!" I said at the beginning of the speech. "Our choice of which road we shall follow will involve all that has been accomplished in the past through the determined efforts of our forefathers to provide us with a good system of public schools; it will also involve the future of our children and our children's children. Make no mistake here! Let there be no misunderstanding! We hold in our

minds and hearts the past, the present, and the future of our
beloved state."

I pointed out that the Supreme Court's decision did not forbid
a dual system of schools in which the children of each race
voluntarily attended separate schools and had never said that
any state must set up a single school system, mixing the children
of both races. Federal Judge John J. Parker, chief judge of the
United States Court of Appeals for the Fourth Circuit and a
native North Carolinian, had said that the Constitution "does not
require integration. It merely forbids discrimination."

Attorney General William B. Rodman, whom I had appointed
to succeed Attorney General McMullen when the latter died, had
urged all local school boards to set up committees to study problems created by the court's decision and the Advisory Committee
on Education made the same recommendation. Both the attorney
general and the advisory committee felt, as I told my audience,
that the court would probably not interfere with the operation
of the schools that year and that the schools should continue to
operate on the same basis of enrollment as had been used in the
past.

Speaking directly to the Negro citizens of North Carolina, I
said:

Any stigma you may have felt because of laws requiring segregation in our public schools has now been removed by the courts.
No right-thinking man resents your desire for equality under the
law. At the same time, no right-thinking man would advise you
to destroy the hopes of your race and the white race by superficial
and "show-off" actions to demonstrate this equality. Only the
person who feels he is inferior must resort to demonstrations to
prove that he is not. . . .

My earnest request of you Negro citizens of North Carolina is
this: Do not allow any militant and selfish organization to stam-
pede you into refusal to go along with this program I am proposing in the interest of our public schools; take pride in your race

by attending your own schools; and make it clear that any among you who refuse to cooperate in this effort to save our public school system are not to be applauded but are to be considered as endangering the education of your children and as denying the integrity of the Negro race by refusing to remain in association with it.

Let there be no mistake or misunderstanding about this thing. Those who would force this state to choose between integrated schools and abandonment of the public school system will be responsible if in the choice we lose the public school system for which North Carolinians of both races have fought so hard and find to our eternal sorrow the personal racial bitterness which North Carolinians of both races have avoided so successfully. We must as whites and Negroes work together to solve this problem. Men of both races of good will and faith will be needed and must be had!

This appeal for voluntary action generally met with good response. There was criticism on the part of some white people, a number of Negroes, and the NAACP. Kelly Alexander, state president of the NAACP, said in Charlotte following my address that his organization "did not recognize in the governor's address any evidence of a plan or program acceptable to the majority of freedom-loving Negroes in North Carolina to desegregate the public schools."

In the days that followed I suggested to the members of the Governor's Advisory Committee on Education that they promote in every school district and community in North Carolina a program of encouraging the voluntary choice of separate schools; that members of both races be invited to take part in organizations to encourage such voluntary action and to improve race relations; and that each organization compile and make available factual material that would show that voluntary separate school attendance was both feasible and desirable. I publicized the program at every opportunity and once took it to a Negro audience.

On August 26, 1955, I spoke before approximately one hundred members of the North Carolina Teachers Association assembled for a leadership conference at Shaw University in Raleigh. I replied to some of the criticisms that had been directed against the voluntary program and declared that I was not in any sense asking anybody to give up his constitutional rights in supporting such a program. I assured the teachers that the basis upon which I asked their cooperation in my program of voluntary separate school attendance was the overriding need to preserve the public schools in order to promote the welfare of the children of both races.

The reaction of the Negro teachers was obviously unenthusiastic, and they responded with only a brief, polite ripple of applause at the end of the speech. Still I felt pretty good about it until Woodrow Price of the Raleigh *News and Observer* came up to me on my way out of the building. "I think," Price said to me, "your speech has had about as much effect as a tennis ball slammed against a brick wall."

In early November, reaction against the voluntary approach was more pronounced as I spoke at the Founders' Day program of the Agricultural and Technical College of North Carolina at Greensboro. Although my talk was primarily on the progress made by the college and had nothing to do with the segregation question, the overflow audience of students and Negro townspeople was obviously unfriendly. They did not stand, as was customary in North Carolina on occasions attended by the governor, when I entered.

The address was interrupted at two points. The first was a discourteous snicker, highly audible, that came early in the speech. The second—a shuffling of feet—came near the end of my talk and was so pronounced that I stopped speaking. Turning to President F. D. Bluford, I asked if I should continue or stop. He disappointed me by saying, "Suit yourself." I turned back to the audience and completed the address.

I realized that Dr. Bluford was somewhat on the spot but I was stunned and disappointed at his lack of courage. He should have stopped the first demonstration, which he could have done by a word or wave of the hand, and when I stopped the speech and turned away from the audience to ask him what I should do, he should have arisen to the occasion. I was not discussing integration-segregation—no reference was made to it. I was, as governor and chief budget officer of the state, outlining what had been done for A & T by the state and telling how many millions of dollars had been poured into A & T's development.

What happened was a discourteous thing to a state's governor, a discourtesy to the office itself. Dr. Bluford could have asked for courtesy and respect and not lost anything concerning any beliefs he had on segregation. But he failed to measure up. Realizing the stress and strain of those days, I hold no resentment.

Later an attempt was made to find the cause of these discourtesies. Some of the students were quoted as attributing them to my pronunciation of the word "Negro." They said it came to their ears as "Nigra." I did not, however, knowingly mispronounce the word. The interruptions were obviously premeditated and were probably instigated by opponents of the voluntary segregation program. I later received apologies from President Bluford, members of the faculty, several student organizations, and a number of individual students.

However, the feelings which caused the interruptions of the speech at A & T College in Greensboro did not accurately represent North Carolina's Negro citizenry. In the fall of 1955 North Carolina's schools opened without serious incident. There was complete and voluntary separation of races.

The North Carolina Advisory Committee on Education continued its work during the fall and winter and with the approach of spring in 1956 began drafting its report to the people. Legislators, at my invitation, came to Raleigh in small groups for conferences on the committee's recommendations. On April 5, the committee convened in Chapel Hill and presented its report to the people. In it the committee recommended that local school authorities be empowered to abolish public schools and that tuition grants be provided children not wishing to attend integrated schools. It further recommended that I call a special session of the General Assembly during the summer to allow that body to consider the constitutional changes that would be necessary to put these proposals into effect.

The next day I told the press I would follow the recommendations of the committee and would call a special session of the General Assembly. My reasoning was that the voluntary plan and the 1955 Pupil Assignment Act might be sufficient to meet the state's needs but that it was necessary to make plans for "safety valves" in case they were needed. The special session was called for noon, Monday, July 23.

Then began the job of preparing for the special session. The "safety valve" legislation was being prepared by Attorney General William Rodman's office with the aid of the Department of Public Instruction. Mr. Rodman had the assistance of Bob Giles, an able attorney who later became a member of my staff. The ideas proposed by the Pearsall Committee, as the Governor's Advisory Committee on Education was popularly called, were discussed back and forth across the state. Our concern at the time was that the legislators did not pre-judge the legislation which would put the committee's proposals into effect. The seven Pearsall Committee members, Attorney General Rodman, Assistant Attorney General Robert Giles, and Ed Rankin of my staff, and I met with Senate President Luther Barnhardt of Concord and Speaker of the House of Representatives Larry Moore to discuss ways of informing the legislators of the contents of the legislation being prepared.

It was decided that this issue was so emotional and so technical that it was best not to discuss it at public meetings for the time being. The only way to explain the proposals was to meet with the members of the General Assembly and talk to them without their having any preconceptions or prior knowledge of the plans. Since we felt this could not be done in the open, a series of four so-called "secret" meetings were held for the legislators in the weeks preceding the special session. These briefing meetings were held for the convenience of the legislators in different areas of the state—at Rocky Mount, Kinston, Lexington, and Waynesville. The first meeting—held at Kinston—had been bugged but the wires were found before the meeting began. Other meetings were guarded to keep uninvited people away.

Committee Chairman Pearsall and I, together with the attorney general, sat down with the elected representatives of the people at these sessions and showed them what was being considered. In turn, the legislators gave their views. The meetings were good. I do not recall anything said at any of them that could not have been said before anybody. Without the press present, however, the legislators discussed things more freely perhaps than they might have otherwise. This round of briefings, plus the round in April after the committee made its report, helped the legislators to be better informed on matters to be considered than any other General Assembly in the state's history.

On Saturday, July 14, 1956, I went before the people to explain the legislation prepared for the General Assembly. Attorney General Rodman and I held a news conference in Raleigh and at the same time a similar report was presented in Asheville by Committee Chairman Pearsall, Paul Johnston, my administrative aide, and Assistant Attorney General Robert Giles.

We made it clear that the plan was designed to discourage attempts by the NAACP and other groups to force integration, and at the same time to discourage demands for more drastic steps such as a complete shutdown of the state's public schools. I was very hopeful that under the plan not a single public school would ever have to be closed. Eight bills were prepared for the General Assembly. These were:

Bill No. 1—An amendment to the state constitution authorizing education expense grants for private education and local elections to suspend local public schools.

Bill No. 2—An act providing for a general election in September on the expense grants and local option amendment and amendments proposed by the 1955 General Assembly on other matters.

Bill No. 3—An act entitling children assigned to public schools attended by children of another race and against the wishes of their parents to apply for state funds for educational expenses. Such funds would be available only for education in private nonsectarian schools when it was not practicable to reassign such children to public schools not attended by children of another race.

Bill No. 4—An act authorizing local school administrative units to suspend the operation of one or more of the public schools under their jurisdiction.

Bill No. 5—An act changing the state compulsory school attendance law so that it would not apply to a child assigned to a school attended by a child of another race against his wishes.

Bill No. 6—An act to allow the education expense grants to be paid out of the state's contingency fund until the 1957 General Assembly convened.

Bill No. 7—An amendment to the Local Option Act, Bill No. 4, making technical changes.

Bill No. 8—A resolution of protest, charging that the United States Supreme Court "is usurping powers of the states and the people."

The plan made the closing of schools in a given area possible but difficult, and at the same time made the setting up of private schools possible but difficult. The board of education of any school administrative unit or of any subdivision of any administrative unit could call a local option vote if it received a petition signed by 15% of the voters. If a majority favored suspending the operation of a school, the board of education would close it. If an election were called, it left the decision of whether or not to close the schools directly with the parents of the children involved. Children, white and Negro, in such a local option unit would not be entitled to attend any other public school, but would be entitled to receive local and state funds under the education expense grant provision.

To re-open the schools in an administrative unit or any subdivision, a board of education could call for an election on re-opening a school, after it received a petition of 15% of the voters requesting that it do so.

The proposals were moderate, but some North Carolinians did not like them. The State Congress of Parents and Teachers came out in opposition to the proposals and put forward its own recommendations. They were essentially the same but they did not contain the tuition grants or the local option features of the Pearsall Committee recommendations. The NAACP also came out in opposition to the proposals and promised "all kinds of attacks" on them. Others opposed the proposals because they wanted measures to close up the schools more easily if they could not be kept segregated.

I was, of course, not surprised at the action of the NAACP. Many of us, however, were concerned and frightened over the attitude of the PTA leadership and its negative action. I do not think they represented the point of view of the rank and file, but their stand was dictated by a few extreme individuals. The PTA— and we told this to their president, Mrs. John W. Crawford of Raleigh—hurt rather than helped our chances to keep the schools open with their more liberal, impractical point of view which most of us felt that the General Assembly would not accept.

The special session of the General Assembly convened at noon Monday, July 23, 1956. It immediately passed a joint resolution inviting me to address a joint session. At 8:10 that evening the two houses convened and I went before them to present my recommendations. I told the legislators flatly: "We face tonight one of the greatest crises which North Carolina has ever experienced and affecting at this moment the lives of more than a million children."

I referred to the April 5 report of the Pearsall Committee and its fundamental premises that the people of North Carolina would not support mixed schools and that the saving of our public schools required immediate action. To do nothing would destroy our public schools. And, I assured the legislators, "We are going to use every legal means we can devise to insure that the effects of what we feel is an erroneous decision by the Supreme Court are not forced on our state in a fashion which could deprive us of one of our dearest possessions, namely our public schools. It is to that end that we are assembled here in special session."

I explained the eight bills briefly and emphasized that the two "safety valves" of school attendance grants and local option were joined together in one constitutional amendment because it was felt that both were needed to give our people the protection they needed. I stressed also that the bills were completely permissive in nature. The proposed constitutional amendment could be adopted and all of the other bills enacted, and there would not necessarily be any change in the school assignment of a single child, no educational expense grants paid, and no votes on suspending schools taken anywhere in the state. The whole legislative package was designed for the people to have if it should ever be needed. It was in truth "safety-valve" legislation.

The plan was compared with others offered. Immediate closing of a school by accumulative action on account of integration would obviously deprive the people of any say so in the matter. On the other hand, immediate integration would, of course, create untold difficulties and would also deprive the people of North Carolina of a choice in the matter. In answer to some who accused the Pearsall plan of permitting integration, I pointed out that the plan did not forbid integration. To do so in light of the Supreme

Court's decision would be void on its face and no protection whatever.

There were those who proposed that we do nothing and let the tide of events carry us where it would. The end result of this course of action or inaction could easily have been integration with no choice and no relief, with the consequence of our schools being starved to death for lack of legislative and public support. I told the General Assembly:

It is my firm conviction that your Advisory Committee has recommended to you the best possible course of action at this time. So let us . . . reason together and find, if we can, a common ground for the salvation of our schools. I know there are extremes on this issue: those who would go far to the left, and those who would get equally as far to the right. It is neither fear nor lack of conviction that makes me stay nearer the middle; it is a sincere desire to be the governor of all the people of whatever belief, of whatever extremes, and to lead as best I can the state in a moderate fashion to help solve this problem pressing down upon us. . . .

And now, ladies and gentlemen of the General Assembly, those of us who have struggled with this responsibility through these past several years place the matter in your capable hands. . . . The proposed bills have been hammered out with your help and advice. . . . We have done the best we knew how to devise a sensible and acceptable plan for your consideration. . . . Yours is the power to accept it as is, to modify and change it as you desire, or to discard it completely, if you see fit. I know that you realize the vast amount of thought and work and prayer that have been given to the program we are submitting to you, but you as individual legislators will, of course, vote as your conscience dictates.

Immediately following the address, the two houses of the legislature met in their respective chambers and the eight bills proposed by the Pearsall Committee were introduced. Senator Lunsford Crew and Senator William Medford introduced them in the Senate, and Representative Cloyd Philpott and Representative

Edward Yarborough introduced them in the House of Representatives. The introducers were, of course, all members of the committee. All eight of the bills were sent to a special committee "of the whole."

Hardly had the proposed Pearsall plan been introduced before an opposing bill was introduced by Representative Byrd I. Satterfield of Person County. Written, we understood, by Dr. I. Beverly Lake, the former assistant attorney general who represented the state during the United States Supreme Court hearings on school desegregation, the bill would have abolished the constitutional requirements for public schools. It would have required the General Assembly to provide for the education of all children of the state by maintaining public schools or by providing grants to parents of children enrolled in private schools. This bill, too, was sent to the committee.

Public hearings on the Pearsall Committee proposals began before the joint committee the next day, Tuesday, and were carried over a statewide radio and television network. People from all walks of life and from all sections of the state went before the committee during the three days of hearings. The speakers were about equally divided between supporters of the recommendations of the Pearsall Committee and those who were against it.

One of the major arguments against the proposed legislation was voiced by Douglas B. Maggs of Durham, professor of constitutional law in the Duke University School of Law and a former assistant attorney general of the United States. He predicted the courts would "eventually hold the program invalid." His concern was that "if the program is adopted, discrimination against, and denial of all opportunity for education to white children will be its principal result." He declared that "the whole recommended program is unconstitutional." Dr. Magg's presentation was a crowd-pleaser, but his arguments were countered the next day by Colonel William T. Joyner, Raleigh attorney and a member of the Pearsall Committee. Joyner said the plan was constitutional.

Opposition to the plan also came from the State Parent-Teachers Association. Francis E. Walker of Durham, representing the organization, and others challenged the wisdom and the practicality of the plan. Walker forecast the possibility that a North Carolina child could grow up without any education if the Pearsall plan was adopted. A representative of North Carolina's Negro teachers, Carl E. DeVane, spokesman for the legislative commission of the North Carolina Teachers Association, opposed the recommendations and called for school integration as "official policy."

The Reverend Maurice A. Kidder, president of the Chapel Hill-Carrboro Ministerial Association, called the plan "hypocritical, coercive, and hopeless to the people who most need encouraging." J. W. Wheeler, a Durham banker speaking on behalf of the "Negro Committee of One Hundred Counties," told the legislators that the Pearsall plan would "undermine and destroy" the public school system. Harry Golden, author and publisher of the *Carolina Israelite*, called the plan "dangerous" and criticized us for not opening what he termed "a line of communication with the leadership of the Negro race."

Among those speaking in favor of the Pearsall plan was Julian Allsbrook of Roanoke Rapids, a former state senator and spokesman for the Patriots of North Carolina Incorporated, a pro-segregation organization. He told the legislators that the white people of the state would not support integrated public schools. Jack C. Woodall, legal counsel for the Durham United Political Education Council, said his organization believed in the leadership of the governor and said the plan was a step toward continuing support of public schools in North Carolina.

There were many other speakers during the hearings both for and against the Pearsall plan. Disregarding for the moment the pros and cons of the arguments, I think there was much merit in Colonel Joyner's appeal to the legislators to "let the people make the decision" on the plan. He said that the plan offered "steps we think proper to meet a situation that may arise, and in all probability will arise." Noting there were extremists on both sides of the question, Colonel Joyner said, "I hope that no schools would close under the plan. I plead with you to let us not take an extreme position. Let us take a moderate position."

The major opposition to the Pearsall plan came from the measure introduced by Representative Satterfield on Monday night. At the hearings Tuesday, Dr. Lake told the legislators that while the "Pearsall plan is basically good it does not go far enough in controlling situations that might arise." He warned them "not to freeze into the constitution a single plan for the education of your children" and urged that the legislatures of the future be given the power to "deal with the problem in the light it will be presented in the future." Lake said the Satterfield amendment should be adopted to give the legislatures of the future control of any situation that might arise.

Senator Robert Morgan of Harnett, who was later to manage Dr. Lake's campaign for governor, introduced the Lake plan in the Senate on Wednesday morning. Later at the hearings Senator Morgan said the Pearsall plan would tie the hands of the General Assembly but that under the Lake plan, "if we made a mistake the legislature could change it." Senator Ralph H. Scott of Alamance, one of the co-signers of the Lake plan in the Senate, supported it because, he said, "we need a chance to get a second thought. This bill . . . may or may not be it."

Late that Wednesday afternoon I called a press conference and reported that the Pearsall Committee had considered proposals similar to Dr. Lake's a hundred times during the year of its study and had rejected them all. As I said at the time, I was completely confident that the Pearsall plan would be adopted by the legislators.

Other opposition developed in the legislature, and for the next two days the air was thick with amendments and new proposals.

They came from both sides, and they ranged from those that were patently vindictive to those that were well-intentioned even if ill-advised or impracticable. All of them fell by the wayside. The State House of Representatives on Thursday night in a short session gave overwhelming approval to the Pearsall plan. With very little discussion, the representatives gave rapid approval to the seven bills and the resolution protesting the United States Supreme Court's desegregation decisions. The bill proposing constitutional amendments for local option on school closing and state-paid tuition grants to private schools passed the House with only two negative votes. These two "no" votes were cast by Representative Satterfield of Person, who felt the legislation was too weak, and by Representative Dan K. Edwards of Durham, who felt the legislation was too strong. The next morning, Friday, the Senate unanimously passed the eight-point program and that afternoon, after five days, the special session of the General Assembly ended.

The 168-to-2 vote in favor of the Pearsall Committee proposals was most remarkable and confirmed my great confidence in the wisdom of the committee's approach to the problem created by the Supreme Court's May 17, 1954, decision. The shortest session in the history of the General Assembly of North Carolina did one of the most important jobs in the legislature's history in submitting the proposals to the people.

Between the time the members of the General Assembly went home and the September 7, 1956, referendum on the Pearsall Committee's proposals, the opposition to the local option and tuition grant features did not subside. If anything, the opposition was intensified. Mrs. John W. Crawford of Raleigh, state PTA president, was most vocal in her opposition and said on several occasions that the North Carolina Congress of Parents and Teachers could not agree with the Pearsall plan because it "could destroy our public schools and could force the integration of the races." She urged its defeat at the polls.

Support, however, was not lacking for the Pearsall plan. The State Board of Education's ten white members endorsed the plan; the directors of the North Carolina Education Association declared themselves in support of its proposals; and more than two hundred speakers took the stump to urge the ratification of the constitutional amendment embodying the Pearsall plan.

Dr. Charles Carroll, as superintendent of public instruction, and the top school man of the state, was a key man. His support for the plan was needed. I am sure he was torn by doubts as to which way to go for he had a very difficult time in making up his mind that he would publicly support the Pearsall plan. The superintendent, like many elected officials, preferred not to take sides, especially on hot issues. He did, however, after much urging, come out in support and his support was extremely helpful.

Dr. Carroll said that the proposed amendment was the "best" immediate action that could be taken to deal with the school segregation issue. State Attorney General George B. Patton, who had succeeded Attorney General Rodman, said the "safety valves" were needed for the protection of the public schools and added that "the beauty of the plan is that nobody has to do anything" with the proposals. President John D. Messick of East Carolina College at Greenville said the plan "provides a compromise action that is best for all people, white and colored."

Holt McPherson, editor of the *High Point Enterprise*, was named to serve as chairman of a Governor's Committee for the Public School Amendment. Ralph Howland of Elkin was named publicity director. The committee campaigned vigorously. In addition to directing a speakers' bureau of some two hundred persons, the committee had printed and distributed some fifty thousand copies of a pamphlet urging the people to vote for the amendment. The committee's operations were financed by private contributions.

I spoke for the amendment at every opportunity and, the night before the referendum went before the people, over a statewide

"Well, if you knows of a better 'ole, go to it!"

television and radio network. I emphasized again, "No more serious issue has faced North Carolina in several generations, and it is up to you, as individuals, to help make it possible for your state to get through this period of grave crisis."

I pointed out again to the people that the proposals of the Pearsall Committee were completely permissive in nature; that they did not remove any child from school nor did they close any schools but they did give the voters of a community the right to do so if need be; that the duty of the state and the General Assembly to provide public schools would remain the same with the only difference being that a community through local action could suspend or re-open its schools as local conditions might require; and that without adoption of the proposals there would be no safety valve to take care of conditions that could become devastating.

In closing my address, I added, "Our public schools need and deserve your support in this critical hour. We ought not, indeed we must not, leave our schools unprotected to be shaken and possibly destroyed by forced integration. Our plan will give to the local communities in North Carolina, as well as to individual parents, an orderly and lawful means to meet the problems which will likely be imposed upon us. In my humble opinion, the safety and well-being of public education in North Carolina demands the passage of the Special Session School Amendment. I urge as strongly as possible that you vote FOR this amendment."

The vote of the people on the Pearsall plan on September 8, 1956, was gratifying. In one of the heaviest votes ever cast in a special election in North Carolina, 471,657 voters favored the amendment to the state constitution and 101,424 were against it, giving a vote of over 80% for the plan.

All of the one hundred counties in North Carolina voted for it. Counties in both the eastern and western sections of North Carolina rolled up substantial majorities in favor of the amendment. One county, Greene, approved the Pearsall plan by a whopping 27-to-1 vote. In the forty-four counties east of Raleigh, where the percentage of Negroes is highest, the vote was 7-to-1 in favor of the proposals. The vote was almost as impressive in the western counties where there are fewer Negroes. The greatest opposition numerically was registered in the urban counties, but approval of the amendment in these areas was still decisive. Winston-Salem was the only city of any size that voted against and the margin there was five in a vote of nearly nine thousand.

I was tremendously pleased and impressed by the vote. The campaign's non-partisan approach was a major factor in the victory. In the light of the violence and turmoil over then current token integration in Tennessee and some extreme legislative measures taken in other states, North Carolinians could take pride in their solid endorsement of a moderate approach to the explosive problems resulting from the decisions of the United States Supreme Court.

With the approval of the amendment to the state constitution to authorize local option elections to close schools in "intolerable situations" and provide public school tuition grants for children not wishing to attend integrated schools, North Carolina had completed its basic policy for public school operations under the Supreme Court's May 17, 1954, decision.

Actually, the state's policy was three-fold, and each prong of policy, though adopted on the state level, was for the use of local areas where segregation-integration problems would arise. The policy included: the Pupil Assignment Act, passed by the 1955 session of the General Assembly, which gave local school boards complete authority in the assignment of children to public schools and made the decisions of the local school boards final as to the schools to which pupils were assigned; the voluntary segregation plan which we advocated in August, 1955, calling on citizens to attend separate schools; and the Pearsall plan with its "safety valves" of local option and tuition grants.

Under the Pupil Assignment Act schools in three North Carolina cities—Charlotte, Greensboro, and Winston-Salem—were voluntarily integrated in the fall of 1957. Although my views on integration were well-known, I emphasized in the week preceding the opening of the schools that the people of North Carolina would not tolerate any lawlessness or violence in connection with the token integration. The integration was accomplished with nothing more than some heckling and one incident of rock throwing. There were no large crowds and no demonstrations. Some white people asked that their children be reassigned to non-integrated schools and this was allowed. In the following years, other North Carolina schools integrated without violence. No schools have been closed.

The problem continued throughout my administration and will probably exist for many years to come. I am very proud of North Carolina and the way it has met this problem, which is one of the most serious it has ever faced. The people were wonderful in their restraint, their moderation, their love for our schools. Working together with true humility of spirit, we in North Carolina made a contribution of which we and our children can be proud.

CHAPTER V

Segregation and
the Nation

THE South in general found an unsympathetic ear in the Republican administration in Washington and sharp and unfavorable criticism from national news media as it worked to solve the problems created by the Supreme Court's decision on school segregation. Fortunately, we in North Carolina were able, as I have just shown, to formulate a moderate approach to keep the peace and at the same time not to defy the court. Most other southern states were not as successful, but possibly they could have averted some of the trouble that developed had the administration then in Washington been a little more considerate.

While we in North Carolina were struggling to preserve the peace and our system of public schools, our efforts were almost completely ignored by northern news media in their search for the more sensational and the more tragic news items. During this time I made several speeches outside North Carolina on what our state was doing. Most were never reported outside my own state.

As a case in point, in June of 1956, while on a six-day industry-hunting expedition to New York City, I was invited to speak before the New York Rotary Club, in which I had served as president in 1946 when I was living in New York. The subject of the talk—segregation—was selected by the club from a list presented them. There was a magnificent audience, packing the grand ball-room of the Hotel Commodore. In attendance were between three hundred and four hundred Rotary Club members from all over New York City, plus representatives from thirty-five states and fifteen overseas nations.

It was a calm and reasonable talk on the segregation problem and North Carolina's approach to the Supreme Court decision. I told them I did not agree with the court's decision and added that, although the other states represented at the meeting might not have the school problem, they might at some other time have on their hands a Supreme Court decision they believed bad. At the end of the thirty-minute talk, I received a standing ovation.

Advance copies of the speech had been sent to all New York newspapers, press associations, and other media. Two representatives of the *New York Times* were present with copies of the speech in their hands while I was speaking, and as I was walking away from the rostrum they came to me with several questions. I gave them full answers. I was pleased that they were interested and more pleased that they were going to tell the story. Despite all of this, however, the next morning there was not one word printed on my speech on a difficult national issue.

A contrasting incident occurred when school boards in Greensboro and Charlotte voluntarily approved token integration at schools in those cities. Negroes entered the Greensboro schools without any trouble or disorder, and the next morning the *New York Times* carried the report of it on page thirty-four in just a couple of inches of space. They apparently did not treat this as news because it was not bad news. The day after the Greensboro schools opened, the Charlotte schools opened. In Charlotte there was no trouble with the school children, but a truck driver's wife taunted some young people and asked them to throw some icicles which had dropped from a passing ice truck at the Negro pupils as they went by. This incident was carried on page one of the *New York Times* with a three-column picture, which I understood the photographer had re-enacted because he did not catch it the first time, and a story on how bad things were in Charlotte.

Several months later, I made a talk to a large group in Orlando, Florida. I told this group, which represented people from all over Florida, of these experiences with the *New York Times* and called the paper by name. I added that this kind of newspaper bias only made it more difficult for those of us who were attempting to find solutions to an already difficult problem. It was hard not to have the support of a great newspaper like the *New York Times*, but it was even harder to put up with such a lack of honesty from a great newspaper.

After the speech I received a call from the editor of the *Orlando Sentinel*. He had been in the audience and expressed interest in the incidents I had related. He was planning to carry an editorial on my speech and wanted to make sure I could back up my statements. I could, of course. He carried the editorial, and soon after I had a letter from Turner Catledge, editor of the *New York Times*, in which he asked for the complete story. I gave it to him and told him how ashamed I was of his paper. He said he simply could not tell why nothing was carried on the New York speech and he lamely tried to explain that they had so much news that they had to pick and choose. He said they had probably made a mistake in judgment. I agreed.

Much good for all concerned could have been accomplished had the national press been fairer. For example, I was invited at a later time to make a speech at the Harvard Law School Forum and there I approached the problem pretty much as I had done in the New York Rotary Club speech. At Harvard we had a distinguished audience and a distinguished panel, including two law professors. I found that the audience and other members of the panel had over-simplified the problem and had assumed that all states were disobeying the law if they did not have Negro children attending white schools.

I quoted the opinion of Judge John J. Parker, chief judge of the federal Fourth Circuit Court of Appeals. He said, "What it [the court] has decided and all that it has decided is that a state may not deny to any person on account of race the right to attend any school that it maintains. . . . Nothing in the Constitution or in the decision of the Supreme Court takes away from the people freedom to choose the schools they attend. The Constitution, in other words, does not require integration. It merely forbids discrimination." His opinion made quite an impression.

The reaction of the Harvard audience was very encouraging. I wished then that audiences all over the nation could have been reached in a calm and reasoned manner on the subject. It could have been done by the national news media. It never was.

During my time as governor, I made it a point and stuck to it not to comment upon or criticize what was being done or contemplated by any other state on the touchy subject of integration. The Southern Governors' Conference, which includes the states from Delaware down through the deep South and westward to Texas and Oklahoma, had also made it a point not to discuss the subject at its meetings. I was chairman of the Southern Governors' Conference in 1957-58 and as chairman was the presiding officer of the session held at Sea Island, Georgia, in September, 1957. This was the time of the Little Rock incident.

Arkansas Governor Orville Faubus, who had already called out the National Guard to curb violence and block integration at Central High School in Little Rock, was the center of attraction as the southern governors gathered for the meeting. At preliminary events in Atlanta, Governor Faubus was cheered at his every appearance, and the press and other communication media followed him wherever he went.

The reason for his popularity outside of Arkansas—his handling of the Little Rock situation—was regrettable. Governor Faubus is a man of fine appearance with a pleasing personality and a good mind. He is perhaps a liberal and I believe he was pushed into the integration situation by powerful forces that he had neither the ability nor the courage to resist. And because of circumstances, he led his people the wrong way. Some schools in Arkansas had already been integrated and the local school board of Little Rock had worked out a plan for integrating some Negro children in the schools. Extremists gained control of the situation there and Governor Faubus went so far as to call out the Arkansas National Guard to prevent integration. He said he was afraid of bloodshed.

When we arrived at Sea Island, Governor Faubus immediately called a press conference. This violated a rule that every governor knew the conference had. A governor was not supposed to call a press conference of his own but was supposed to set up press conferences through the chairman of the conference and the conference secretary. Further, it was traditional that the chairman of the Governors' Conference hold the first press conference in order to set the spirit of the meeting and outline the conference program. Despite the rules Governor Faubus called his conference purposely ahead of mine, which had been previously arranged. His was fully attended, of course, and he received much attention.

At my press conference I told the press that the governors were not going to discuss the school integration situation in any of the official meetings of the conference. We did not discuss it at the meetings. However, the subject was on everybody's mind and was discussed constantly by people outside the official meetings. Everybody was concerned over what was happening in Little Rock.

The situation there grew worse and before the Southern Governors' Conference was over the inevitable happened. President Eisenhower, from his vacation retreat in Newport, Rhode Island, ordered the paratroopers to Little Rock. The action was taken almost without warning. It was a drastic move and, as many of us thought at the time and since, it was a foolish, unnecessary move.

Although it was nearing the end of its session, the Southern Governors' Conference authorized a committee of five to see President Eisenhower and to ask him specifically to withdraw the paratroopers from Little Rock. That was our only assignment. I was made chairman of that committee, and named to it were Governors Leroy Collins of Florida, Frank Clement of Tennessee, Theodore McKeldin of Maryland, and Marvin Griffin of Georgia. Governor Griffin later refused to serve and we were left with a committee of four.

I immediately put in a call for the White House and then began to wait for an answer. We went in to lunch at Sea Island with the reporters pressing for news and for an answer as to when we would see the President. I told them of the call I had put in to the White House and added that I was sure we would get an answer soon. I believed that we should go to Washington immediately and considered it entirely possible we would go directly from Sea Island to see the President. How little did I know the President and his desire for golf. The White House had been left apparently with an almost complete delegation of responsibilities to staff people who evidently did not know of or appreciate the gravity of the situation affecting Little Rock.

During the lunch I kept pushing the Washington call for an answer. Finally as I came out from lunch I had to tell the press that the White House staff could not reach the President or did not want to bother him because he was playing golf. His staff had reported to me that the President would be back in Washington the first of the following week. The delay of several days was arrogant neglect. We could have gone to Newport or Washington and seen the President. Other governors at the conference felt the same way. Governor Faubus had returned to Arkansas. There was nothing else we could do at the time. We went home!

The next few days were long ones. The newspapers, the radio, and the television reported the terrible incidents that were occurring in Little Rock. The whole country was agog, and the world was getting reports and gossip that were destroying the reputation of America. And it was all because a governor had taken a wrong stand and because the President of the United States had also taken a wrong stand.

At the end of September, the Southern Governors' Conference committee met in a Washington hotel suite on a Monday morning before our scheduled meeting with the President at the White House early that afternoon. It was a private meeting and we tried to hammer out a statement to submit to the President. It was decided by the committee that, as chairman, I would present the statement for the committee. Everyone, however, would be free to participate in the discussion. During the morning we were also in contact with the White House and it was decided the discussion with the President would not be on legal matters.

At the White House we were received by Sherman Adams, assistant to the President. In a fairly blunt tone, Mr. Adams told us how we should handle ourselves with the President and then told us who was going to be in the conference. In addition to the four of us, Mr. Adams said the participants would be Frank Bane, secretary of the National Governors' Conference; Attorney General Herbert Brownell; Howard Pyle, assistant to the President, former governor of Arizona, and our liaison with the White House; and himself.

Immediately I took exception to Mr. Adams' list and pointed out that in our telephone conversation that morning we had agreed upon who was to attend the conference and at that time it was decided that Mr. Brownell would not attend. I then added that there would not be a meeting if he were present because we had had a clear understanding with the White House that the discussion would not be on legal matters. We were not there to tell the President he did not have a legal right to send the paratroopers to Little Rock and under these conditions Mr. Brownell was not needed. It would do no good to have him present. Mr. Adams was obviously furious. He excused himself almost without apology, came back in a few minutes and agreed Mr. Brownell would not attend the conference.

President Eisenhower received us cordially. He then began reading a document that had been prepared for him. As he paused during the reading, I broke in and said, "Mr. President, as chairman of this delegation, I am authorized to say one thing. We are simply asking that you remove the paratroopers. We are not questioning your legal rights to send them in. We believe, however, it was bad to send them in and worse to keep them there."

The President then told us about the experience he had had with Governor Faubus a few days earlier at Newport. This was before the governor had called out the Arkansas National Guard and before the President had sent in the paratroopers. That meeting had been arranged by Congressman Brooks Hays of Arkansas who wanted to see peace in his state and the school situation settled. However, an agreement could not be effected between Governor Faubus and the President.

After the southern governors' committee had discussed the problem further with the President and his advisors, Mr. Eisenhower agreed that, if we could get a proper statement from Governor Faubus, assuring that order would be maintained and that force would not be used against students who had been ordered to integrate, then he, the President, would order the paratroopers out of Little Rock. His statement made us feel good. From recent contacts with Governor Faubus, we understood that we might be able to work out something. We felt this would be a victory and believed we could persuade Governor Faubus to do what the President had requested.

Leaving the President and settling down in a conference room, we began to work out the proposed agreement. Mr. Adams brought in a draft that Mr. Brownell had evidently given him. The draft was pretty in its language but it was extremely critical of Governor Faubus and made certain legal points as to the rights of the President to send in the paratroopers. We were able to persuade Mr. Adams to leave out certain of these things and to direct the agreement on the part of Governor Faubus to do what the President had requested. This was, of course, to see that order was maintained and that any of the students who wanted to be in school would not be molested. We finally agreed on a draft of the proposal.

Just as we finished drafting the proposal, President Eisenhower stuck his head in the door of the conference room and said, "Governor Hodges, gentlemen, I want to say to you that you are dealing with an uncertain person in Governor Faubus. You want to be sure that he agrees to what you are proposing." We assured him that we understood the agreement and added that we were certain Governor Faubus would agree to the proposal we had drafted.

Frank Bane and I immediately got Governor Faubus on the telephone and read him the proposed agreement. Governor Faubus made one suggestion and we agreed to make that change. I told the governor that Bane was on the extension and was hearing what we said. Then I asked him if the draft was satisfactory. Governor Faubus said it was and added that he was willing to go along with it. I asked him then if he would confirm this by wire. He said that he would. He asked that the proposal be sent to him by wire and added that he would send it back to us within a few minutes with his approval. "That's fine, Governor Faubus," I declared, "We appreciate it very much and the whole world will be pleased."

The southern governors' committee was pleased with Governor Faubus' decision to approve the proposal. The White House was pleased and the press was waiting. The President's press secretary, James Hagerty, asked that we come into his office to hold a press conference. His office was packed. I read them the proposal, told them of the agreement with Governor Faubus, and that we were now just waiting for his confirmation. Outside the White House a battery of microphones and cameras were set up and I again gave an interview. I emphasized, however, that until the confirmation came from Governor Faubus nothing was official and final. Many of the news corps ignored my warnings and before long the story was out that the Little Rock crisis had been settled.

We went back to the hotel and waited. As we discussed the situation we mentioned the President's warning several times, but we pushed aside the only doubt we had in the light of Governor Faubus' promise to send his approval of the proposal by return wire. We waited an hour, but no message came. I then started the most mysterious and frustrating evening I have ever spent. I was on the telephone for two hours, talking with the governor's office, with his confidential secretary, with his administrative assistant, in fact with practically everybody but Governor Faubus. His office said repeatedly he would call me "back in five minutes." He never did, nor did he ever send a wire approving what he had promised to approve. He never contacted me at all that night or later.

President Eisenhower called, however, between 9:00 and 9:30 P.M. to tell me that Governor Faubus had sent a message to the White House. In it, the President said, Governor Faubus had indicated that he as an individual, not as governor, would do nothing to interfere with a court order. The President told me that Governor Faubus' message was unsatisfactory because there were too many ways Governor Faubus could get around it. The President added that he could not be bound by the agreement that the southern governors' committee had drawn up unless Governor Faubus agreed to it.

I told the President I could not agree with his keeping the paratroopers there. I thought, and I still do, that it would have been better had he ordered the paratroopers out of Little Rock with the warning that if advantage was taken of their absence he would immediately send them back in. However, under the terms of our afternoon agreement I could not disagree with the

President's refusal to go along with the proposal. I was furious at Governor Faubus for his failure to accept a telephone call or to live up to his word. I felt as if I had been on a mountain top trying to aid a fellow man and he had pushed me off a cliff.

Later that evening two of us of the southern governors' committee went on a nationwide broadcast that had been set up to hear of the Little Rock situation and our conference with President Eisenhower. The other two members of the committee declined to go on the air after the agreement failed. I told what had happened, what the problem was, and what the possible consequences might be.

That ended the Little Rock, Governor Faubus, and President Eisenhower episode as far as I was concerned. The whole painful and damaging experience of Little Rock made me thankful that we North Carolinians were anxious to work out our own problems resulting from the anti-segregation decision in an orderly and peaceful manner and in such a way that the federal government would have no cause to send paratroopers to our state.

Despite the difficult time I had explaining the North Carolina approach to the people in other sections of the United States, in November, 1957, I was asked by the United States Information Agency to make a statement on our position in a Voice of America broadcast. The press conference type of interview was later carried over the air to many foreign countries in several languages. It was hoped that our view on the race question would aid in counteracting some of the feeling that was then being stirred up in foreign countries by the Little Rock integration crisis and similar episodes. I later received many congratulatory letters from various parts of the world on the broadcast.

The interviewers during the broadcast were Dr. Diadados Yap, editor of the Manila, Philippines, *Chronicle*, and Jay Jenkins of the *Charlotte Observer*. In answer to a question from Jay, I told of North Carolina's approach to the problem, and then Dr. Yap

asked me to explain "what steps are being taken to solve gradually
this question of integration so that the peoples of Asia, who are
colored people, will get the best idea of just what the stand of
a United States governor is in connection with this problem?"
I answered that I knew there was deep concern all over the world,
but that much of it was because of misunderstanding. I explained:

We in this state and this country are not against any race; we
are not trying to do anything that is bad. We have for a hundred
years lived under a certain arrangement of separate schools where
the states wanted them that way. This recent Supreme Court decision was a very sudden one. It takes a little time to work it out.
There have been acceptances of mixed schools in a very great
number of border states. If given time, if people think right, if
they cut out their race prejudice and hatred in their hearts, then
we will have an understanding in this country just like you
would have in any other country of the world. These things we
would like to have, but it takes time and we cannot do it overnight, and we can't do it by law.

In answer to other questions, I noted that, for a number of
reasons, the average salaries of Negro teachers in North Carolina
were higher than the average salaries of white teachers, and that
we had more Negro teachers in North Carolina than in all the
New England states, and New York, Pennsylvania, and Delaware
put together. As to the school buildings, I noted that the Negroes
actually had better ones because so many of them had been built
recently and that the Negro students were taken care of completely, just like anyone else. The Negro race had made tremendous gains in North Carolina, too. Skilled jobs had opened up
for many Negroes, North Carolina had the largest Negro insurance company, the largest Negro bank in the world, and there
were many evidences of a prosperous Negro middle class.

When asked if I felt the North Carolina approach to the race
problem would be followed generally in other parts of the South,
I answered:

I wouldn't want to say because I can't speak with authority on what is happening. I am just hopeful of this, that I feel that a great majority of the southern people feel as I do, that although their personal feeling may be one thing, they want to obey the law. They want to see Negroes come along rapidly. They want to see their economic status bettered, and I believe that there are literally millions of southerners that feel the same way. Unfortunately, because of the treatment of the press and other situations, we have had a misunderstanding, and we find that some of our extremists in the South are speaking out and giving their own impression of what we believe in.

As the interview drew to a close, I pointed out that the race problem was not limited to the southern area of the United States or even to the United States. There are, I added, such problems all over the world, but "if you have it in your heart to be good to people, you will bring them along just as fast as they can take it." The moderator of the interview said, "In other words, Governor, this problem is certainly not restricted to areas of the southern United States," and I answered: "Not at all." He asked then how I thought it would be worked out. I said:

I would just like to say that we tried in this country twenty-five years ago what is called a noble experiment of prohibition. We tried it for awhile and we had a mess and we finally corrected it. I say this, that if the federal government or any government, wherever it is in the world, tries to push something over and the people are not prepared for it, it will not work. Now, I think the thing for us to do in this country wherever we have this problem is to work it out the very best way we can, always having in mind trying to get along, and I think our whole governmental machinery must understand that we are dealing with human beings and must work slowly and gradually and with good spirit.

There were several other incidents either directly or indirectly stemming from the race situation that received much attention during my administration. One of these involved touring segrega-

"Who touches a hair on yon kingly head—!"

tionist John Kasper of New Jersey who came to North Carolina in August of 1957 when several of our schools were preparing for token integration. At the time Kasper was free on bond awaiting sentence for a criminal contempt of court conviction for interfering with peaceful school integration at Clinton, Tennessee.

I was asked to comment on his visit during one of my weekly news conferences. I replied that I did not know Mr. Kasper, did not care to know him, and added, "From what I have read and heard, I don't think we need him in North Carolina." I stated that "without judging whether recent actions by some local school boards are right or wrong in accepting or rejecting Negro applicants, I want to emphasize that the state and the people of North Carolina will not tolerate any lawlessness or violence in connection with this problem."

Mr. Kasper came to North Carolina anyway. He was jeered from the courthouse lawn in Winston-Salem, but did talk to small groups in Greensboro and Charlotte. Few people paid much attention to him. He was greeted with expressions of displeasure by newspapers, state and local officials, and even by organized segregationists in North Carolina. Mr. Kasper did not stay in North Carolina too long.

Another of these incidents involved the Ku Klux Klan, which became active over the race issue. Oddly enough, however, the incident that brought the Klan to my attention involved not Negroes but Indians. Early in January, 1958, the Klan had a rally at Maxton in Robeson County. Klan Wizard James "Catfish" Cole of Marion, South Carolina, came over the line to appear at the rally, and quite a crowd of hooded figures had gathered to see another cross burning.

A "war party" of Lumbee Indians, incensed by recent cross burnings reportedly directed against their race, swooped down on the rally, screaming and shooting rifles and shotguns in the air. The Klansmen ran for cover and sought safety in ditches, behind cars, and by just plain running. Cole was arrested for inciting a

riot—some of the Klan members had come to the rally armed—
and was later sentenced to prison. Soon after the Indian raid,
there were rumors that members of the Klan, including a number
from South Carolina, were planning another rally in North Carolina. No one was killed at the Maxton rally, but the next time
everyone might not be so lucky.

In a public statement I declared that the Ku Klux Klan had
shown itself to be an organization of violence and intimidation
that would lead to public disorder. I warned the Klan leaders and
the few citizens who might have been beguiled and misled into
joining or giving aid to the Klan that North Carolina's citizens
would not tolerate lawlessness. North Carolina's citizens, I declared, do not want or need an organization whose creed spawns
hate and violence. I pointed out that our sheriffs, police chiefs,
and all local law-enforcement officers would do a good job in
maintaining law and order, but, if they needed any aid, state
officials and agencies stood ready to assist them. There was no
more violence stemming from Ku Klux Klan activities.

In the fall, there was a series of school bombing hoaxes in various communities in North Carolina. Irresponsible people would
call up school officials—mainly at schools that had been integrated
—and report that a bomb was in the school. Naturally, the schools
were emptied and police went in to search the schools. No bombs
were found. However, the disruption and confusion resulting from
such unlawful acts could not be condoned or shrugged off. Each
anonymous bomb hoax was a threat to the security and peace of
our state, our communities, and our entire public school system.

I appealed to every citizen of our state, young and old, to do
what he or she could to prevent any further bomb threats to our
schools. Parents were asked to make certain that their children
understood fully the serious consequences of making such anonymous calls. At the same time, law enforcement agencies brought
in new tracing equipment to detect telephone calls very quickly
and to apprehend the guilty people. The misguided people—either

students who wanted to get out of school or older people who thought such acts would end the limited integration—soon stopped making these threatening calls.

The most overplayed and one of the most interesting and troublesome situations that we faced during my term of office was the sensational Monroe "kissing case." The "case" developed from an incident that occurred in a culvert in the town of Monroe. A little white girl was playing with some other children, including two Negro boys. According to the story told, the Negro youths trapped the little girl in the culvert and would not let her out until she kissed one of them. It was very difficult to get the true facts of the case, but the boys were apprehended and taken before the juvenile court judge. The boy who had forced the kissing had been in trouble before. His mother was aware of these problems but, according to reports, showed no interest. However, the news media demonstrated great interest in the case with results I shall never forget.

The youths were committed to one of our correctional schools, which are among the best in the nation. As the news sped around the world, a campaign of misrepresentation against North Carolina and its court system was started and it stirred reaction almost everywhere. With a little pushing on the part of a few people more interested in publicity than fact, the incident was sensationalized and many of the facts were forgotten as the story spread around the world. My office received hundreds of critical letters and cables from various European countries and other parts of the world, including one from a prominent London clergyman. I insisted that each letter be answered fully and completely and that the person who wrote the letter be requested to write to us further after he had received the explanation and the facts of the case.

This effort on the part of myself and my staff helped the situation somewhat. But much damage had been done, at least temporarily, to North Carolina's good name by the few whose personal positions were bettered by misrepresenting the facts in the case and by those who were extremists on the race question. The truth could never catch up with the distorted story. The two Negro boys served brief terms in the correctional institution and were released. The instigator of the "kissing" incident, whose family had moved to Charlotte, was arrested soon after his release from the correctional institution by Charlotte police on a morals charge, involving a young Negro child.

During the last year of my administration, the sit-in demonstrations started in North Carolina. Greenboro was the first city hit by the sit-ins, but they quickly spread to other cities in North Carolina and the United States. In the movement, Negro and sometimes white students would go into a store that served Negroes at regular merchandise counters but would not serve them sitting down at the lunch counters. To protest this, the students would sit at the lunch counters and wait for service. As they were not served, they continued to wait and pledged to do so "until we are served." There were demonstrations and counter-demonstrations. Violence was held to a minimum but always there was the danger that it would spread.

We put a great deal of time on this problem, first from the standpoint of law and order. We had been fortunate in North Carolina in avoiding the extreme incidents that occurred in other states. Speaking solely of my concern for law and order, I made it perfectly clear that I had no sympathy whatsoever for any group of people who deliberately engaged in activities which any reasonable person could see would result in a breakdown of law and order as well as interference with the normal and proper operation of a private business.

I strongly concurred with a statement by Gordon W. Blackwell, then chancellor of the Woman's College of the University of North Carolina at Greensboro, who said that "in a place when tangible progress is being made in leveling many of the unequal places in democracy, I believe the common cause of better race relations has been set back" by the demonstrations. "The tensions that have been generated now threaten the good relations that have existed between segments of our population," he added. "The good will of substantial elements in the community has been jeopardized to the cause of improving race relations. . . . All of this might have been avoided had negotiation been attempted in the first place."

While the demonstrations continued, my office worked behind the scenes over a period of months in an attempt to work out a peaceful solution. We believed that there was some difference between retail establishments that offered to sell the Negro things in every department except their lunch counters and establishments that never served Negroes at any time. My office talked with representatives of national chain stores and pointed out to them some of the fallacies of their position in the matter. We argued that they had some responsibility for leadership both from the national and local levels through their management. These talks may or may not have done any good.

Generally these demonstrations and counter-demonstrations were peaceful. Some of the firms concerned did open up their lunch counters to members of all races, and the situation gradually quieted down. I do think that North Carolina again set an example in the way it worked out this troublesome problem of the sit-ins. The people rose to the occasion, and cooler heads of both races prevailed and did the good job that is characteristic of the people of our great state.

I want to say again that I am extremely proud of North Carolina and its citizens for the way in which it is handling its integration problems and other social and economic problems that confront it. Wherever I go, either in the United States or abroad, I hear complimentary remarks about North Carolina and the way it meets and seeks to solve problems of this type.

CHAPTER VI

Pushing Politics
Off the Highways

I HAD been sworn in only a few days in the fall of 1954 when I had my first official meeting as governor with Highway Commission Chairman A. H. "Sandy" Graham of Hillsboro. Oddly enough, this meeting came about because of a problem at the State Art Museum. State Treasurer Edwin Gill, who was working with the Art Museum project, came by my office and said the Art Museum group was having a problem with the Highway Commission chairman in connection with the Highway Building, which joined the Art Museum. As I recall, it had something to do with a connecting door. Mr. Gill asked if I would go over with him and a committee to see the chairman of the Highway Commission. I agreed.

Mr. Graham and I had been good friends, both on a personal and political basis, up until the previous year or two, but since that time I had seen very little of him. In my opinion, he is one of the most forthright and honest men in the state. At times, he can be a little stubborn, but, of course, there is nothing wrong with that. The Art Museum people discussed with the chairman of the Highway Commission the connecting door. Mr. Graham was somewhat imperious and let me and the committee know he was running the Highway Commission. The implication was that it was somewhat apart from the governor's control—or the control of anyone except his commission.

In the next few days, the question of air conditioning and other improvements to state buildings came up in discussions with various department and agency heads. The statement was made to me by another department head that the Highway Commission had put air conditioning in its building and did anything else it wanted to without having to check with the Budget Bureau. I was amazed. Immediately the budget officials were called in and they said that this was substantially correct. In spite of the fact that the Highway Commission was spending over $100 million a year, I was told the highway officials never spent more than a few minutes with the Budget Bureau when they were having their budget reviewed. The reason for this, I assume, was that the Advisory Budget Commission and the Budget Bureau were primarily interested in the general fund that supported the other departments of the state.

As long as the Highway Department officials could point out that their revenues from gas, licenses, and other special sources would not leave a deficit, they could do pretty much what they wanted to, according to the reports I received. Some of the other state departments, which might spend only $1 million to $10 million, would have to fight the Budget Bureau for every nickel of it. For instance, the Wildlife Commission, which theoretically should be far more separate from the regular state budget than the Highway Commission, had to justify anything it did and was even refused a good carpet for its director's office because the Budget Bureau considered it too expensive.

Meanwhile, I had been reading in the papers about an extensive study that had been made by a group of consulting engineers for the Highway Department. It had cost $110,000 and was to determine the state's road needs of the future. That was about all I knew until one day in January, 1955, Mr. Graham came into my office flashing a report in his hand. "We want your support for a $150 million bond issue for building some primary roads," he said. "I won't even sit down. This has all been worked

"Mind if I look under the hood first?"

out and I just want your permission." I asked him to sit down, told him I could not move quite that fast, and said that I would like to have more information.

I told him I wanted to check his proposed program as I was checking everything else in preparation for the budget message for the soon-to-convene General Assembly. Noting that the $150 million bond issue was not in the budget message, I told Mr.

Graham that I would send certain questions over to him about the proposal. And, I added, the bond issue seemed to be, on the face of it, totally unnecessary. He sat down, stayed much longer, and apparently was not too happy about my reception of the bond proposal. Later we had an exchange of views in writing.

In the next few days, I learned that the State Highway and Public Works Commission had employed the New York engineering firm of Parsons, Brinckerhoff, Hall, and MacDonald to make a survey of the state's highway needs. On the basis of this firm's report, the Highway Commission proposed to spend $610 million in the next six years to modernize primary highways and bridges. The proposed $150 million bond issue, plus a raise in truck and auto taxes and fees, was to help bear the cost of the program. In view of its importance and the publicity given to it, I did not discuss it in my regular budget message to the General Assembly but sent a special message to the two houses on January 20, 1955.

The unsatisfactory answers I had received from Mr. Graham to my inquiries about the project further convinced me that much of what the commission had recommended was, to say the least, premature. As I told the legislature in the special message: "I must and do recommend that there be no authorization for a highway bond issue at the present time." As to the proposed methods for meeting the increasing highway revenues, I added, "I am unable to express an opinion other than that, on the surface at least, some of them seem to have merit." The message concluded with these three paragraphs:

As I have previously emphasized, highway problems are one of my chief concerns, and you may be assured that I shall make every effort in support of a highway program which I feel is satisfactory. In the meantime, I would like to advise with the Roads and Finance Committees of the House and Senate in studying our whole highway set-up, including the present operations and the Highway Commission's plan for the future.

In my opinion, it is time that the highway fund be handled

as an integral part of state government and not as a separate, un-integrated enterprise. It has been suggested that the State Highway and Public Works Commission ought to have its expenditures and its programs carefully reviewed and approved by the Budget Bureau just as any other agency of state government. It is now spending $200 million each biennium, or one-third of the total cost of the entire state government. State budget officials ought to know more about the highway management and its plans, both current and long-range. The Highway Commission should submit its budgets in the same detail that is required of all other agencies. I propose, in the interest of the state as a whole, that the Highway Department be treated in the same manner as other departments of the state government.

I should also like the aid of the General Assembly in devising means whereby the Highway Commission will be encouraged to function as an agency dealing with the highway needs of the state as a whole and not as fourteen more or less autonomous units. Until this takes place, we are not likely to have long-range planning or statewide highway construction designed to provide a state highway system such as I believe is wanted by this legislature and the people of the state as a whole. Naturally, I would want to have the Highway Commission's advice and assistance in all of these matters.

Instead of the long-range highway building program proposed by the Highway Commission, later during the session I suggested that the state undertake, for the time being at least, a program of road building in two-year stages on a pay-as-you-go basis. The reasoning behind this was that at the end of two years, some of the doubtful factors—such as the new federal road program and toll road feasibilities—would probably be definite enough to permit a review of the necessities of our highways in a manner that could be expected to give the 1957 General Assembly a solid foundation upon which to build a long-range program.

Along with the two-year pay-as-you-go suggestion, the highway commissioners were requested to prepare and make public specific projects that would be undertaken during the coming two years. They complied with this request and, for the first time in a generation, interested North Carolinians knew in advance the locality and nature of primary highway construction that was to take place during the immediate years ahead.

During the early months of 1955, I continued to study the operations of the State Highway Department. In checking into this matter further with David Coltrane of the Budget Bureau, I found that biennium after biennium the chairman of the Highway Commission would present a budget showing the same, or approximately the same, revenues projected for the next two years as had been approved in the preceding two years. And practically no questions were ever asked about the budget proposals of the Highway Department. Sometimes it took as little as fifteen minutes to pass a $200 million highway budget.

There was, of course, a reason for this presentation of a budget which projected about the same revenues for one biennium as had been approved for the past biennium. All monies collected beyond the "official estimate" of the Highway Commission chairman's budget went to the governor as a "governor's surplus fund." In many cases, we were told, this "governor's surplus fund" was used for political purposes. This was a great windfall for the governor. I doubt if many roads were built with any of this money on a strictly political basis or if any of the roads so built were not needed. But it was certainly evident that in several administrations such funds had been used for political influence.

A prominent political appointee, then in state government, told me that he had worked in a previous campaign, and in order to get his vote and influence in the next gubernatorial election, the governor asked him where he wanted his road built. And the man told me that he picked out a place on his farm where a road would bring him the greatest added value. The man further told me that the governor then issued instructions to have the stakes put down exactly where his friend had requested it, and that the road was built.

This incident could be multiplied many times and, I was told, by more than one administration. I have no charges to make, but it was generally understood that this kind of thing was done. There were cases in which the stakes were put down and then taken up after the primary or after the election. I do not know of a case of outright dishonesty on the part of any state officials or highway commissioners in connection with the building of highways in North Carolina, but there definitely had been too much favoritism and, until recent years, very little forward planning.

Others were concerned about politics in the Highway Department. During the 1955 General Assembly I was approached by many legislators who said that they would like to change the organization of the commission from divisions to a statewide system and also would like to change certain commissioners. They thought these changes should be made at once. This, however, was not the proper way to bring about changes, even if they were badly needed. My suggestion was that we leave the Highway Commission in the hands of its present chairman and members of the commission until their terms expired and meanwhile have a group of legislators and other citizens study the Highway Commission set-up fully and make recommendations before any action was taken.

The General Assembly followed my suggestion and authorized a study group for highway matters. It was my pleasure to appoint the Honorable Claude Currie of Durham, many times state senator and president pro-tem of the Senate, as chairman of the study commission.*

This commission worked very hard at its assigned task. It

* Other distinguished citizens named to the study commission were Senator T. Clarence Stone of Stoneville, Representative James Stikeleather of Asheville, Representative Carroll Holmes of Hertford, Representative B. T. Falls, Jr., of Shelby, Harold Makepeace of Sanford, and John G. Clark of Greenville.

visited every highway division in the state, talked at length with the chairman and every member of the State Highway Commission, reviewed the work of the department, and generally made a careful, thoughtful study of the problems facing the highway agency. The study group had the services of a full-time staff man and they spent many days in meetings and discussion before it was ready to make a preliminary report.

The study commission in its preliminary report pointed to a statute, section 136-1, which read: "It is the intent and purpose of this section that all of said Commission and the chairman shall represent the State at large and not be representative of any particular division. It shall be the duty of the Commission as a whole to select the road projects to be constructed or reconstructed which now or shall constitute a part of the primary highway system of the State. The intent and purpose of this section is that there shall be maintained and developed a State-wide highway system commensurate with the needs of the State as a whole and not to sacrifice the general State-wide interest to the purely local desires of any division."

The report then stated that the people of North Carolina had a right to expect that the Highway Commission operate on a state basis as outlined in the statute, instead of a divisional basis as was the practice at that time. The study group explained that there had been a gradual departure from the principles set forth in the statute over the preceding thirty years. Keeping this statewide approach in mind, the study commission gave me a tentative recommendation that the State Highway Commission be reduced from its then fourteen members to a much smaller statewide policy-making group, with an outstanding man as an executive-administrator to run the organization under the policy set by the commission.

I agreed with this approach as being more in keeping with the proper management of a state agency spending over $100 million a year of our tax money. The statewide approach was important.

The fourteen members of the Highway Commission had been selected to represent the fourteen divisions in the state, and these divisions were tied together with the engineering divisions of the department. This meant, in effect, that to a very great extent the highway budget was split fourteen ways and that each commissioner was a king in his own division.

The final suggestion for reorganizing the Highway Commission was that no commissioner have an assignment or responsibility or authority in any area or any engineering division. Because of his place of residence he would naturally be carrying on public relations and counseling highway people in his area. But he would not have the authority alone to build a road or even change a road.

The recommended executive-administrator would be a full-time director instead of a full-time chairman. He would presumably be a man of experience in engineering, planning, and administration. He would be responsible for the work of the Highway Department and would report to the commissioners, who would be responsible only for over-all policies. This made up a strong but essentially simple organization that would get the job done and give the greatest service to the greatest number of people.

Another major change in the Highway Commission's activities was in the area of secondary roads. Instead of being left to the complete discretion of the Highway Commission, the study group recommended that the construction and maintenance of secondary roads be put entirely on a priority basis determined by formula. Every secondary road throughout the state would be checked and a point system would be set up that would rate each road by such factors as traffic density, number of houses served, use of road by school buses, and other aspects of public convenience. The development of each road would be determined by its total rating.

Every mile of road would be listed and would have a priority number in its particular county. A list of the roads would be posted in the courthouse of each of the hundred counties so that any citizen, with or without influence, could, by looking either in his newspaper or in the courthouse, find out if and when his road would be paved. He would not have to get somebody to do it for him. And his influence—or lack of it—would not be a factor any more on whether a road would be paved.

There was a good deal of debate in the 1957 General Assembly over the proposed changes in the Highway Department. But it finally was adopted by both the Senate and the House of Representatives and became law. The statute required that the state be divided into geographic areas without regard to engineering division boundaries, and that one or more commissioners be made responsible for public relations generally in each area.*

Colonel William T. Joyner was named chairman of the new Highway Commission and his appointment was well received over the state. He served only a short while, however, and then resigned for personal reasons. The Honorable Melville Broughton, Jr., was named to succeed him and he continued in that position throughout my administration. W. F. Babcock was named director of highways. He was at the time of his appointment professor of transportation at North Carolina State College in Raleigh and was a consultant to about fifty towns in the state on their highway planning and traffic problems. He was exceptionally qualified for the new position.

Harold Makepeace of Sanford was appointed director of secondary roads to give his full time and attention to the state's vast system of secondary roads. He had managed my campaign for governor in 1956 and I knew I would be accused of playing politics with this appointment. Nevertheless, I appointed him because I knew how completely honest he was and how well he worked with people. He was given specific instructions to pay

---

* With this in mind, I appointed to the Highway Commission Colonel William T. Joyner of Raleigh, Ralph Howland of Elkin, E. L. White of Wilmington, Fletcher Gregory of Weldon, Cutler Moore of Lumberton, Robert Bunnelle of Asheville, and Lee White of Concord.

no attention to any proposition made to him on a political basis.

He owed nothing to anybody, including the governor. Harold emphasized this, as it was reported to me sometime later, when people from my own county of Rockingham were asking him to build a road for them. It apparently was not justified under the point system and he told the Rockingham people so. And he added, "I'm not going to build the road. I don't even care if Governor Hodges gives me instructions to do it."

It was a difficult job to sell initially the idea of an impersonal selection of rural or secondary roads to be built or improved. It was my conviction that North Carolinians, even those who might not get their pet projects taken care of, would support a system of road building as long as they were satisfied that all requests having to do with roads were decided on the same basis for everyone without favoritism or political bargaining. Harold Makepeace and his group, backed by the Highway Commission, did a great job of selling this concept—and acting on it.

We were able to make the point system work, because the man in the street—the average Tar Heel—believed in it. The average man did not mind getting a "no" to his own request if he was sure he was being treated like everyone else, and if he was sure that someone else with political influence would not have an advantage over him. It naturally took time and energy to sell this idea to the people because they had been used to talking to the neighborhood commissioner and getting his "yes" or "no" answer.

The difference between the two systems, and the unfairness of the old division system, is shown by the record. Under the old division system, in one county where a highway commissioner lived over 90% of all the secondary roads had been paved. In another county with a different political situation and where no commissioner had ever lived—I believe this was Wilkes County—only a small percentage of the roads had been paved. Under the statewide point system, this latter county got several hundred thousand dollars in one year, while the county that had previously been given preferences because of its commissioner got practically nothing because it did not need it.

The new seven-member Highway Commission, headed by Chairman Broughton, held hundreds of meetings with county commissioners and other groups all over the state to discuss the secondary road system and the planning of all roads. In the latter part of 1959, the Highway Commission came out with a fifteen-year plan of roads for North Carolina, and it covered every mile of primary road in the state. Mr. Babcock was one of the nation's experts in highway planning and he spent countless hours with his aides in going over the whole highway system in North Carolina, especially the primary system, to see where we could get the most for our money.

The change in the State Highway Commission to one with a statewide concept and the addition of the point system in the secondary road system were big steps forward for North Carolina. They were not accomplished without some hard feelings. I found great resentment on the part of the commissioner from New Hanover County because I would not reappoint him to the new Highway Commission of seven members. Nearly all of the other fourteen commissioners were perfectly willing to retire, as I had purposely allowed them to stay on for the full lengths of their appointments by Governor Umstead, but one or two of them had other projects they wanted to finish and they resented my not putting them on the new commission.

After very careful consultation with the study commission and with friends in the General Assembly and elsewhere, I had come to the firm conclusion that I could not afford to appoint any of the old commissioners to the new Highway Commission. This decision I made in spite of the fact that several of the fourteen commissioners were very close personal friends of mine. That this decision was correct, we found out later, because in many cases various people came to the new commission or to me and said, in effect, so-and-so promised us he would build our road and we want you to make good on his promise. We pointed out to them that we would build the roads according to needs, that such a commissioner had no right, under the law, to make a promise, and that the law was still on the books after thirty years. It did not do any good to point out to these people that commissioner after commissioner disregarded this law, and it had become the tradition to divide the roads up by letting commissioners have such power. Again, I want to say I do not know of anybody who actually was dishonest in building roads and I do not know that any roads were built that were absolutely unnecessary, since North Carolina's road needs were so great—but the system certainly was not fair nor was it well administered.

Many of my friends could not understand that I would not make a little exception in their case. They would say, "My friends in the governor's office in the past did not hesitate to do me a favor." My reply: "I can't make any exception, otherwise the system breaks down. You simply have to abide by the procedures and rules set down for the state as a whole." Most of those who tried to get favors came to respect me for taking that position, but there were several who were quite disgruntled and who remained sullen and somewhat unfriendly for the remainder of my term.

It is, of course, possible to make regulations that are so strict that they would be ineffectual and silly; and it is entirely possible that where a system is set up, as we set it up, that requires absolute equality and the treating of everybody alike, perhaps an appeals board should be created to reconsider decisions about roads which had been turned down on the technical point system. But I would hate to see the state get away from the broad and basic principle that roads should be built on needs rather than influence. And I think the great majority of people are happy to abide by a regulation or law if they feel that they are treated like everybody else.

I recall an incident that occurred fairly early in my administration that illustrates the need and the desirability for a state or a chief executive to have a principle and a rule that applies to all alike. Paul Johnston, who in the early days of the administration had an office at the rear of my office, came in the door smiling and said, "Governor, I've just had an interesting telephone conversation with a man from New Jersey." Paul had received a telephone call from a man who said, "I'm Senator So-and-So from the State Senate of New Jersey, and I was traveling in your state of North Carolina on U.S. 301 going north beyond Rocky Mount and one of your patrolmen gave me a ticket. I'm just calling to tell you to have Governor Hodges fix it for me." Paul remonstrated mildly and said, "This isn't the kind of thing we do in North Carolina." The man said, "I said you ask Governor Hodges if he wouldn't handle this for me because I'm Senator So-and-So." Paul said, "If you'll let me open the door leading to his office and hear me tell him, you can hear the explosion."

The man hung up, but before he did, Paul had had a chance to say to him, "Things like that are not done in this administration in North Carolina and it's not done in North Carolina generally. You will probably be surprised to know, Senator, that we have a senior United States senator who was given a ticket for speeding in North Carolina, we had a congressman from North Carolina who was treated likewise, that the secretary of state, I believe it was, had the same experience, and the governor's own son was recently given a ticket for traveling thirty-five miles in a twenty mile speed zone." In spite of all this information, the senator said he thought the governor would take care of him and that was when Paul referred to the explosion.

After I had been in office a short while, a very prominent member of a state board who had been appointed by either Governor Umstead or Governor Scott called me up and said, "Governor, I have a very special friend, prominent in my community, who has lost his driver's license because of drunk driving, and we'd like to get it restored." I called the man by his first name and I said,

"You know very well that I wouldn't do a thing like that." He said, "Governor, I've done it a half dozen times before." "Well," I said, "you'll never do it while I'm here. I wouldn't restore a license that had been taken away on a lawful basis by the court for anybody in the state, including my own family." And I never did. I think my fellow citizens will be glad to know that we practically never had a request after that—the word got around the state.

The State Highway Patrol and Ed Scheidt, the director of motor vehicles, and those under him who were in command of the patrol knew that the governor was supporting them, that he would not allow favoritism, that he would not ask for special favors. I believe that almost immediately there was a boost in morale, a greater feeling of pride and prestige in them because they knew they were with an organization that was backed up. True, they knew they were having trouble with certain courts and certain judges and certain solicitors, but on the whole the administration was backing them.

Not directly connected with this kind of thing but as a total result of its outstanding work, the State Highway Patrol won several national prizes for best administration, best enforcement, and best education of the public on safety. I have been with the highway patrol in many states and never have I dealt with any or had experience with any that matched the North Carolina Highway Patrol. It is high-grade; it has a great spirit, a wonderful morale. It would be a sad day if any of these were impaired. Law and order, law enforcement, equality before the law, the principle of treating everybody alike, all these things go to make a great state. North Carolina is well known as that kind of a state.

As lieutenant governor, I had become acutely aware of another problem involving the Highway Commission. This was the question of separating the state prisons from the Highway Commission. The prisons had been an appendage of the Highway Commission since the early 1930's. During those tough days of the depression, the prison system had been joined with the Highway Department as one of the many things the state did to cut down on the cost of government. Some of these depression reorganization measures turned out to be good, but others did not. Putting the prisons under the Highway Commission was one of the latter. The prison system had been run by the highway people with very little attention to good prison administration or modern penal methods. Their primary goal seemed to be to keep the nearly ten thousand prisoners busy, most of them working on the highways and streets of the highway system.

Generally speaking, a good job had been done as far as it went. There had been few difficulties and practically no riots or serious disturbances. But our prison system was not building people. Prisoners were being brought back over and over to serve time. And after they had served their time, they were sent out without much training or much hope. The highway people were, of course, primarily interested in highways and the politics connected with these highways, and not in the prisons or the prisoners.

With this in mind, the 1953 General Assembly had asked its Commission on Reorganization of State Government to consider the feasibility of separating the prison system from the State Highway Commission. The commission was studying this matter in November, 1954, at a meeting in Chapel Hill the Friday after I was inaugurated as governor. I stopped in on my way to Leaksville and found that the commission was about ready to complete its deliberations and that its members had decided, after a discussion some days before with Governor Umstead, that they would not recommend prison separation.

This discouraged me because it looked as if the advice and consent of the governor had caused them to decide to take the easy way out. It was a tough proposition, but certainly one deserving thorough study and consideration. I asked the commission at this meeting if it would not make a report without prejudice on the matter of prison separation. That, at least, would allow me to appoint a special commission from the legislature to study cost of separation and to make further recommendations. The commission was extremely kind to the new governor and agreed to do so.

In its report, the commission found two major obstacles in the way of immediate and complete separation of the prison system from the Highway Commission. One was the problem of finding suitable employment for the prisoners, and the other was the problem of financing the prison system from the general fund in the event that complete separation were accomplished. The commission concluded, too, that any improvements in the prison system which could be achieved independently during the coming biennium could also be achieved by operating the prison system within the Highway Department.

In my message to the General Assembly on January 6, 1955, I stressed the importance of this report and joined with the commission in recommending certain interim measures. They were designed to continue the improvement of the prison system. Among the measures was one to transfer administrative and executive powers and duties from the Highway Commission to the prison director, with administrative rules and regulations to be approved by the Prison Advisory Council as well as by the Highway Commission and the governor.

The director of prisons would be appointed for a four-year period, starting one year after a new governor came into office. He could be removed only after notice and for cause. The director would have the power to appoint subordinate prison personnel, and supervisory workers would be forbidden to engage in political activity or collection of party funds. These recommendations were introduced in the General Assembly in early February. The measure had my backing along with that of the Highway Commission, the Prison Department, and legislators generally. It was enacted into law without any particular opposition.

It was a step in the right direction, but the complete separation of the prison system from the Highway Commission was needed.

The Commission on Reorganization of State Government recommended that continuing detailed studies be made, particularly as to costs of the present operation, to determine the feasibility of complete separation. The resolution by the General Assembly directed the chairman of the Highway Commission, the chairman of the Prison Advisory Council, and the director of prisons to determine the feasibility of separation and to submit a report to me for transmission to the 1957 General Assembly. These three officials engaged the Institute of Government of the University of North Carolina to coordinate this research and prepare reports upon measures taken, results obtained, and facts determined. Mr. Lee Bounds headed the institute's study and did a most thorough and commendable job on this report and in helping with our prison problem generally.

Work on this study got underway immediately. The Highway Commission began estimating its requirements for prison labor and products over the predictable future, devising a formula for fixing a fair rate of pay for prison labor hired and identifying property that would be transferred to a separate prison system. The Prison Department assumed the responsibility for determining, with the assistance of the Prison Advisory Council, the number of prisoners for whom constructive work would have to be found in the years ahead and the potential market for prison labor and prison products. The Prison Department also worked on budget estimates for the prison system operating under the Highway Commission and a second set of budget estimates for a separate department.

Long-range planning for the prison system was not easy because there was no satisfactory method of predicting changes in the size and composition of the inmate population. At that time, 1956, there were in our state prison system 9,700 male prisoners. Of three estimates made, the medium one predicted there would be 11,300 male prisoners in the system by 1960, 13,100 by 1965,

15,100 by 1970, and 17,400 by 1975. These figures were not very encouraging, but they were presumably realistic and had to be considered carefully in any long-range planning for the Prison Department.

The general statutes declared that it is public policy to provide for the gainful employment of all able-bodied inmates of the state prisons. Priority for the labor of male inmates was given to road work, and all who could be economically employed in such work had to be so employed with the State Highway Commission. Inmates not needed on the roads could be used for work on prison farms, prison industries, forestry work, or hired to other state agencies, counties, or municipalities.

In years past the Highway Commission had found work in road maintenance and related activities for as many as eight thousand male prisoners. As long as road work required a great amount of hand labor the use of prisoners on this scale was economically feasible for the state. By the mid-fifties, however, machines could do a better job in less time and at a lower cost on most operations formerly performed with hand labor. It was estimated that not more than six thousand prisoners could be economically employed in road work in 1956, although another one thousand were being accepted by the Highway Commission because other employment could not be found for them at the time.

Prison industries—as long as they did not compete with private industry—were recognized as being able to serve a useful and profitable part in the operation of our prison system. A survey which the state made recommended that we recognize that well-equipped and well-managed industries manufacturing products of good quality for sale under the state-use system were profitable to the state and valuable as vocational training for prisoners; that we establish a division of industries in the Prison Department under a qualified officer responsible directly to the director of prisons; and that we develop a diversified industrial system manufacturing products for sale to state, county, and municipal institutions and agencies and by vigorous salesmanship take full advantage of the legitimate market they represent.

Soon after these recommendations were made improvements began in prison industry. Production increased substantially. A re-invigorated soap plant was put into operation and the metal plant got busy handling license tags. A new sewing room was constructed at the Woman's Prison. In an effort to step up the production of our state-use industries, as well as the sales of these prison products, George Randall, Jr., of Mooresville, a former member of the General Assembly from Iredell County, was employed to work with the Prison Department as a special consultant in the prison industries field. It was his job to promote sales of products and services, coordinate production, and investigate possibilities for new or expanded operations.

In the period between the 1955 General Assembly and that in 1957 the Prison Department improved greatly. However, it was still under the control of the Highway Commission. Our desire to separate the prison system from the Highway Commission continued because the prison system needed its own board members instead of having to depend on the scanty attention it received from the highway people. People about the state, in this period between sessions of the General Assembly, were beginning to see the need for this. They told their legislators about it.

The effort to separate the state prison system from the Highway Commission supervision was successful in the 1957 General Assembly. A bill was enacted that created an independent prison system. It set up a State Prison Department and transferred to it all powers of prison control and management and all prison properties formerly held by the Highway Commission. In spite of our recommendation that the cost of the prisons be borne by the General Fund, the Highway Fund remained the source of monies to meet prison expenditures in excess of earnings. The transfer was officially made July 1, 1957.

The Prison Advisory Council was abolished. A seven-member

policy-making State Prison Commission and a full-time director
of prisons responsible for administrative management of the
prison system was formed. Colonel William F. Bailey, appointed
director of prisons under the Highway Department in 1953, was
appointed as the first director of the new Prison Department.
Later George Randall, who had became chairman of the Board
of Paroles, was named to the position when Colonel Bailey resigned.

Putting the prison system under its own board took away the
political flavor and raised substantially the morale of the prison
staff. It also gave us a start toward some real rehabilitation work.
The majority of the prisoners continued to work on the roads;
but others began to do forestry work, and others, in increasing
numbers, were employed in prison industries and agriculture on
prison farms. Others could be used under contract with any person or group of persons for forestry work, soil erosion control and
the like, if the work was certified by the director of the Department of Conservation and Development. The prisoners would still
be under the supervision and control of the Prison Department.

The 1957 General Assembly also authorized the State Prison
Department to grant work-release privileges to misdemeanants
under the recommendation of the sentencing judge. The plan
allowed a prisoner to work on a regular job outside the prison
provided he spend each night and each week end in jail or in
prison. The plan had been developed after a study of a system
in Wisconsin, which left it up to the counties to use or not use
the Work Release Program. In North Carolina, we went a step
further and enacted the program on a statewide basis. North
Carolina was the first state in the union to offer this opportunity
to prisoners on a statewide basis but other states soon saw the
merits of the program.

The Work Release Program was relatively weak in 1957 but it
was a beginning. It was tried first in a few carefully selected

camps with suitable facilities close to the major cities, and then only on an experimental basis. It was a start on a good plan. The 1959 legislature realized this and expanded the law considerably. It allowed prisoners with a prior record to take advantage of the program, including felons with up to a five-year sentence. The Board of Paroles, as well as the courts, was authorized to recommend prisoners for the program. This action, of course, expanded the program quite a bit.

For a prisoner to be eligible for the Work Release Program, he had to be an honor-conduct-grade prisoner or be qualified to be in that grade, and his record in prison had to be good. The director of prisons had to approve his application. The approval came after the prisoner secured or maintained employment with a reputable firm or person. The jobs were all investigated by the Prisons Department. The prisoner continued to be housed at a prison unit or other facility near his place of work and was released only during the time he was actually at work.

A prisoner working under this plan received the same pay from the employer as any other worker doing the same type of work. However, the prisoner was required to turn over his pay to the superintendent of the prison unit, and he, in turn, sent the pay to the supervisor of prisoner job placement who turned it over to the prison accounting office for disbursement. The Prison Department kept a part of the prisoner's salary for maintaining the prisoner and for transportation to and from his job. The charge was $2.25 a day for maintenance and $1 a day for transportation. The prisoner received enough of his earnings for personal expenses. The remainder went to support his dependents and pay debts he might owe; and any balance was put in a trust fund to be turned over to him on his release.

The Work Release Program has grown by leaps and bounds. In 1957 and 1958, because of the limited scope of the program, only a few inmates had the opportunity to take advantage of it. In the fall of 1958, a prisoner job placement section was created in the

Prisons Department and Garland B. Daniel was made its supervisor. The following year, 1959, the scope of the program was enlarged and forty-five prisoners were placed in the program. In 1960, sixty-five more inmates were placed on jobs. It was beginning to grow and in 1961 there were 240 prisoners placed in the program. Because of seasonal employment and other factors, the average number under the program has been between 125 and 150 prisoners at one time.

The earnings of the inmates under the work-release program are impressive. They earned $1,902 in 1957, $5,449 in 1958, $33,655 in 1959, $55,549 in 1960, and in 1961 their earnings jumped to $137,469. The economic value of the program has been much more than this figure. The prisoners working under the program pay their own expenses in prison, they relieve the Welfare Department of some, if not all, of the expense of supporting their families, and they pay off their debts. For every hundred inmates working under the Work Release Program, it is estimated that the state saves about $250,000 annually.

It has many other advantages, too. From the employer's standpoint, the program assures him good and dependable workers, who show up for work on time and who do not have any Monday morning problem because of a too-long weekend. For the members of the prisoner's family, it is a source of pride because, in many cases, it ends their complete dependence on welfare and gives them hope for a better future after their loved-one is released from prison.

The big advantage of the Work Release Program is, of course, to the individual prisoner. Its rehabilitation value is tremendous. The inmate under the program is out working on a regular job and is paying his own way. He has a sense of security as well as a sense of responsibility. And, too, it gives the prisoner a strong hope for the future. In many cases, he has the job when he is released from prison. Even if that job is not waiting for him he has a new faith and a new confidence in the future. This faith and confidence was exhibited in a letter to the supervisor of the Work Release Program, Mr. Daniel, from a prisoner who worked under it. It read, in part:

Dear Sir,

This is a word of thanks to you and your assistants for the recent consideration given me. I am now on work release, and I cannot express in words my appreciation to you . . . and the Parole Board. As I cannot express my appreciation in words, I shall express it in my work. The faith and consideration you have placed in me shall not be in vain.

I shall do my best to make parole so that I can go to college. I have determined in my heart to pay my debt to my state and clear my name by asking God for his forgiveness.

Again may I thank you, sir, and thank God for you and your consideration.

That letter and others like it are worthy tributes to the Work Release Program. The program can be expected to almost double in size annually during the next few years. It will mean untold savings to the state and to the counties, and it will offer much for the prisoners and their families. The true worth of the Work Release Program, however, will be measured by the number of North Carolinians who determine in their hearts to pay their debt to society, clear their names, and make contributions as useful citizens to their state. This program, started in such a modest way, may turn out to be one of the most significant things done by the state in human rehabilitation and in common sense handling of its prisoners.

CHAPTER VII

The Business
of Being Governor

THE campaign I waged for lieutenant governor, which brought me into state government, was the only political fight of consequence I had. Although I was never really accepted by the political pros of the state, I hope and believe that they respected me and my service to North Carolina. L. Y. "Stag" Ballentine, our experienced agriculture commissioner, took great pleasure in boasting that he was a politician whenever someone said to him that "Governor Hodges is not a politician."

Of course I was a politician and still am; but I believed and usually practiced an accepted axiom: "Good government is the best politics." This does not mean I was above politics or was not interested in working through or with politicians. Actually, I did this regularly but tried not to make a public show of it. I felt then as I feel now that I could do a better job quietly and with less show of partisanship. This was true in the state and on the national scene, especially since much of my work was with industrialists and businessmen, many of whom are independent and too many of whom are Republicans. I have never tried to make out to any of them that I was anything but a loyal Democrat, and they all knew that.

An example of this came when we were trying to get a large

plant to locate in the state. I had a call from the president of the company and he said, "I see you (it was during the national campaign of 1960) are going all the way with those fellows, and I don't like it." I answered him, "You are considering building a plant in North Carolina. Don't you like the way I have tried to handle things in the state and don't you think the state has a good business climate?" He said he was quite satisfied. "Well," I continued, "I shall continue supporting the Democratic ticket because I believe in the party's principles and I want to help in every way I can to see that the party gives the best service to the nation." Yes, the plant was built in North Carolina.

In one of the eastern counties during the latter part of my administration, I asked to meet with the county executive committee of the party. The chairman of the committee is supposed to have said, "Well, he is starting mighty late." We met, however, and had a good political meeting. Still, the chairman was right in a way. I simply had not taken the time on my hundreds of trips to all parts of the state to visit all the political leaders.

It is true the political pros did not accept me, but there were several outstanding exceptions. One of these is the present United States Senator B. Everett Jordan, who was state Democratic chairman when I ran for my first public office. I discussed with him almost everything of a political nature, and the same was true of John Larkins and Woodrow Jones, both of whom served as state Democratic chairmen. Certainly my legislative liaison selections were leading politicians and able ones—John Larkins, Joe Branch, and Joe Eagles.

I also worked very closely with the state's leaders in the State Democratic Executive Committee meetings and at the State Democratic Conventions. Except for the segregation issue, there was never any really important difference between me and any of the county political leaders. And differences over the segregation issue involved only a few people. Because it made sense and would help me in my work as governor, I kept in close touch with all our congressmen in Washington. I kept them advised of important plans and developments and sent them releases and speeches for their information.

At the close of the 1955 General Assembly, I went straight to work on the many appointments that came out of new legislation and the many, many appointments or reappointments to regular standing boards and commissions. For example, a governor during a normal four-year term has the privilege and the responsibility to appoint over one thousand state officials, judges, department heads, board members, and commissioners. At the time I became governor, he also had to appoint eight hundred justices of the peace—I was able to have this abolished by the General Assembly —and twenty-eight thousand notaries public. More, there are approximately one hundred officials, including department heads, board chairmen, executive directors, and others that the governor must appoint and who are responsible directly to him.

Announcements of my appointments were not as slow as they would have been under a governor who had gone through political campaigns and who had to be extremely cautious about whom he named to various positions. When I became governor, I was in the rare but fortunate position of not owing anybody anything politically. I had made no pledges or obligations—it had been unnecessary for me to make any. This was true when I was lieutenant governor, and it has remained true because of the way I came in as governor. It was, I emphasize, an almost ideal situation and very few governors in history have been so fortunate.

I made it a strict point to select people for the various boards and commissions, old and new, based on fitness, ability, and dedication to state service. My philosophy in appointments was that, all things being equal, I would generally appoint people active in the Democratic party. I did not reward party workers or friends unless they were qualified. I only appointed those I felt to be of the highest caliber—men and women who would do the best job for North Carolina.

Some old-time politicians in the Democratic party accused me of not paying any attention to politics or to party rules and traditions. They accused me of not counseling with Democratic leaders in the counties and the precincts. These charges were not true. I did check on all important appointments with the state chairman of the Democratic party. I checked on many, many appointments with the local and county Democratic leaders. And on appointments where I felt I had to go ahead, I notified these leaders in advance by letter or wire of what I was going to do. I admit very freely that I did not take the time a more politically minded governor would have taken to visit around and take counsel with local party leaders.

I was especially careful about getting only the finest men for the judiciary. I knew that this branch of the government should be above politics. Even though our judges are elected by the people, I knew that when governors appoint judges to fill vacancies, they usually stay in office as long as they wish or until they die. I felt that one should be extremely careful in the appointment of people to the judiciary. The 1955 General Assembly authorized additional Superior Court judges, so early in my administration I had the privilege and honor to appoint eleven Superior Court judges and four special judges.* The men I selected had character and ability, were generally younger men who could give long service

* The eleven new Superior Court judges were Hugh Campbell of Charlotte, C. W. Hall of Durham, J. Frank Huskins of Burnsville, Malcolm Carlyle Paul of Washington, Hubert E. Olive of Lexington, Malcolm Seawell of Lumberton, William J. Bundy of Greenville, P. C. Froneberger of Gastonia, Hamilton Hobgood of Louisburg, Raymond Mallard of Tabor City, and L. Richardson Preyer of Greensboro. The special judges who were reappointed by me were George M. Fountain of Tarboro, Susie Sharp of Reidsville, W. A. Leland McKeithan of Pinehurst, and George B. Patton of Franklin. The following year when Patton resigned I appointed J. Braxton Craven of Morganton to succeed him. Preyer and Craven are now federal judges, and Judge Sharp is the first woman to be a North Carolina Supreme Court Justice.

to the state, and could and would improve the administration of court procedure.

Back in 1952, when I was first considering entering the race for lieutenant governor, Mrs. Hodges had expressed concern about my getting into the game of politics. I had already made up my mind and I told her: "I will do the best I can, and I will not worry about what I have done after I have made the decision. Neither will I let criticism make me lose sleep or my health." I followed this rule and I am happy to say that Mrs. Hodges co-operated fully and never complained about my work or my attitude toward the job. She is a good sport.

With this personal philosophy, when 1956 came around, I was enjoying the job to the hilt, and I had started enough things that I wished to see through to want very much to run for re-election on my own. I was encouraged by many of the political and business leaders throughout the state as well as a host of friends. This was particularly true among educational and women's groups. I was never quite sure that year who might run for the Democratic primary for the governorship on the race issue, and that was the only thing that disturbed me. I was not so much worried about getting beaten in the primary as I was about having a campaign on that issue. I did not think it would help the state to have this a campaign issue as it became in many other southern states. My opponents did not raise the issue.

I did not turn to the professional old-time political group to handle the campaign although I was in touch with most of them and most of them helped. I asked my friend, Harold Makepeace, who, with Bill Shope of Weaverville, had done the most active work for me in the lieutenant governor's race, to become my state campaign manager. He accepted and did a tremendous job. He worked in the headquarters with Paul Johnston, Bob Giles, and Ed Rankin of my staff, and Hugh Morton, Al Resch, Mutt Burton, Ben Trotter, and others. They raised about $30,000 for expenses and had enough to return about 25% to contributors at the end of the campaign. On a television program in New York a few months after the campaign, Will Rogers, Jr., told of our returning part of the funds and described it as a "unique and crazy kind of politics."

Although my opponents were worthy people, I had the distinct advantage of being in office and of being in the middle of several state programs that the citizens evidently wanted to see finished, if possible. In the Democratic primary in May, 1956, I received a vote of 401,082, while Tom Sawyer received 29,248; Harry P. Stokely, 24,416; and C. E. Earle, Jr., 11,908. All three of my opponents in the primary were from Charlotte. In the November general election, I received a vote of 760,480, while Kyle Hayes of Wilkesboro, my Republican opponent, got 375,379.

The business of government never slowed down for the primary or general election campaigns. I was in the midst of budget discussions preparing for the approaching legislature. In my State of the State biennial message to the General Assembly on February 11, 1957, I presented a proposed budget of over a billion dollars. It was the first in the history of North Carolina. I concluded that message with a description of a vision which I believe can be the North Carolina of the future. This "North Carolina dream" was and is:

I see a land of thriving industry of many kinds—manufacturing, agricultural, research; with plants distributed throughout the state —east, west, north, and south, set well apart on our countryside and in well-planned small towns and medium-sized cities, drawing their workers from all the surrounding areas, without the slum conditions, the polluted air, the unmanageable congestion, and the other unwanted characteristics of the present typical American industrial center. This is a land where all workers are land owners and home owners, rather than modern-day cliff dwellers cramped in gloomy rented flats and furnished rooms; a land with prospering farms producing many different crops and no longer dependent for their existence on a one-or-two-crop market. I see in every

---

community well constructed, modernly equipped and modernly run schools, staffed by adequately trained and adequately paid teachers, supported by an enthusiastic people who demand nothing less than the best for all children. This is a land where all citizens have sufficient economic opportunity, spare time, and education to enjoy the best there is in life through private pursuits supplemented by public cultural and recreational facilities. And in this land, looking out over all else, there are towers of colleges and universities—for it is an enlightened land—and the spires of many churches—for it is a moral land.

This is the vision, the North Carolina dream. And it is not an unattainable thing. We have a great heritage, with past leaders who have shown us what courage and faith and hard work can do. We have the people, and the natural resources to turn this dream into eventual reality, if we but work and continue to have courage and faith in our own abilities. You and I, in the all too few years remaining to any of us, can do no more than lead our state a little of the way, but if we do this, and hand over to those who come after us the courage and the faith which were handed to us, then, God willing, this vision of North Carolina will become her destiny.

This vision of North Carolina's future was shared by many members of the General Assemblies with which I worked. In my opinion, the three legislatures during my administration were composed of outstanding representatives of the people. They worked long and hard on behalf of North Carolina, and they performed many worthwhile and long-lasting services.

In 1957, for example, the General Assembly—as I have already recounted—separated the Prisons Department from the Highway Department and the Highway Department was revamped for better service to the people. A Department of Administration was established and I named Paul Johnston as its first administrator. Teachers and state employees were given raises and a School Finance Study Commission was authorized. The state's first steps into a community college program were made, a study commission on a legislative building was authorized, loopholes in the welfare program were plugged, and needed aid was provided for the state's mentally ill and mentally retarded.

In the area of taxes, the 1957 legislature changed the allocation formula that aided the industrialization program. An important change to many Tar Heels removed the 3% sales tax from farm machinery parts and allowed an additional one-cent-per-gallon refund to farmers and other non-highway users of gasoline. More than 111,000 Tar Heels—small farmers, small business proprietors, and wage earners who supplemented their income from other sources—received a $650,000 tax reduction as a result of the standard deduction privilege being extended.

The state's total budget for the 1957-59 biennium, including funds from all sources, was more than $1 billion. Almost one-half of this amount was for the state's general fund, which finances the operations of schools, mental institutions, health and welfare activities, and general government. Slightly more than 70% of the general fund or more than $384 million went for education at all levels. Over $400 million in state and federal funds went into the highway program during the biennium.

In February of 1959, to my third and last General Assembly, I recommended another far-reaching legislative program, and most of those recommendations were approved. Another raise was provided for state employees and teachers, a minimum wage law was enacted, and vaccination against polio was required before children could enter the public schools. The legislature extended by eight weeks the length of time during which unemployment benefits could be paid, approved an important recommendation for the establishment of a State Department of Water Resources, and provided for a new legislative building. A point system for determining when the Department of Motor Vehicles could suspend the driver's license of those who were convicted of several violations of the motor vehicle laws was also enacted.

The greatest single item, as always, was the budget. For the

"*Please—be nice to the poor li'l kitty*"

1959-61 biennium, the 1959 General Assembly made general fund appropriations for current operations of over $582 million, an increase of approximately 14% over the previous biennium, and highway fund appropriations of $271 million, which was an increase of approximately 5%. When federal funds were added to all state funds, the 1959-61 state budget amounted to $1,264,252,-531. It was another record.

For public welfare, the 1959 General Assembly appropriated from state funds about $21 million. It was an increase of 17% over the preceding budget period expenditures. However, the program called for a reduction in the minimum needs of the aged and disabled, and during the session I was accused of taking away funds for poor people and sick people. In the spring of 1960 the matter became something of a political football and among candidates for public office there were calls for a special session to restore "cuts" in the welfare payments.

I would be the last man to take anything away from those who needed it. The increase in welfare funds by the 1959 General Assembly, in addition to providing for the expected increase in case loads, provided for a continuation of the average monthly payments for the various programs at rates not less than those applying during 1958-59. There were reductions in the minimum figures, yes, but the dollar amount of the welfare payments to the aged and disabled was never lowered. In fact, the dollar amount increased.

During the 1959 General Assembly, I did not recommend any additional taxes although state services continued to increase at a rapid rate. The Advisory Budget Commission and I determined that a good state budget could be worked out for the coming biennium, with increases for practically every state function, without imposing new taxes upon the citizens of North Carolina. This was done through the withholding plan for income tax payments, which I recommended and the General Assembly approved.

The withholding tax plan meant that the people had to pay in

1960 their 1959 taxes and, by installments, their 1960 taxes. This applied to just about everybody. Corporations had to make returns for their employees and send the money directly to the state. The federal government had, of course, for years been using basically the same system. There was practically no criticism of our action except on the part of a few politicians who were just against the governor. There were misgivings on the part of some persons about using the pre-payment of income tax for the current budget, since it would not recur.

The withholding system brought in a windfall of about $27.5 million for the biennium. This made it unnecessary for the 1959 General Assembly to raise taxes. And it not only meant that North Carolina received tax on the current pay-as-you-go basis, but that it added to the tax rolls many thousands of people who for some reason or another had never before made a tax return. This was strange. After the withholding system was put into effect, we began to get returns from people who sent them in for several years back. Their consciences must have bothered them.

Critics of the system told us that the state would have to make up this tax money in the next biennium, since we were only borrowing it from that period and using it for current expenditures. I disagreed. I thought the state would grow and that this would take up any slack we might have and that North Carolina would not have to have any additional taxes to meet the needs of the ever-growing state services. I was right. The budget prepared for the 1961 General Assembly during the last months of my administration did balance without calling for new taxes. The 1961 General Assembly, as was its privilege, added a special program to the budget that necessitated an increase in taxes.

As for the withholding system, it was a step forward. In the months after the 1959 General Assembly went home, I talked to many people and the majority confirmed my belief. They preferred that a small amount be set aside from their weekly or monthly pay checks to take care of their state income tax rather than be confronted with the necessity of one large payment in April of each year.

"It is enough to say that employers can afford it, employees deserve it, and the state's economic progress demands it." With this statement from my biennial message to the 1959 General Assembly, the last battle for a minimum wage law for North Carolina workers was joined. In May of that year, after much lobbying against a minimum wage law and debate over a bevy of proposed crippling and killing amendments, the General Assembly enacted a seventy-five-cents-an-hour minimum wage law. Effective January 1, 1960, it brought increased wages to more than fifty-five thousand additional Tar Heel workers. This was the first minimum wage law enacted by a state in the southeastern United States and was one of the most important forward steps taken by North Carolina while I was governor.

The passage of the minimum wage law came after defeats in seven previous General Assemblies going back for a period of twenty years. It was first attempted in 1939 and then regularly each session from 1947 to 1957. Governor Kerr Scott and Governor William Umstead both had recommended minimum-wage legislation to the General Assembly. Labor Commissioner Frank Crane and his predecessors A. L. Fletcher and Forrest H. Shuford had spoken out for it, as had many private groups and individuals. Opposition, particularly from small businessmen, had always impressed legislators with the supposed disadvantages of a minimum wage and such legislation never got very far.

In the 1955 General Assembly, as I was just picking up the reins of the government after the death of Governor Umstead, a minimum wage measure calling for a fifty-five-cents-an-hour minimum was introduced. This was a very meager minimum. Still, it was too much to suit a majority of the members of the legislature, and it got nowhere at all. However, the defeat of this minimum wage bill made me realize more than ever the definite

162   *Businessman in the Statehouse*

need of such a law in North Carolina. I determined to do something about it.

On February 12, 1957, I went before a new General Assembly with my biennial message. I had just recently been inaugurated to my own term as governor. In that message to the legislators I declared, "One of the essentials of prosperity is widespread purchasing power in the hands of the people. A minimum wage will help provide this by raising the level of our very low income earners." I did not mention a figure at that time, but soon after I let it be known I would favor a minimum wage bill that would not exceed seventy-five cents an hour.

There appeared to be a growing sentiment in both the Senate and the House for the adoption of a minimum wage. A number of the legislators made statements to the press that they favored or would "not oppose" a seventy-five-cents-an-hour minimum wage. I felt such a bill would definitely have a chance of getting out of committee, where the 1955 minimum wage proposal had died. In the meantime, Representative Jack Love of Mecklenburg County introduced a one-dollar-per-hour minimum wage bill. Many people, including me, felt that this was just too big a step for the state to take at that time. Besides there was little chance that the legislature would approve a minimum wage that high.

Senator R. Lee Whitmire of Henderson County introduced the administration's seventy-five-cents-an-hour minimum wage bill in the Senate on March 21, 1957. It contained provisions to exempt workers engaged in agriculture and dairying, domestic servants, outside salesmen on commission, workers who customarily received tips and gratuities in addition to wages, and workers whose pay consisted in part of food and lodging. The bill also provided that the commissioner of labor be authorized to set lower minimums for handicapped workers. It would have benefited an estimated ninety thousand North Carolina workers.

After expected discussion and debate, the minimum wage bill was given a favorable report by a Senate committee and then passed by the Senate. Sent to the House, the bill was referred to the House Committee on Manufacturers and Labor. There it stayed. A quick parliamentary maneuver tabled the bill in that committee, ending all chance of passing a minimum wage bill for that session. If the measure could have gotten back to the floor of the House, it might have been a different story. The defeat of minimum wage legislation was one of my big disappointments of the 1957 General Assembly.

There was nothing we could do but wait for another General Assembly and try again. There were two minimum wage bills introduced in the 1959 General Assembly. On February 4, the first day of the session, Representative Dwight W. Quinn of Cabarrus County and Representative J. M. Phelps of Washington County introduced the first one. It called for a seventy-five-cents-an-hour minimum wage and provided for a number of exemptions, similar to those included in the 1957 minimum wage bill. It was sent to the House Committee on Manufacturers and Labor.

Just over two weeks later a second minimum wage bill was introduced in the House by a trio of freshmen representatives. These were Sam J. Burrow, Jr., of Randolph County, Steve Dolley, Jr., of Gaston County, and Frank N. Patterson, Jr., of Stanly County. Their bill provided for a minimum wage of $1 an hour and had basically the same exemptions as the seventy-five-cents-an-hour bill. It provided that the provisions of the bill would not apply where an employer had three employees or less. This bill was also sent off to the House Committee on Manufacturers and Labor.

In late March the committee held a public hearing on the two minimum wage bills. It became apparent at this hearing that the key differences were not between the supporters of the two bills, but between proponents and opponents of minimum wage legislation. At this hearing, Commissioner of Labor Frank Crane delivered the major argument for a minimum wage for North Carolina. He stressed that a minimum wage bill would help the state's economic prosperity as well as provide a livable wage for many thousands of Tar Heel workers.

A number of other people from various sections of the state spoke in favor of a minimum wage bill. One of these speakers was J. B. Long, Alamance County commissioner and a Burlington retail merchant. Under a minimum wage law, Mr. Long knew he would have to pay his employees more money, but he saw the need of such a law and spoke out in favor of it. He declared that workers who would be aided by such a law had no lobbyists to speak up for them. In fact, he added, "most of them live on Misery Hill, between the county jail and the county home."

An array of speakers against any minimum wage bill appeared at the hearing. Raleigh attorney J. C. B. Ehringhaus, Jr., representing the Small Business Committee of North Carolina and the Hotel Association, said small businessmen were against the minimum wage. W. W. Taylor of Warrenton, a former legislator, also spoke against a minimum wage bill and said it would work a hardship on small stores, particularly those in the rural areas of the state. The committee, of course, took no action on the bills at the hearing.

Action was taken by the House Committee on Manufacturers and Labor at its meeting on April 2, 1959. There was such a large turnout of anti-minimum-wage lobbyists at the committee session that Representative Burrow later declared, "You could hardly see the committee for the lobbyists." In fact, he and Representative Dolley threatened to introduce a bill in the House to ban hired lobbyists from breathing down legislators' backs during committee votes. Despite the presence of so many lobbyists, however, the committee went on with its work.

The bill introduced by Representatives Burrow, Dolley, and Patterson was amended to allow a minimum wage of seventy-five cents an hour instead of $1. Then opponents of minimum wage law made their move, and by a seventeen to sixteen vote eliminated all of the exemptions from the bill. The strategy was to extend the bill's coverage to every worker in the state, including farmers. This, of course, would have kept legislators from rural counties from voting for it. Then Representative Quinn moved that consideration of his bill be postponed indefinitely and that the other bill be reported favorably. There was a sixteen to sixteen tie on this, and Committee Chairman Edward Wilson of Caswell County had to cast the tie-breaking vote. He voted that the seventy-five-cents-an-hour, no-exemption bill be reported favorably.

A week later, the bill came to the floor of the House of Representatives. The amendment doing away with all the exemptions was brought up first. Representative Ashley Murphy of Pender spoke against this and moved the amendment be tabled. This motion carried by an eighty-eight to twenty-three vote and the exemptions were once again back in the bill. Then on the motion of the committee chairman, Representative Wilson, the House approved the amendment lowering the minimum from $1 to seventy-five cents an hour. Then a parade of amendments began. Most failed, but some passed, including one by Representative Roland Braswell of Wayne to have the minimum wage bill apply only to concerns that employed six or more instead of four or more.

Finally after three hours, the previous question was called, and the minimum wage bill came up for its important second reading. On a roll call vote, sixty-two representatives voted for it and forty-eight against it. There were three pairs. There was an objection to the third reading and it was carried over. There was a lot of work done in the next few hours by proponents and opponents of the minimum wage bill.

The bill did not come up again in the House until the following Tuesday, April 14. Again the amendments came, and debate seemed endless. Because of a Finance Committee hearing, the House adjourned without taking any action on the bill. The next day there was another parade of amendments; twenty-four were introduced. Some of these were introduced in good faith, but others were put in with the hope they would cause the minimum wage bill to be killed. After a half-hour recess in mid-afternoon, the House settled down for a session that lasted until after six o'clock. Finally, the vote on third reading was taken. The minimum wage bill passed sixty-six to thirty-nine, including pairs, and was sent to the Senate.

The Senate Committee on Manufacturing, Labor, and Commerce met to discuss the minimum wage bill on April 28, 1959. Commissioner of Labor Frank Crane went before this committee with an appeal for the adoption of the bill. He pointed out:

The benefits which a minimum wage will bring to the people affected and to the state as a whole are manifold. An employee working 40 hours a week at 75 cents an hour will have earnings of $30 a week or $1,500 a year. Such a minimum wage will lift that employee 12.5 per cent above our 1958 per capita income of $1,333. It will bring a basic standard of living to many thousands of our citizens who have no other guarantee of even a semblance of a living wage. It will provide a substantial, non-inflationary boost to the economy of the state.

Far from "hurting" small business or putting people out of work, this legislation is most unlikely to have anything but a beneficial effect upon the overwhelming majority of small enterprises. As passed by the House, this bill exempts any business employing less than six workers. As for the establishments which it covers—as well as those who will reap all of its benefits without being covered—this bill will provide additional buying power which will be channeled straight back into the purchase of goods and services. Businesses paying the higher wages set by statute will immediately receive the money back again in the form of increased sales and profits.

Far from creating unemployment, this bill will help to provide additional jobs for workers in the production of food, clothing, shelter, and services which the affected workers will buy with their increased incomes.

The Senate Committee gave the minimum wage bill a favorable report, and the next day, April 29, 1959, it came to the floor of the Senate. At the request of a senator, however, action was delayed for a week. It came up again on May 6, and there was some discussion on certain points. In the end, however, the Senate voted forty-three to six to pass the minimum wage bill on its second reading. The next day, May 7, on its third reading the vote was forty-two to six, and North Carolina had its first minimum wage law.

The seventy-five-cents-an-hour minimum wage law went into effect January 1, 1960. It had a direct boosting effect on the earnings of some fifty-five thousand workers. The wages of this group increased an estimated $300 per year for each worker. This created new purchasing power in this group amounting to $16.5 million a year. Included in this group were workers in variety stores, department stores, grocery stores, restaurants, laundries, and dry cleaning establishments, maids and other custodial workers in hotels and motels. For these fifty-five thousand Tar Heels, it was a wonderful way to start a new year.

Another step in minimum wage legislation was made by the 1961 General Assembly, with the support of Governor Terry Sanford's administration. The 1959 minimum wage law applied to firms that had six or more workers on the job. After much debate, the 1961 General Assembly changed the law to apply to firms that employed four or more workers. Because of their action, some nineteen thousand employees of small retail and service businesses in North Carolina came under the provisions of the seventy-five-cents-an-hour minimum wage law as of January 1, 1962.

The minimum wage legislation during my administration helped Tar Heel families to help themselves. It helped to increase the purchasing power where just such an increase was most needed. And, in addition, the minimum wage was another way to help raise the low per capita income of the state. The minimum wage in the state is proving to be, as I predicted early in 1959, something that employers can afford, employees deserve and need, and something that North Carolina's economic progress demands.

Unlike many governors of North Carolina, I was not a lawyer. Nevertheless, from the beginning of my service as governor I had a great interest in our courts and in all aspects of the administration of justice. Quite early I became concerned with the vital need for improvement in the administration of justice. Despite a long and complete study and the proposal of a sound constitutional revision concerning the judicial branch, definite constructive action was not taken by the General Assembly during my administration. A start was made, however, and the 1961 General Assembly approved a "court improvement" bill for submission to the people for approval.

My campaign for court improvement started in the summer of 1955. The General Assembly that year had provided for eleven additional Superior Court judges and four special judges, all to be appointed by me to serve until the next general election. I made my selections and the swearing-in ceremony was set for July 1. This was the largest number of judges ever authorized and sworn in at one time in the history of the state. In addition to the fifteen appointees, nearly all of the incumbent Superior Court judges and six of the seven Supreme Court justices were present for the ceremonies in the Capitol.

I took this opportunity to make a few remarks about the administration of justice in North Carolina. I said, in part:

The courts, as you well know, are the bedrock upon which good government must be built. In spite of my own high regard for the judiciary of this state, however, I cannot help but say to you that I am convinced that, generally speaking, whether it is correct or not, the courts do not now occupy the same high place in the minds of the average citizen that they once did.

Justly or unjustly, it is often remarked that courts are too technical, too slow, and too expensive, and that the decisions which are made are in too many instances dependent upon the skill or oratory, or popularity, of the lawyers, and too little dependent on the merits of the case.

I pointed out that these criticisms were, at best, only partially justified because many people did not realize that the judiciary of English-speaking countries had been designed for hundreds of years for the protection of our most precious freedoms and rights. However, I warned the judges that "only by self-analysis and correction can the courts and the bar hope to hold the respect and confidence of our people and . . . it is of fundamental importance to a free society that the courts and the bar do hold this respect and confidence."

I suggested that the judges and the bar install better procedures, by de-emphasizing unnecessary technicalities, by refusing to put up with dilatory tactics, causing cases to remain on dockets for months and sometimes years, and by always keeping in mind the fact that the State of North Carolina is an interested party in every lawsuit and its interest demands expeditious settlement of every case. I also suggested that an improved system of public relations, by which the public would be informed that many tedious procedures are absolutely necessary for the protection of human freedoms, would do much to help the people to understand and respect the courts.

In June, before the swearing-in ceremony for the judges, I spoke in Asheville at the annual meeting of the North Carolina Bar Association. I talked along the same lines at the Bar Association meeting and requested its president to appoint a special study committee to make recommendations to the governor and the chief justice of the Supreme Court as to methods for further improvements in the administration of the court system in the state. To my delight, the North Carolina Bar Association accepted my challenge to recommend improvements to the court system and appointed a study committee.

J. Spencer Bell, an attorney of Charlotte and a past president of the Bar Association, was named chairman of the committee.* The committee had the jawbreaking name of "The Committee on Improving and Expediting the Administration of Justice in North Carolina." Its name was no larger than its task.

The committee began its work carefully. Mr. Bell told me that to do the job as it should be done would require an answer to this broad question: Is the system of courts we have in the state adequate; and if not, why not, and what should be done to make it so? We realized at the outset that before a satisfactory answer to all the facets of this question could be expected, the true facts concerning our existing court system would have to be ascertained. Next had to come a careful analysis of the facts and the formulation of recommendations based on the analysis. And finally, the recommendations had to be implemented if we were to show any real results.

To gather the facts needed, of course, would take a great amount of field work and research by a competent staff. This phase of the program was expected to take at least a year. To analyze the facts would require not only the professional competence of the Bar Association Committee but other members of the association and other professional groups, such as the Judicial Council, the General Statutes Commission, and the State Bar Council. To formulate proper recommendations would also require the help of these groups as well as interested leaders in the state. It was estimated that the analysis and recommendation stage of the study would take at least six months.

* Other members, all attorneys, were Joel B. Adams of Asheville, David Clark of Lincolnton, Shearon Harris of Albemarle, Francis J. Heazel of Asheville, Howard Hubbard of Clinton, Thomas H. Leath of Rockingham, Wallace Murchison of Wilmington, William B. McGuire, Jr., of Charlotte, James M. Poyner of Raleigh, John C. Rodman of Washington, Beverly S. Royster, Jr., of Oxford, William L. Thorpe of Rocky Mount, and William F. Womble of Winston-Salem.

The final stage of implementing any recommendation would require the combined efforts of all of these groups, plus the interest and support of an informed public. All in all, there was a lot of work to be done. I hoped that some action on court improvement could be taken by the 1959 General Assembly, then two and a half years away. I urged the Bar Association committee to work with this target date in mind.

In addition to work, such a project needed a substantial amount of money. Soon after the committee was formed, we began looking for a source for the funds necessary to do the job as it should be done. At the North Carolina Bar Association Convention in the summer of 1956, I was able to announce that approximately $70,000 had been secured from private foundations. These foundations were the Richardson Foundation of North Carolina and New York, the O. Max Gardner Foundation of North Carolina, and the Martin Cannon Family Foundation of North Carolina. The money was made available to the Bar Association and in turn to the committee studying the administration of justice in North Carolina.

In the following months Mr. Bell's committee did a tremendous amount of work. The Institute of Government at Chapel Hill was most helpful. As a result, we made the most thorough study of our courts in the history of the state, and one of the most complete studies of the courts of any state that had been made at any time, anywhere in the United States. When the basic research studies were being completed and readied for consideration by the court study committee in 1957, the president of the Bar Association appointed a number of laymen to work on the committee * with the lawyer members.

* Members on the revised committee who were not on the original committee included John Archer, J. Murrey Atkins, D. G. Bell, Henry Brandis, Jr., Fred Fletcher, Ashley B. Futrell, A. Pilston Godwin, Jr., P. K. Gravely, T. N. Grice, R. O. Huffman, William H. Murdock, G. Harold Myrick, Woodrow Price, Robert W. Proctor, William Snider, and John W. Spicer. Members of the original committee who remained on it were Bell, Harris, Adams, Clark, Heazel, Hubbard, Leath, Murchison, Poyner, Rodman, and Womble.

The committee presented the report of its findings and recommendations, including a constitutional amendment, to the 1959
General Assembly with the request, from the North Carolina Bar
Association, that the legislators "permit the people of our state
to vote upon this amendment." The report was no surprise. The
people of the state had had the opportunity to become acquainted
first with the tentative and then the final conclusions of the committee. Before the 1959 legislature convened, Tar Heels had had
the opportunity to discuss thoroughly the proposals of the
committee.

Many things were brought out and emphasized in the report.
One was that in one year the justices of the peace in the state
had handled over eighty-eight thousand cases, in which their fees
were not collected unless the defendants were found guilty. There
was but one characterization for such a system; this was not
justice—this was a travesty of justice. On the Superior Court level,
there were some administrative and organizational problems as
were evidenced by the growing backlog of cases awaiting trial.
The recorders' courts about the state varied widely in every
respect, including the fees and costs that were charged.

The general recommendations of the Bar Association committee
were:

1. Combine all North Carolina courts into one organization to
bring uniformity and co-ordination to the administration of justice.

2. Make the chief justice of the North Carolina Supreme Court
the executive head of the statewide court system.

3. Give the Supreme Court the power to make the rules for
the mechanics of operation of the courts and for trying cases in
them, and the responsibility for keeping these up to date.

4. Provide for a uniform method of selecting judges and trial
magistrates for the local courts, below the Superior Court level,
throughout the entire state, to help insure unbiased and prompt
judgement in all cases brought before such courts.

The Bar Association committee objectives, if adopted, would

have required a revision of Article IV of our state constitution. The committee had provided a suggested draft of the judiciary article of the constitution and that had been circulated widely over the state. (The Constitutional Study Commission had also given careful consideration to the problem of our court system and had also made suggestions for the consideration of the General Assembly, including a revision of the judiciary article of the constitution.)

There was a terrific battle over court improvement in the 1959 General Assembly. Senator Bell, who had headed the Bar Association committee, along with many others, worked hard to get the court improvement legislation enacted. There were, however, many well-meaning people in both the House and the Senate who did not agree with the recommendations. Some of these were sincere; others just simply were determined there would be no changes in the old system.

One of the major differences was on the question of where the responsibility should be vested for continuously observing and examining the entire court system and for taking action to remedy administrative defects when found. The Bar Association Committee had recommended that it be vested in the Supreme Court of North Carolina. There were many legislators who felt it should be vested in the General Assembly. These legislators felt that if control of the courts was vested in the General Assembly, it would be closer to the will of the people.

It was my contention that both the Supreme Court and the General Assembly were elected by the people and both were responsible to the people. The major question then was which of these branches of our government could carry out the responsibility of judicial administration most effectively. I thought the responsibility should be placed in the Supreme Court. It was almost continuously in session and it was intimately and solely concerned with the business of the courts. As the state's highest appellate court, and by the nature of its duties, the members of that court thought in terms of statewide interest. It seemed to me that with proper administrative help, the Supreme Court was better fitted to carry out the task of court administration than was the General Assembly.

Opponents of this view believed that once control by the Supreme Court was put in the constitution, the General Assembly would be restricted even if the approach was ineffective or was found to be generally unacceptable to the people. It was my recommendation that the responsibility be vested in the judiciary, with the provision that a revision could be exercised by the General Assembly by a three-fifths vote of the Senate and the House, without a vote of the people. And, too, under the Bar Association Committee's recommendations the General Assembly would retain the power to determine the number of judges, to fix all court fees and costs except those of the appellate court, and would have over-all budgetary supervision of the courts.

There was no court improvement legislation enacted during the 1959 General Assembly. The Bar Association Committee's recommended constitutional amendment was introduced in the Senate and sent to the Committee on Constitution. This committee reported favorably a substitute bill which was amended once on the floor and passed its second reading. After that it was postponed indefinitely. The provisions of the amended bill were then incorporated in another bill revising the entire constitution. This one passed the Senate but, after its judicial article was amended in the House, it was postponed indefinitely.

Fortunately, the idea of court improvement did not die there in the General Assembly in 1959. Following the session, the Bar Association Committee began meeting again. It took the Senate-passed version of the court bill and studied it to determine what changes, if any, the committee should recommend in it for introduction in the 1961 General Assembly. After this, the revised bill was studied by a legislative committee of the Bar Association and a bill embodying a modification of the Bar Association court study committee's revised text was readied for introduction in the next General Assembly. Fortunately, too, Governor Terry Sanford had, while he was running as a candidate and after he became governor, taken a strong position in favor of court improvement.

In late April, 1961, a much-compromised bill to provide North Carolina with a "unified and uniform" court system was rushed through both the Senate and the House. The final compromise in the long debate was reached when opposing factions agreed to leave the control of the lower courts with the General Assembly rather than put it in the Supreme Court. The major change from the existing court system would be a uniform system of inferior courts throughout the state to replace the hodgepodge system.

Under the compromise, the General Assembly would provide for an administrative office of the courts to carry out the provisions of the act. It would be responsible to the legislature. There would be few changes in the present set-up of Supreme and Superior Courts in the state. On the inferior court level, however, a complete change would take place within ten years. The General Assembly would divide the state into districts, with at least one court in each county. The district judges would be elected by the people for four-year terms. Magistrates would replace the justices of the peace, and would be appointed by Superior Court judges on nomination of county clerks of Superior Court. The General Assembly would prescribe their powers and their jurisdiction.

With the approval of the General Assembly, court improvement still had to be approved by the people through a constitutional amendment. Originally it had been scheduled to be submitted in 1961, but because of a capital improvements bond issue vote it was postponed until 1962.

The compromise bill accomplished the major objectives of the Bar Association Committee. It fixes the responsibility for the judicial product and provides for a uniform system of courts throughout the state. All parties are to be commended for the adoption of the court improvement legislation. All North Carolina will benefit from it, and I hope Tar Heels will vote for it.

CHAPTER VIII

Education–
First on the Budget

EDUCATION is the chief business of the State of North Carolina. Public school education and state-supported colleges provide North Carolina with its biggest and most important problem and opportunity. The financial needs of education make up the majority of our state budget year after year. Since the administration of Governor Charles Brantley Aycock at the turn of the century, North Carolina has never ceased to go forward in public education. Education has been the basis of our economic progress. In this century North Carolina governors have asked for and legislators have continually provided increased appropriations for education.

Teachers' salaries have been raised and raised again. Most of the former small and inadequate schools have been consolidated into larger units and replaced by what may almost be called palaces of education. North Carolina has for a long time transported to and from school more children than any other state. In brief, despite its low per capita income, the state has put relatively more into education and made a greater proportionate effort for education than have most of the more wealthy states.

An example of this and one of North Carolina's most courageous steps of the past half century was what we did near the bottom of the great depression of the 1930's. When many of our local governmental units were defaulting on their bonds, when many of our teachers were unpaid, when numbers of our schools were threatened with closing, instead of retreating and giving way to despair, we resolved upon and carried through a far-reaching program. Our state government took over the operation and maintenance of all the public schools and went so far as to guarantee an eight-months term in every school district of the state.

This move during the depression probably saved our schools, but it also planted the seed for one of our greatest educational problems of the late 1950's and 1960's. For when I became governor in the mid-1950's, the chief problem—other than the emotional segregation-integration issue—had to do with school financing, especially teachers' salaries. The problem was emphasized by too few classrooms and continually increasing enrollments. We were constantly concerned over whether or not our schools were keeping abreast of the time in their programs and their outlook. Our problem was similar to that in other states, but it was different because of the actions taken by our state during the depression.

One of the depression legislatures had even forbidden by statute any locality's spending supplementary money for school teachers' salaries. It had left all of the payment of the salaries to the state. A later legislature—at the urging of the Honorable Frank Graham, I understand—repealed the statute forbidding local supplements for public school education. There was a rebirth in the following years of local effort to supplement and to improve the state level of support for public education. This local effort, however, was small and was limited almost entirely to city school units. Local school officials lacked an incentive.

Following my recommendation, the 1957 General Assembly authorized the appointment of a commission to study public school financing. The commission was authorized to make a study of all problems of public school financing and to appraise the future role of the state and local units in support of the public schools. The commission was required to make a report of its findings and recommendations to the governor, the General Assembly, and the people.

O. Arthur Kirkman, state senator from High Point and a great friend of the schools in North Carolina, was appointed to head the study commission.* It was an excellent commission, representing local government, the legislature, the public, and the schools, and its members worked very diligently.

C. P. Spruill of Chapel Hill, a distinguished professor and economist, was engaged by the commission to help in the study and recommendations. The commission's report stated:

Education in North Carolina is a constitutional responsibility of the state government. It is a primary function of the state. The state may meet this obligation by delegating a part of the responsibility and authority for the educative process to other units of government. A proper utilization and combination of the efforts of the people at various governmental levels is required if North Carolina is to furnish her sons and daughters with an education adequate to their needs and commensurate with their ability.

To obtain this "proper utilization and combination of efforts," the commission proposed a participating program that was designated the incentive fund plan. Counties could join or refuse to join as they saw fit. The formula for each county's qualification was based on the county property valuation (economic ability) and the average daily membership in the schools. To qualify for each $10.00 of state money, the amount of money that a county would have to put up would run from $1.95 in the case of Bertie

---

* Others named were Lloyd C. Amos of Greensboro, Representative H. Clifton Blue of Aberdeen, Cecil W. Gilchrist of Charlotte, Mrs. Charles E. Graham of Davidson County, Representative George Watts Hill, Jr., of Durham, H. A. Mattox of Murphy, Faison W. McGowen of Kenansville, and L. Stacy Weaver of Fayetteville.

County, for instance, to $10.00 in the case of Durham. Thus the
state's poorer counties were assured of much more state help,
proportionally, than the richer counties. If the plan had been put
into operation, there would have been available for teachers'
salaries and other current expenses $10 million each year from the
state; and if all counties had participated another $6.4 million
would have been available yearly, or over $16 million the first
year.

Although the commission had not been given instructions as
to what kind of report to bring in, its recommendations in principle were quite similar to my own views. I felt strongly that
we ought to encourage localities to support the schools—especially
through teachers' salaries—and that the schools should not be
completely dependent on the state. I had been deeply concerned,
and I am still deeply concerned, at the attitude taken by our
people in the 1930's when they forbade local support. I was more
concerned at the little progress that we had made since the 1930's
in getting supplemental support from the localities. A few communities were doing something fairly substantial, but of the 174
school units in the state, only half were doing anything, and in
most cases their contributions were extremely modest.

The incentive fund plan was a giant step in the right direction.
As might have been expected, however, there was considerable
misunderstanding of its purpose. Some people charged that it was
an effort to unload the state's burden on the counties. The commission denied any such thought and I agreed with them. In my
biennial message on February 5, 1959, I said that "I, for one, do
not desire to see the state 'unload' the burden of public school
financing on the counties." And, to reassure everyone that such
a burden would not be transferred at some future time, I suggested that some clear standards be set up in the law as a means
of measuring the state effort—past and current.

For example, the state could have continued its present support
with increases proportionate to growth in school population, plus

a cost-of-living grant at each biennium, or some similar specific provision. Definitely the state should have continued to support a strong statewide system of public schools of whatever number of grades and for whatever number of months the General Assembly might determine. The school incentive fund was intended to provide something extra.

The school incentive plan died on the vine. By the time the report came before a legislative committee, there was little support for it. Many of the legislators were from small and comparatively poor counties that would have benefited most from the plan. Nevertheless, they felt they simply could not afford to back legislation that would cause the localities to assume *any* portion of the school financial needs beyond what they were already doing—namely, school construction.

Somebody should have come out swinging for the incentive plan. I wanted to go in person before the committee and argue the case for the plan just as I had done in a previous session before the committee handling the water resources program. I discussed the matter very fully at a breakfast meeting at the Mansion with the lieutenant governor, the speaker of the House, and chairmen of the committees, including the one handling this bill. They did not think it had a chance and urged me to refrain from going before the committee. I was finally dissuaded from doing it. I later regretted that I had let them talk me out of it.

Many state and local school officials privately knew and believed that the recommendation of a school incentive plan was sound, and several of them told me it would have to be enacted sometime if our schools were to develop as they must. But they did not have the courage to speak out and did not come forward to support the measure when their support was needed. There were some exceptions to this and a few—but very few—officials did speak out in favor of the plan.

I am afraid I did not do my homework well enough on the school incentive plan. If I had realized that the sponsors of the plan and school officials who had talked to me favorably about the plan were not going to come out in the open and support it, I would have approached the matter differently. It was a mistake for us to allow the plan to be presented so early. And once it had gotten to the committtee, it was a mistake to allow a vote to be taken on it. Our General Assembly, like so many other assemblies of its kind, follows tradition. When a piece of legislation has been killed, usually quite a long time passes before the same legislation or similar legislation will be introduced again. The school incentive plan had not been properly sold to the people; we had not done enough explaining or educating; we had not checked enough key people to know what the reaction would be.

As I see it now, it would have been far better if we had withdrawn the recommendation or not put it in at that time, but carried it over for another two years to the next General Assembly. Meanwhile we could have been telling the state about it, getting information about what was happening in other parts of the country, what the tax rates were in other towns and cities for schools, and showing the people the real problem facing North Carolina. It might also have been desirable to find some index of county wealth and ability to pay that was fair but more easily understood. The formula in the commission's report was rather complex, and this may have contributed to the defeat of the plan.

I still think there is considerable merit in a school incentive plan or something of a similar nature and that such a plan is a good part of the answer for the future of our schools in North Carolina. It would mean more money to enrich and supplement the state's continued good minimum. Cities and towns in other states supplement state funds for education, and for that reason many can afford to pay teachers more money than North Carolina schools can afford to pay. North Carolina is now almost the only state in the nation trying to get practically all of its money for teachers' salaries from the state treasury. This should not be. Communities and counties should be allowed and encouraged to do a better job of supporting schools, if they are willing to pay for it. By working together at local and state levels we in North Carolina can improve education for all our children.

Like every other North Carolina governor—and I suppose every other governor in the United States—I had the problem of the teachers' lobby. The teachers are more powerful than many people think, and their lobbying puts the individual members of the General Assembly on the spot while they are running for office and after they get into the General Assembly. The governor of another southern state telephoned me one night and said that he was sick at heart over his situation. This governor's state paid a much higher average salary than was being recommended for teachers in North Carolina, Tennessee, and many other southern states. Despite this and the fact that he had gone overboard for increasing still further his teachers' salaries, he had taken terrific abuse from the legislative galleries and from teacher organizations that were not satisfied even with the large increase he had recommended for them. He made the point that many other people make. It is that the teachers do not emphasize the child or the future of the state, but ask each legislature only how much more they are going to get.

Teachers in North Carolina, as well as in other states, need pay raises. But professional school people have a great responsibility. And their failure to solve some of their own problems, or their unwillingness to face up to some of them, has created in my mind and in the minds of many legislators and citizens serious questions as to whether or not our school people are willing to be judged by the service they render and the quality of public school graduates they turn out. Many people feel that too many professional school people prefer to come to the General Assembly every two years for an extra amount of money across the board regardless of the quality of teaching, regardless of merit.

I do not want to be misunderstood because I think our schools are doing a good job. But they could do a better job and with what they have. Many legislators in the General Assembly have told me the same thing. During my administration many school people said they preferred no raises at all to any raises based on a testing program. Merit rating plans were opposed by practically all the leaders of the profession.

There was more to the problem than just higher teachers' salaries. As I pointed out time after time, too many of our young people were dropping out of colleges because they were not prepared well in our high schools, too many students were dropping out in our high schools because they were not well prepared in the graded school. I summed up my point of view in an address before a statewide Conference on Teacher Education in Raleigh on April 29, 1960:

Notwithstanding the fact that North Carolina has within its resources met the quantitative challenge in providing more school houses, more classrooms, more teachers, I am afraid that we have, until recent years, tended to neglect that second very important facet of the educational challenge, namely, quality.

The clear clarion call of Governor Aycock for a rebirth of interest in and emphasis on education recognized not only the need to extend to every child the opportunity for education, but also recognized the need for quality in education. Remember the admonition of Aycock that it is "the right of every child to burgeon out all that there is within him." This right cannot be fully realized unless we also achieve more quality in education.

By my own conscience, I worked hard to improve our schools, our educational standards, and our programs during my term as governor. The state's concern over teachers' salaries was evidenced in the 1957 General Assembly when the legislators provided a 15% pay increase to public school teachers and added a contingent 1.09% to be paid at the end of each year of the ensuing biennium if revenues were sufficiently high. They were. Two years later, the General Assembly approved another pay raise for teachers. This one raised their salaries another 5% contingent upon the availability of funds. As before, these funds became available and were paid to the teachers. (Teachers received another, larger pay boost from the 1961 General Assembly.)

During the 1959 General Assembly, the legislators began to look to the future of education, and three special commissions were formed to study and to make recommendations. These were the Commission for the Study of the Twelve Months' Use of Public School Buildings and Facilities, the Commission to Study the Public School Education of Exceptionally Talented Children, and the Commission for the Study of Teacher Merit Pay and Implementation of a Revised Public School Curriculum. And the State Board of Education was directed by resolution to study teacher evaluation, rating, and certification and to report its findings to the 1961 General Assembly.

Throughout my administration, it was my ambition to impress upon people generally the need of a good school system. I made many speeches on the development of education in North Carolina and described the state's future needs. I worked to build a strong State Board of Education that could create and direct educational policy, do the best with what we had, and urge the local units to do more. And across the state there developed among the people a desire to improve the quality of education. People realized that the quality of teaching and the quality of the challenge which each child can find through those open doors of our schools had to be of a high order.

Much of this was accomplished, not by the professional educators but by the lay public. I said as much to the school superintendents at a meeting in Durham in December of 1956. I told them it was necessary to form a statewide citizens' committee to push the development of the schools to the point that our state deserved. This citizens' committee was later formed and Holt

McPherson of High Point became its chairman. He has done a fine job. At the first meeting of this committee, I first saw Dallas Herring of Rose Hill in his best form in discussing from the heart his philosophy of education. I had the pleasure and honor later of appointing Dallas Herring to the State Board of Education and later of recommending him as chairman of that important board—a position in which he served with dedication and distinction.

It will probably be some years before the professional classroom teacher believes that I had a sincere interest in schools when I was governor of North Carolina. I will let the future take care of this opinion. Public school education in North Carolina during my administration, as it had before and has since, continued to move forward toward that dream that Governor Aycock pictured for it back at the turn of the century. I am confident of the future of education in North Carolina and North Carolina's future in education.

A major strengthening of educational opportunities for North Carolina's young people and an attractive feature for expanding industry was the establishment of industrial education centers across the state. These centers were designed to fill two needs. One was to train North Carolinians for better paying jobs in industry and the other was to make the state more attractive to industry by providing a skilled labor force. From either an educational or business viewpoint, the idea of industrial education centers was sound at its outset and held an ever-growing promise for the future. Despite this, there was strong opposition to the centers that almost succeeded in defeating the program.

Behind the idea of the industrial education centers there was the desire for better opportunities in life for Tar Heels. North Carolina in the mid-fifties was moving rapidly from a rural to an urban economy and, if Tar Heels were going to come off the farm and go into industrial jobs, the gap in their training had to be bridged. Vocational courses in the public schools were attempting to bridge this gap, but most of these courses simply were not adaptable to the needs of industry already in the state or that of industry which we wanted to come to North Carolina. With better vocational and industrial training, many of our young people would have the opportunity to stay in North Carolina and earn a better living for themselves and their families.

In the early days of our attempt to attract industry to North Carolina, we found that new or expanding industries looking at prospective sites in North Carolina asked about the quality as well as the quantity of the labor supply. The answer we had to give was not satisfactory to either our prospects or ourselves. We determined to do something about the quality of our labor supply in North Carolina, and the industrial education center plan offered the most progressive solution.

The idea was presented to the 1957 General Assembly with a request for $2 million to implement the program for the centers. Dr. Charles Carroll, state superintendent of public instruction, did not think too much of the idea and largely because of his inaction the program made little headway. It lingered before the Joint Appropriations Committee until one afternoon during the latter part of the session. That afternoon things happened pretty fast. A motion was made to kill the plan for industrial education centers, and it was seconded and passed. The idea seemed dead and it probably would have stayed that way for another two years had it not been for a couple of young legislators.

Senator Richard Long of Person County and Representative George Watts Hill, Jr., of Durham County were sitting together at that meeting of the Joint Appropriations Committee and, after its defeat, continued to wonder about the merits of the idea. Finally, the two young men came over to see me and, for the first time, were told of the many opportunities such a program held for North Carolina's future. They immediately realized the importance of the program and determined to do something about it. Working with vigor and a purpose, Long and Hill succeeded in reviving the request for industrial education centers and got it back into the budget. The General Assembly, however, appropriated only $500,000 for the plan, and this was appropriated to the Department of Administration rather than the Department of Public Instruction. This indicated a lack of confidence in state educational leadership.

A careful study of industrial education as it related to the needs of North Carolina's citizens and their opportunities for employment within the state began almost immediately. The study caused the State Board of Education to conclude that realistic industrial education was beyond the means of local boards of education. Industrial education, the board found, was more expensive than general education. And in many cases local boards were turning to cheap vocational courses, such as bricklaying and carpentry, whether they were needed or not, as the only solution within their means. In such cases employment opportunities—the only true criteria for any program of vocational education—were forced to become secondary.

In the spring of 1958, the State Board of Education requested that all interested local boards of education conduct a survey of the job opportunities in their occupational areas. Where a need could be objectively justified, the local boards were asked to submit a request that their unit be considered for a system of regional schools to be called "Industrial Education Centers." According to the proposal, the state would furnish equipment and pay the cost of instruction. The local boards would furnish buildings and offer realistic educational opportunity to both qualified high school youngsters and adults in the skilled trade and technical areas.

Not too long after that, forty-three of the most populous areas submitted requests for these regional schools, and the State Board approved eighteen as showing a valid need. Of these, seven * submitted evidence that they were financially able to construct buildings and were approved by the Board of Education and the Advisory Budget Commission.

By the fall of 1958, these seven units were building or letting contracts for the construction of $2,350,000 in new buildings. These units alone could provide a new educational opportunity for an estimated 8,100 North Carolinians. Thirteen additional counties † were later approved as sites for the industrial education centers, and construction on the centers was to begin just as soon as the necessary local and state funds were available.

Community reception of the centers was wonderful and school officials quickly became enthusiastic over the program. The centers were financed in various ways and with various combinations of local, state, federal, and, as in the case of Davidson County, private funds. In every case, the centers were designed to fit the needs of not just the community or the county in which they were located, but the whole area and the state. They offered only courses for which there was a demand, and the curriculum was such that it could be adjusted to meet specific needs of employment. In fact, any new plant locating in North Carolina could look to the industrial education centers to provide it with qualified people capable of operating its equipment efficiently.

The courses offered at the centers had two main purposes: training for initial employment and improving the skills of persons already employed. In each of these areas many courses of study were offered. The various programs included the training of machine operators, craftsmen, technicians, and supervisors. Courses offered included such skills as auto mechanics, drafting, printing, refrigeration servicing, tool and die working, and textile process-

* These units included the counties of Guilford, Wayne, Wilson, New Hanover, Rockingham, Alamance, and Durham, and the co-operating cities of Greensboro, High Point, Goldsboro, Wilson, Leaksville, Burlington, and Durham.

† Catawba, Mecklenburg, Gaston, Buncombe, Cumberland, Forsyth, Davidson, Randolph, Lee, Wake, Lenoir, Rowan, and Pitt.

ing, to name only a few. Included among the hundreds of different updating courses were courses in electrical code work, heat treating, precision measurement, and color television servicing.

To enroll in the industrial education centers, Tar Heels had to meet minimum standards for the course to be taken, including a good general education. The only cost to them was for books and supplies. The centers offered the courses at hours convenient to students, and in some cases the centers opened early in the morning and closed late at night. The opportunities offered by the centers were recognized immediately by men and women across the state. By the end of my administration, enrollment in the centers then opened had jumped to over twenty thousand. In some cases, the centers were too small for the number of students that wanted to enroll. And the best part of it all was that the program was just beginning to grow and develop.

Within a few years, when all twenty of the presently proposed centers are completed, enrollment may even exceed fifty thousand annually. Some of these Tar Heels will be trained for industries already here in North Carolina. Others will be trained especially for new and expanding industries that want to come to North Carolina. The industrial education centers were an investment in North Carolinians and already that investment is paying off. Bigger dividends are still to come.

In the area of higher education at the beginning of the 1950's, North Carolina operated a loose and haphazard confederation of state-supported colleges and universities. Some wondered how there could be any efficiency in such a set-up. Others, including me, were concerned about the future effects of the indicated great increase in enrollments at our colleges and universities. We were also concerned about the unnecessary duplication of curricula by the separate colleges, under the urging of ambitious presidents or faculties.

To seek a solution to this problem, the 1953 General Assembly provided for the appointment of a seven-member commission on higher education. Its duties were to make a comprehensive study of the organization and operation of each of the state-supported institutions of higher education and to make recommendations for improvements to the 1955 General Assembly. The study commission * was headed by Victor S. Bryant of Durham.

This study commission made a most comprehensive and courageous report. It concluded, as some others had partly realized, that North Carolina was not getting the results in higher education which might have been expected in view of the amounts of money being spent. The report said: "This state ranks much higher nationally on effort put forth than on results achieved." The commission pointed to a number of reasons for this situation:

One is the unjustified duplication of programs and functions by the institutions. Such duplication in specialized areas of learning is expensive and wasteful. There is no provision for an effective allocation of functions at the present time.

Another situation lies in the present method of appropriating funds for the support of the institutions. Accurate analysis of financial requests from institutions requires that uniform systems of student and fiscal accounting be installed so that valid data on which to base decisions concerning the wise division of available funds may be secured. The collection and analysis of these data call for an agency equipped to render such service and to recommend to the fiscal agencies of the state a budget for higher education which is educationally sound and in the state's best interest. Such control is essential if the allocation of functions is to be effective.

The members of the study commission also concluded that "logical and sound planning for the future of higher education in

---

* Its membership included F. L. Atkins, Dudley Bagley, E. Y. Floyd, L. C. Gifford, Grace T. Rodenbough, and Fred S. Royster. After some delay, the commission employed Leonard S. Powers, professor of law at Wake Forest College, as its executive secretary.

the State of North Carolina is one of its more important concerns."
The report continued:

Perhaps the situation which is most alarming in state-supported
higher education in North Carolina is this lack of planning for the
future. The many problems which the increased college enrollment in the next fifteen years will precipitate furnish eloquent
argument in support of the need of long-range planning. Plans for
dealing with non-resident applicants and for stimulating the production of public school teachers should be made. Planning concerning the extent to which the state can afford to offer expensive
graduate and professional programs for which there is little demand is essential. The recent decision concerning segregation calls
for plans concerning the future of the Negro institutions. The
separate institutions now independent and un-co-ordinated obviously cannot perform this planning function, for it requires some
agency with a statewide view and over-all jurisdiction.

It was natural that the recommendation of this study commission would be to form a state board of higher education that
would correlate and co-ordinate the activities of all state-supported colleges. The idea was not to keep them from growing, but
to see that they grew intelligently and properly, and to see that
they spent no more of the citizens' money than was needed. Following the recommendation of this study commission, the 1955
General Assembly established a nine-member State Board of
Higher Education with authority to determine the general functions and activities of each institution and to co-ordinate their
operations so as to avoid duplication and overlapping in the educational effort.

On June 30, 1955, I appointed nine members to the first Board of
Higher Education.* D. Hiden Ramsey was elected chairman of

* These included Santford Martin, Mrs. T. R. Easterling, Reginald L.
Harris, W. J. Kennedy, Jr., Charles H. Reynolds, William F. Womble, Robert
Lassiter, Jr., L. P. McLendon, and D. Hiden Ramsey. Mr. Martin and Mr.
Harris soon resigned because of ill health and were replaced by Dallas Her-
ring and E. L. White.

the board. Early in 1956, the board appointed Dr. J. Harris Purks, Jr., then acting president of the University of North Carolina, to the position of director of higher education. Dr. Paul Apperson Reid was made assistant director. Both went to work March 1, 1956.

The Board of Higher Education wasted no time and, when the 1957 General Assembly convened, the board had a host of important measures to sponsor or support. One of the most important was the Community College Act, which provided a plan of organization and operation for community colleges and authorized the levy of taxes to support them. This will be discussed in more detail later in this chapter. Another measure sponsored by the board revised the charters of nine of the state's twelve senior institutions. The charters were brought in line with the activities of the colleges and were changed in emphasis consistent with the board's plan to promote the development of a system of higher education.

A scholarship loan fund for prospective teachers was provided under a bill supported by the board. It provided for three hundred regular scholarship loans in the amount of $350 each in the first year of the biennium and six hundred scholarship loans in the second year to be awarded to prospective teachers. Another four hundred summer school scholarship loans of $75.00 each were provided for the biennium. This loan fund provided a big boost to many prospective school teachers in North Carolina.

The Board of Higher Education also proposed a revolving fund for the construction of dormitories. The legislature did not follow this recommendation exactly but did establish a revolving fund for the construction of self-liquidating college facilities and appropriated nearly $6.7 million for specific projects. Other measures backed by the board included the issuance of revenue bonds to provide for student housing and appropriations totaling nearly $51 million. The General Assembly appropriated over $49 million of this for the institutions.

Two years later, during the 1959 General Assembly, the Board of Higher Education did not support or sponsor as many different measures as it had in 1957. Most of its work in that session was in the area of appropriations. The University system and the colleges requested nearly a third more for the 1959-61 biennium than they had in the 1957-59 biennium. The Board of Higher Education cut these requests down to about 17% more, and the Advisory Budget Commission cut them to only about 6% more. The legislators, however, increased the requests until they were an estimated 18% higher than those of the preceding biennium. Nearly $60 million was appropriated for higher education.

In addition, the 1959 legislature had for consideration the board's ten-year capital improvement recommendations. These called for nearly $90 million for the 1959-69 period. The board recommended that about $33.5 million of the total be made available by the General Assembly. The legislators approved just over $22.2 million. Of this, nearly $18.7 million was included in a special bond issue authorized by the General Assembly. This was a good cause, which I enthusiastically supported. Later a Citizens Committee for a Better North Carolina was formed and in October of 1959 most of the issues, including that for higher education, were approved by the people.

The 1959 session of the legislature also saw a compromise worked out to a question raised by the consolidated University of North Carolina concerning the authority and responsibility of the Board of Higher Education. Committees representing the Board of Higher Education and the trustees and administration of the University met and agreed upon certain amendments to the act creating the board. The changes, relating to roles in the control and management of the University and in its future development, were incorporated into the act.

The members of the Board of Higher Education continued to work and plan for the future during the remainder of my administration. After Dr. Reid resigned as assistant director of the board to return to the position of president of Western Carolina College, Dr. James E. Hillman was appointed assistant director. Dr. Purks went on a leave of absence from his duties as director of the board and later resigned. Dr. W. W. Pierson, former dean of the graduate school at the University of North Carolina, served as acting director of the board for a while. Then on September 1, 1961, Dr. William G. Archie, a former dean of Duke University and of Wake Forest College, was named director of the Board of Higher Education. The fine work of the board never ceased from the day it was created. And I hope for the sake of the state and our institutions of higher education that the board will be supported and not thwarted in its very serious responsibility of insisting on quality instruction with the least possible duplication of effort.

Many alumni of the state schools, out of zeal or loyalty or prejudice, objected to the Board of Higher Education's activities and power, just as many people from the University's branches had objected and still object to the consolidation that was put in by Governor Max Gardner in the early 1930's. The issues were well aired in meetings of college boards and in the newspapers, and I think the state understands better than before what the function of the Board of Higher Education is and ought to be.

It took a great deal of courage on the part of Chairman Ramsey and later Chairman L. P. McLendon and their board members to make some of the plans and statements that they did. They were trying to see North Carolina as a whole; they were trying to give to North Carolina and its citizens the best college and university system that it could get for its money; they were trying to prevent duplication of courses, of programs, of degrees. They were also trying to prevent the building of empires on the part of certain college presidents and boards which might be jealous of other colleges and, in particular, jealous of the University. We found little of this among the Negro colleges and their alumni, but much among the others. The board went right ahead with its plans and its programs because it knew that it was thinking in terms of the state as a whole.

One of the chief things that the Board of Higher Education and those of us who favored its work had in mind was the preservation of the consolidated University of North Carolina. It was not a matter of school loyalty but the simple recognition of the fact that the University is the capstone of higher education in the state and ought to grow in strength, influence, and prestige through the years as it has in the past. The board had plenty of evidence that some of the other college presidents were presenting new programs for courses and degrees that were impinging on the fields and responsibilities of the consolidated University. They were doing so without consulting anyone but their own trustees, who could not be expected to judge the worthiness of such programs objectively. This kind of thing happens in other states, of course, and some of them may be rich enough to afford duplication, but North Carolina, with the limited amount of money available to it, could not. Those of us who supported the Board of Higher Education did so because the board could channel these new programs where they belonged. This did not mean taking away an existing program from any college, but simply having an objective board with an over-all point of view review changes before they were made.

When you have three good four-year state colleges such as we have in Western Carolina, Appalachian, and East Carolina, headed by able, dedicated, strong, and ambitious presidents, it is natural to expect them to want to expand. Their competitors in other states are doing it. And on the face of it, it seems sensible to add courses and degrees to the extent that it is convenient for the students of their localities. But if carried too far, this kind of unregulated proliferation (as the academicians put it) could result in a duplication of expensive teaching skills, libraries, laboratories, and other facilities that would wreck the entire system of state-supported higher education. This is especially true in the field of graduate studies and in the teaching of law, medicine, and the other higher professions. The consolidated University is equipped and staffed to work in these fields, and it should be the place to which graduates of the other institutions go to further their education.

In this connection, I would like to testify that wherever I have been in this country I heard nothing but praise for the University of North Carolina and for the quality of work that it has done and is doing. If we by carelessness or by failure do not support both in money and in influence the consolidated University, we can hurt the state as a whole. I have been asked a score of times by people from other states and by correspondents and public officials, "What is the secret of North Carolina and its progress as compared to its sister states in the South? Why does it seem to be so liberal or so moderate. Why doesn't it do as the other states have done?"

These were hard questions to answer, but I have said generally that it is because of our educational system as a whole—good teachers' colleges, both white and Negro, fine advanced institutions, both for white and Negro. But basically it is because in the old days before other colleges were built up to serve the regions within the state, the University of North Carolina established in its graduates a desire for public service in the community and in the nation. It tried to be of service to the state in intellectual leadership; it tried to challenge its graduates, its alumni, and the citizens generally to see the state's needs as a whole, to look at all sides of a question.

The education-minded 1957 General Assembly also provided a plan of organization and operation for community colleges throughout the state. This Community College Act, providing for state assistance for the support of such institutions, is considered by some to be the most significant step in the field of state-supported colleges since the formation of the consolidated University of North Carolina in 1931. Only time can validate that opinion, but the importance of the community colleges to the state system is already recognized and is continually growing. I am convinced it is a big part of the answer to our college problem.

There had long been talk of community colleges in North Carolina. A study on them authorized by the State Board of Education had been made early in the 1950's by Professor Allan S. Hurlburt as a part of a survey of public education. This study called attention to the need for further development of community colleges and presented a plan for it. It noted the many justifications for creating a system of publicly supported community colleges. Among the more obvious were the need for less expensive higher education than that being offered by the residential colleges, the need for vocational training for beginners in various fields including business, and the need for more adult education within commuting distance.

Less obvious but highly important was the need to preserve the senior colleges as institutions to provide upper division, graduate, and professional work and expanded programs of research. Hurlburt's community college study noted, "The increased enrollment in the senior college by the transfers from community colleges will make it possible for the senior colleges more nearly to meet the ever-increasing need for engineers, doctors, dentists, architects, lawyers, educational administrators, teachers, and professional leaders for all occupational groups."

The report of the Commission on Higher Education, headed by Victor S. Bryant, presented to the 1955 General Assembly pointed out: "The community college may be North Carolina's solution for the problem of the large increase in enrollment that is predicted. Certainly it would advance this state considerably insofar as its relative position in educating its college-age population is concerned."

Coupled with the advantages community colleges offered for

the state were the financial difficulties being experienced by the four struggling community colleges then in the state. These were the Asheville-Biltmore, Charlotte, and Wilmington colleges for white students, and Carver College in Charlotte for Negro students. No state funds were then being provided for the operation of these institutions and each was being financed largely from local funds and tuition. These colleges in the mid-1950's had done a good job, but they were at the point where they had to have some state aid.

At my recommendation the 1955 General Assembly decided to take a limited step into the field of community colleges and approved small appropriations for the Asheville-Biltmore, Carver, Charlotte, and Wilmington colleges. Representative Addison Hewlett of New Hanover helped to achieve this. The reasoning behind this was that these four municipal colleges relieved the demands for dormitories and teachers, and they prepared North Carolina students for advanced study at regular state-supported universities and colleges. The state's grants-in-aid to these four colleges were considered by the legislators to be capable of accomplishing the same results as larger appropriations would for the regular four-year institutions.

After the 1955 session of the General Assembly, the Board of Higher Education studied the various community colleges and prepared to recommend significant increases in the state's grants-in-aid program for the 1957-59 biennium. At the same time, the board could not discover a uniformly accepted definition of a community college. It formed its own and defined a community college as an institution dedicated primarily to the particular needs of a community or an area. There was considerable interest shown in the idea of community colleges after the 1955 General Assembly. Many people, including a number of legislators, became keenly aware of the importance a community college system could play in the educational future of the state.

With this importance in mind, the 1957 General Assembly took up the proposed Community College Act, which included a plan for organization and operation and authorized the levy of taxes and the issuance of local bonds for the support of community colleges. During the discussion on this proposed act, it was emphasized that this act would insure the quality of these community schools which would probably start in many areas of the state in the not-too-distant future. In addition, these colleges could provide education at less cost than four-year schools, both for the students and the state. And, proponents noted, community colleges would have the fellowship and faculty-student relationship that only a relatively small college can offer.

There was some opposition to the proposal. Some educators saw a system of community colleges as a threat to the smaller private colleges in the state. There was also some opposition from members of the board of trustees of the consolidated University of North Carolina, and some did not like to have me—the chairman of the Board of Trustees of the consolidated University—backing community colleges. Some of this opposition stemmed from the early interest the State Board of Education had taken in community colleges. Others felt the diversion of funds from the system of existing colleges to the community colleges would not be wise.

Much of this opposition faded, however, as the proposed plan for community colleges was explained. The community college system would be under the Board of Higher Education and not the State Board of Education. Most of the trustees of the consolidated University came to realize that the community college system could assure quality students for the four-year colleges and University system, and that it would take away some of the pressure on the four-year colleges for finding room for the ever-increasing number of Tar Heels who wanted a college education.

The legislature passed the Community College Act. It provided that the governing board of an existing college could pass a resolution asking to come under the act, providing for the transfer of all assets owned or used by the existing college to the community college, and subject to the approval by the people of the county of an annual tax levy. In counties not having a college supported by public funds which would be eligible for conversion to a community college, the county board of education could, under the act, petition the State Board of Higher Education for authority to establish a community college in the county. Upon approval of the petition by the state, an election would have to be called and the people would have to authorize the levy of a special tax to support, equip, and maintain the college.

State funds appropriated for grants-in-aid to community colleges for operating expenses under the law had to be paid on the basis of a specified sum per student quarter-hour of instruction in a limited college-credit freshman and sophomore curriculum, not exceeding the total of local public or private funds made available annually to the college for operating expenses. All state appropriations for capital or permanent improvements were to be made to the community colleges strictly on a matching basis.

This act opened the door for the development of community colleges in the larger cities and towns of North Carolina. Asheville-Biltmore College, the Charlotte Community College System which included Charlotte College and Carver College, and Wilmington College soon qualified as community colleges under the Community College Act. The state had provided an incentive and these communities took advantage of it. Citizens in these communities voted for local bonds in support of capital improvements which more than matched the state appropriations.

These community colleges continued to make substantial progress in the acquisition of adequate and appropriate sites and in construction of new facilities. In 1960 the Board of Education of Pasquotank County submitted a formal petition that a community college be established at Elizabeth City. Following the compliance of the Pasquotank Board of Education with the requirements of the Community College Act, the essential documents were transmitted to the secretary of state in December, 1960, and on

December 16, 1960, a charter was issued for the college under the name of "College of the Albemarle." It opened in the fall of 1961.

The community college program was actually just beginning when my term as governor ended early in 1961. Already these colleges had justified their establishment. They opened up new opportunities for many young Tar Heels who could not afford to go away from home to attend a four-year college. For example, in the last year of my administration the cost of attending one of the major four-year state-supported colleges was between $750 and $1,000 annually for a North Carolina resident. At all of the community colleges, the annual cost was less than $250. It was quite a saving, and nearly two thousand young men and women were taking advantage of it.

Community colleges someday in the not too distant future will provide an opportunity for education beyond the high school level for many thousands of young men and women—educations they could not afford if they had to "go away" to college. For others the community colleges will provide a good preparation for later and more advanced work in the University system.

Despite the numerous improvements I have described in its system of public schools and state-supported institutions of higher learning, North Carolina's major business, education, is still an uncompleted structure. Great things have been accomplished since Governor Aycock launched his crusade for education at the beginning of the century. But the mid-century has presented challenges to education in North Carolina and the country that could not have even been dreamed of fifty years ago. Every aspect of our educational system demands of all of us continued study, wise planning, and courageous action.

CHAPTER IX

The Research
Triangle

THE heart and hope of North Carolina's industrial future is the Research Triangle. While it is actually a good deal more complex, the Research Triangle should be thought of as basically three things. First, it is an actual tract of land—the five-thousand-acre Research Triangle Park spread over the beautiful central Carolina countryside, which a decade ago was empty pineland and where now a half-dozen laboratories and research buildings are a promise of even more to come. Second, the Research Triangle is the larger area surrounding the park, triangular in shape, with corners at Raleigh, Durham, and Chapel Hill—the homes of three of North Carolina's greatest institutions of higher education, North Carolina State College, Duke University, and the University of North Carolina. Finally and most important, the Research Triangle is an idea that has produced a reality—the idea that the scientific brains and research talents of the three institutions, and their life of research in many fields, could provide the background and stimulation of research for the benefit of the state and nation. In a way, the Research Triangle is the marriage of North Carolina's ideals for higher education and its hopes for material progress.

It should be a matter of pride for all North Carolinians that within less than a decade we have conceived the idea and moved quickly and dramatically to make it a reality. In future years—it may well be sooner than most imagine—our Research Triangle will create benefits that will touch every citizen in our state, as well as many throughout the South and the nation. Certainly North Carolina is in on the ground floor of something really big, and it is to our advantage that we have, in recent years, gone a step further than most states and have actively promoted greater interest in research in all areas of business, industry, and applied science.

The Research Triangle, which is now a reality and which is growing in strength and prestige, was the result of hard work and dedication on the part of many people. It is certainly to the credit of our business, industrial, and educational leaders that efforts to promote and develop the Research Triangle met with their enthusiastic co-operation and encouragement. They saw the economic need of the state and realized early that the Research Triangle could be a means of leading not only the Research Triangle area but all of North Carolina into a future of industrial development.

The idea of a Research Triangle, utilizing the personnel and facilities at institutions of higher learning at Chapel Hill, Durham, and Raleigh, was talked about in several forms during the early 1950's. The late Howard Odum, sociologist at the University of North Carolina, talked of a research institute for the development of southern resources to be operated jointly by the University and North Carolina State College. The triangle idea apparently was voiced publicly first by Romeo Guest of Greensboro, vice president of a construction company. His initial interest was simply that of contracts for his company. He prepared a brochure that pictured the three universities in a triangle, and emphasized their combined potentiality for research work.

Of course, research was being carried on at all three of the institutions. But to have let the matter rest with no more than an indication of the possibility of co-operation among the three institutions, without sitting down at length with the universities' officials and without preparing a much more comprehensive plan, would have let the idea die aborning. Guest was one of the first to realize this. So he talked of the idea of seeking industrial laboratories to locate in the present Research Triangle area with a number of people, including especially Brandon Hodges of Asheville. Hodges saw the Research Triangle as a co-operative venture between industries and the institutions.

The idea was mentioned to me by Brandon Hodges in early 1955 and immediately I saw the potential it held for North Carolina. It was discussed, along with many other ideas, as a means to promote the state and to attract industry. The key to its development was co-operation among the University of North Carolina, Duke University, State College, my office, and the business and industrial leadership of the state. There was a need for organization, and, with North Carolina's future at stake, there was also a need for the maximum amount of action.

A Governor's Research Triangle Committee was formed in the spring of 1955 and the late Robert M. Hanes of Winston-Salem was named chairman.* He accepted the responsibility and spent much time, money, and effort to make this dream a reality, which it became just before his death.

One of the first things that we did was to talk with the officials at the three schools to see what resources they could offer. They had given assurances of support but had noted that they could neither commit their offices nor their faculties to the project. There was a definite need for responsible university people to be

* Other members named to the committee, in addition to myself, were Duke University President Hollis Edens; consolidated University of North Carolina President Gordon Gray; Brandon Hodges; Robert Armstrong of Charlotte, vice president for research of the Celanese Corporation; E. Y. Floyd, director of the North Carolina Plant Food Institute in Raleigh; Grady Rankin, Gastonia textile manufacturer; C. W. Reynolds, assistant works manager of the Western Electric Company in Winston-Salem; and William H. Ruffin, president of Erwin Mills in Durham.

brought into the project at the working scientific level. President Gray appointed three persons from the University at Chapel Hill and three from State College in Raleigh, and President Edens appointed three from Duke to a "working committee."

J. Harold Lampe, dean of the School of Engineering at State College, was named chairman of the working committee.* This working committee was asked to find out how many people on the faculties of the three great institutions were then engaged in research or scientific work and whether there were other research people and facilities in the Triangle area; to write a statement of policies and purposes consistent with the Research Triangle idea; and to begin looking for a full-time executive officer.

A subcommittee of the working committee found that we had nearly nine hundred people in the Research Triangle area who were doing research or scientific work. In addition, this subcommittee's report listed various research facilities, such as laboratories, special equipment, and libraries, located in the area. This survey proved that there were enough research facilities in the area to continue with the project, as well as an academic atmosphere that should in the long run attract people to the Research Triangle area.

Another subcommittee of the working committee developed a statement of purposes, which included:

The basic concept of the Research Triangle is that North Carolina possesses a unique combination of educational and research resources and communications facilities eminently suitable to the

* Other members were D. W. Colvard, dean of the School of Agriculture of State; Malcolm Campbell, dean of the School of Textiles of State; W. C. Davison, dean of the School of Medicine of Duke; Marcus E. Hobbs, dean of the Duke Graduate School; W. J. Seeley, dean of the College of Engineering of Duke; Henry T. Clark, Jr., administrator of the Division of Health Affairs of the University of North Carolina; R. J. M. Hobbs, acting dean of the School of Business Administration of the University; and Gordon W. Blackwell, director of the Institute for Research in Social Science of the University. Arthur Roe of the University was named to replace R. J. M. Hobbs when he retired.

fostering of industrial research. It is not anticipated that the three universities in the Triangle shall engage directly in the conduct of industrial research, except under carefully designed and administered policies. Rather, the principal functions of the universities are to stimulate industrial research by the research atmosphere their very existence creates and to supplement industrial research talents and facilities by providing a wellspring of knowledge and talents for the stimulation and guidance of research by industrial firms.

The working committee also made recommendations concerning the establishment of a research center, the organization of the Research Triangle Committee's work, and the hiring of a full-time staff member to serve as a director of the committee. It was recommended that Dr. George L. Simpson, Jr., professor of sociology at the University of North Carolina and an associate of the late Howard W. Odum, be hired as director. He agreed to take a year's leave of absence from the University to map out a workable program and went to work in October, 1956.

Dr. Simpson made his first report to the Research Triangle Committee and the working committee in January, 1957. In it he proposed that efforts be made to make industry and government agencies acquainted with the research resources and environment of the Research Triangle; that a research park be established, if possible, in the center of the Research Triangle; and that a research institute be established to do contract research for industry and government. The Research Triangle Committee adopted the program.

Efforts began almost immediately to acquaint industry and government with the Research Triangle area. It was done on a professional basis. Brochures giving facts of interest on the area's resources in a number of research fields, such as pharmaceutical, electronic, and chemical, were prepared and sent to officials in thousands of companies across the United States. Dr. Simpson traveled as much as possible to urge people to visit and consider the Research Triangle. He was later joined by a number of faculty members from the three institutions, who traveled about the country "selling" the Research Triangle during the summer. Chairman Hanes provided the extra funds needed to support these travels.

By the fall of 1957, a good beginning had been made in acquainting the nation's business and governmental leaders with the Research Triangle. And several companies had expressed considerable interest in the Triangle area as a possible site for new laboratories they were considering.

The idea of the Research Triangle was growing rapidly on paper by early 1957 and with it the need for a research campus such as had been proposed at the January meeting of the Research Triangle Committee. There were many questions and many problems arising from the dream of a Research Triangle Park. For instance, would residents of an area within the Research Triangle be willing to option their land—and what could be used for money to pick up the options? We began looking for an angel.

People in North Carolina were asked first. However, most Tar Heels at the time did not quite grasp the full implication of the Research Park idea or did not have money readily available for such a project. During a discussion of the project with William Saunders, then State Conservation and Development director, he suggested his friend Karl Robbins might be interested in such a project. Mr. Robbins, who then lived in New York, had owned textile mills in North Carolina and was greatly interested in this state. I had known him for about twenty years.

We invited Mr. Robbins down for a breakfast meeting at the Mansion with Saunders, Simpson, and me. Selling him on the Research Park project was surprisingly easy. I had been talking for only about five minutes when he interrupted me. The gist of his remarks were, "You need not say anything more, Luther. I understand. It is a wonderful idea and a money-maker. I'll back you and will put up to a million dollars in the project." This was a great milestone. Mr. Robbins was well acquainted with Romeo Guest of Greensboro and he engaged Mr. Guest to handle the park matters for him. Guest, in turn, named William Maughan of Durham as land buyer. The project developed rapidly.

A special press conference was called September 10, 1957, to announce plans for the multi-million-dollar Research Triangle Park, on a four-thousand-acre tract in the southeastern corner of Durham County and a portion of Wake County. At that time, Mr. Robbins already had committed about $750,000 in options for land and was planning to spend an additional quarter million for utilities for the area. Although he was not present, Mr. Robbins said in a statement, "North Carolina has been good to me and I am proud to play a part in her future growth." He also pledged to work with the three universities and the Research Triangle Committee in the development of the park area.

The land for the park was near the Raleigh-Durham airport. It had frontage on the Southern Railroad on the east and on the Durham and Southern Railroad on the west. North Carolina highway 54, running from Chapel Hill to Raleigh, passed conveniently through the area and there were direct connections with United States highways 1, 15, and 70. Plans for the development of the park area, which was primarily woodland, were placed in the hands of the laboratory architectural firm of Voorhees, Walker, Smith, and Smith of New York. Actual work on the project was scheduled to begin as soon as the plans were completed. The project was, of course, a long-range one.

Interest picked up in the project. Perry Coke Smith of the well-known architectural firm said in Durham, "Unlike many areas that are of interest to planners because they are so bad, this is of interest because it is so good. Its most notable quality is that there are so many communities of pleasant and livable size in the area not too large to afford the opportunity for common facilities and benefits without congestion or merging." He added that the project "creates opportunities in regional planning that are unique and extremely exciting."

In October, I announced that anyone desiring to invest in the Research Triangle Park could do so. Mr. Robbins had authorized the announcement. A few days later a North Carolina corporation, named the Pinelands Company, was chartered in Raleigh by state and New York financiers.* Its purpose was to convert the four thousand acres in the Research Triangle Park for use by research firms. Romeo Guest was elected corporation president and treasurer, and L. P. McLendon, Jr., Greensboro attorney, was elected vice president and secretary. William Maughan of Durham, commercial forester, was named land manager.

At this point—in the fall of 1957—bad luck hit the Research Triangle. The recession the country was then going through had its effect, and many firms cut back their research programs. Three laboratories then under consideration by firms, whose representatives had visited the Research Triangle Park during the summer, were put off indefinitely. There were other problems, too. It took months to work out the matter of securing water from the City of Durham for use in the park area. Moreover, Chairman Hanes of the Research Triangle Committee became ill in the fall of 1957, and Brandon Hodges died in November.

Nevertheless, work continued. George Watts Hill, Sr., stepped up his participation on the project. George Simpson agreed to extend his leave from the University to February, 1958, and to remain connected with the enterprise as long as necessary. In January of 1958, the Research Triangle Committee announced, through my office, that Pearson H. Stewart of the Institute for Research in Social Science at the University of North Carolina had been

* Stockholders of the new Pinelands Company chose as directors Karl Robbins of New York, chairman; attorney Kenneth M. Brim of Greensboro; realtor Collier Cobb, Jr., of Chapel Hill; realtor Claude Q. Freeman of Charlotte; banker George P. Geoghegan, Jr., of Raleigh; contractor Romeo Guest of Greensboro; banker George Watts Hill, Sr., of Durham; and businessman Allan J. Robbins of New York.

named assistant director of the committee. Stewart, quiet and always effective, had made a very worthwhile study of what the state could do to better withstand the effects of hurricanes, after several of those storms had severely damaged our coastal areas. With the committee, Stewart was to give special attention to the physical planning in the Research Triangle. Meanwhile, Dr. Simpson continued his work to acquaint industry and government leaders with the Research Triangle and what it had to offer and to organize a research institute.

The efforts paid off and in late May, 1958, I was able to announce that Astra, Inc., a consulting and physics engineering organization specializing in atomic energy work, had decided to move its principal office to the Research Triangle area from Milford, Connecticut. Astra was the first research corporation to be brought to the area through the activity of the Research Triangle Committee. Initially the firm planned to be housed in leased premises in Raleigh and later to move into the Research Triangle Park.

The announcement of the movement of Astra, Inc., was both historic and auspicious. Not only was it the first firm brought in by the Research Triangle Committee, but its move demonstrated that the cities and various groups of the area could co-operate for the good of the Research Triangle and the state. The Raleigh Chamber of Commerce, Durham interests, especially George Watts Hill and his son, and North Carolina State College had provided a magnificent example of what could be done by working together. The firm moved to Raleigh in July and, although it was comparatively small in size, it gave our project a big boost and showed that plans for the Research Triangle were materializing.

Money became a problem before too long. Karl Robbins and others had bought the land needed for the Research Triangle Park; and contributions from individuals and industries across

North Carolina, but particularly those in the Research Triangle
cities, had paid the expenses of the Research Triangle Committee.
Now, in the fall of 1958, money was needed to pay for the establishment and development of an institute equipped to undertake
research on a contract basis similar to the Stanford Research Institute in California. Such an institute had been proposed in an
earlier report by Dr. Simpson, who had asked President Hanes to
appoint a special committee to study the many problems involved
—especially problems of co-operation among the three universities.
The committee was appointed.*

For more than a year this committee met often. By the summer
of 1958, however, the committee had worked out a proposal for
establishing a research institute that would work in close co-
operation with the three universities in the Triangle area. Substantial funds were then needed and it appeared that the only
way such a project could be carried through was to find someone
to go out and raise the capital.

Archie Davis of Winston-Salem, chairman and a member of the
board of directors of the Wachovia Bank and Trust Company, was
persuaded to take the job. He had the concept of what was wanted
and what was needed, but after making several contacts with people about the state he developed a bigger and more exciting idea.
He and I flew down to Morehead City where Bob Hanes, president of the Research Triangle Committee, was vacationing. Davis
proposed a solution. It was to discard the idea of a profit-making
land set-up, to buy out Karl Robbins' interest in the Research Triangle Park, which amounted to several hundred thousand dollars,
and to go to the public for contributions.

The proposal meant that one and one-half million dollars would

* It included Paul Gross of Duke University, W. M. Whyburn of the University of North Carolina, J. Harold Lampe of State College, C. W. Reynolds
of Western Electric in Winston-Salem, Robert H. Armstrong of the Celanese
Corporation of New York, and Brandon Hodges of Asheville. When Hodges
died, his place was taken by George Watts Hill, Sr., of Durham. George
Simpson acted as secretary of the committee.

have to be raised. Bob was skeptical, Archie was optimistic, and I was hopeful. We decided to try, and we began a more spirited campaign to buy the land in the park area. Funds from the sale of land in the park were to go to the Research Triangle Committee for its work. It was to be a non-profit organization and no one was to get anything out of it except North Carolina as a whole.

It was amazing! In just a few months time, on January 9, 1959, I joined with Bob Hanes in publicly announcing that $1,425,000 had been contributed by business and industry in North Carolina for the further development of the state's Research Triangle as a center of industrial and governmental research. The funds, raised in the campaign headed and sparked by Archie Davis, were earmarked for three purposes:

1. To establish a Research Triangle Institute to do research work on a contract basis for industry, business, and government.

2. To house the Research Institute in a new building to be started immediately in the Research Park, the center of the Research Triangle area.

3. To purchase the Research Triangle Park, assembled in 1957 and held privately by Karl Robbins of New York City, and pass it to the control of the non-profit Research Triangle Foundation.

This was one of the most significant events in the history of North Carolina. Already the Research Triangle Institute had been granted a certificate of incorporation by Secretary of State Thad Eure. And George R. Herbert, former executive associate director of the Stanford Research Institute in California, had begun his duties on December 1, 1958, as the first director of the Research Triangle Institute. Temporary offices and work space for the Research Institute had been secured in the new Home Security Life Insurance Building in Durham, through the courtesy and generosity of George Watts Hill, Sr.

Dr. Gertrude Cox, founder and director of the Institute of Statistics at North Carolina State College, had already taken part-time leave from that institution to organize and establish a statistics unit in the new Research Triangle Institute, with the support of funds provided by John Sprunt Hill of Durham. This first step had been prompted by the increasing need for all types of statistical control and analysis in industrial research. Already there were other areas of work under development by the Research Institute. It was certainly off to a good start.

The Research Triangle Institute was designed to support itself ultimately through contract research for industry and government. It was to have its own professional staff and its own laboratory buildings. The revenue derived from its contracts was to be used to pay operating costs, buy the buildings and equipment needed for research investigations, and to provide capital for growth. The institute is classified as non-profit and none of the net income may be used for the benefit of any individual or group of individuals.

At the same meeting that set up the Research Triangle Institute, the Research Triangle Committee changed its name to the Research Triangle Foundation of North Carolina and increased its membership from twelve to twenty-five. The membership included the governor, the presidents of Duke University and the consolidated University of North Carolina, Hollis Edens and William C. Friday; an additional representative appointed by each university president; and two members named by the boards of trustees of each university. The remaining members represented major industrial and banking interests in the state.

Officers of the Research Triangle Foundation were elected at the January, 1958, meeting * with Robert M. Hanes as chairman. At the organization meeting of the Research Triangle Institute, George Watts Hill, Sr., of Durham was elected chairman of the board of governors; and George Simpson was named chairman of

---

* Other officers were: Archie K. Davis, president; George Akers Moore, Jr., of Raleigh, vice president; George Watts Hill, Sr., secretary; Thomas W. Alexander of Raleigh, treasurer; and William T. Joyner of Raleigh, chairman of the executive committee. Dr. George Simpson, Jr., of Chapel Hill remained director of the Foundation, and Pearson Stewart of Chapel Hill remained associate director.

the executive committee. And at a meeting of the directors of Pinelands Corporation, the operating organization of the Research Triangle Park, George Akers Moore, Jr., of Raleigh, was elected president.

It was announced during the meeting that the Research Park management was expecting to begin immediately to provide water and other services to the park. The Research Park already had a contract with the City of Durham for two million gallons of water per day. And the State Highway Commission had allocated $150,000 for an access road into the Research Triangle Park.

That day—Friday, January 9, 1959—marked another great step forward in the progress of North Carolina's Research Triangle. The planning initiated at the beginning of the project had come to an end. The goals had been reached, and much quicker than had been anticipated, thanks to the help of many people. The Research Triangle Foundation, the Research Triangle Park, and the Research Triangle Institute had become realities. This was, however, just a beginning; and the state and the nation were to hear much more about the North Carolina Research Triangle in the months and years ahead.

Development began immediately for the Research Triangle Institute under the capable direction of George Herbert. Even before the formation of the institute became public knowledge he had started the work of assembling a staff of highly competent scientists. He noted at the outset that the institute's "natural resource is brains; its output is technology for the improvement of our way of life." He did not predict immediate miracles, however, and stated, "We're building for twenty and twenty-five years from now, not for tomorrow or next week." Herbert also began looking for national research contracts for the Research Triangle Institute.

Until such paying contracts could be obtained, other funds would have to be provided from some source. Even after contracts began to come in, sufficient money had to be provided to balance expenditures until a large enough volume of work could make it self-supporting. It was estimated that at least $500,000, exclusive of equipment and buildings, would be required to get the Research Institute on its feet. That $500,000 had been provided by the Research Triangle Foundation at the outset of the institute. Another $300,000 of the funds raised by Archie Davis were contributed by relatives and business associates of Robert M. Hanes to build the headquarters building for the Research Institute in the park.

There was still money needed for equipment for the institute, and in March, Herbert and George Watts Hill, Sr., went before the Joint Appropriations Committee of the North Carolina General Assembly to ask for $200,000 to purchase equipment. The grant-in-aid on a non-recurring basis already had my backing as well as the blessing of the Advisory Budget Commission and the chairmen of the House and Senate Appropriations Committees. Mr. Hill told the legislators, "The Research Triangle is the best single resource for the expansion of jobs and industries on a state-wide basis; it is a resource that can be put to use through hard work and the application of available and reasonable financial resources." The grant-in-aid was later approved and the Research Institute was ready to move ahead.

In June, 1959, the Atomic Energy Commission in Washington announced it had awarded a $160,400 contract to the Research Triangle Institute under the AEC's isotopes development program. It was the largest of twenty-five awarded to private research institutions and industrial firms. The federal funds were set aside to be used to co-ordinate efforts of the University of North Carolina, North Carolina State College, and Duke University in low-level tracer studies, fission product uses, soil moisture studies, and quality control techniques.

The announcement from the AEC came as no surprise. In September, 1959, Simpson and Dr. A. C. Menius of North Carolina State College had opened negotiations on the project. And nearly two months before Herbert had said it was coming and added that it would be temporarily housed in a building then under construction on Durham Industrial Development Corporation property. The project got underway in the fall.

Also during the summer an operational sciences laboratory was set up in the Research Institute's offices in the Home Security Life Insurance Building in Durham. This type of research uses quantitative measurement and scientific study of cause and effect relationships to aid management of industrial and government activities in making operational or policy decisions. It is aimed at such industrial operating problems as the control of inventories, efficient scheduling of industrial processes, and the planning of economical warehousing and shipping.

In addition, an expansion of the institute's statistics research program was announced. Herbert, after only a few months, was able to report to the Research Triangle Foundation that the institute was conducting projects in three areas of research and had received research contracts totaling approximately $400,000. It had already employed twenty-six staff members. It was still a small beginning but the Research Triangle Institute was moving ahead rapidly.

Meanwhile, progress continued at the Research Triangle Park. An additional three hundred acres of land had been purchased. James B. Shea, Jr., was named by George A. Moore, Jr., president of the Pineland Company, as executive vice president of the Research Triangle Park. He became responsible for the business activities of the park and began to co-ordinate efforts to secure new research facilities for the area.

In late April, Durham made its first step to provide up to two million gallons of water a day to the Research Park as the City Council approved plans to boost the city's water distribution system capacity. Under the city's contract with the Research Park, Durham was to supply the water to the city limits. The Pinelands Company was then to construct a pipeline from the city to the Research Park. The pipeline from the city limits to the park area, a distance of about four and a half miles, began in mid-September. That pipeline cost around $318,000, and was designed to carry up to five million gallons of water daily to the park.

The Research Triangle Planning Commission, which had been authorized by the 1959 General Assembly, started its work with an organizational meeting on September 24, 1959. The commission was designed to recommend action to local governing and planning agencies in Orange, Wake, and Durham counties as well as in Chapel Hill, Durham, and Raleigh. It cannot take direct action. Membership on this commission was largely ex-officio and included the mayors of the three cities and chairmen of the county commissioners of the counties, along with members selected by the local governing bodies and three appointed by me. Pearson Stewart became its executive secretary.

In the coming weeks and months, the Research Triangle Planning Commission was to achieve decisive progress in zoning, in road planning, in stimulating planning where there had been none, and in looking ahead to problems of water, sewerage disposal, and the like. It was and is a significant illustration of cooperative planning by three counties and three cities.

Good things come to those who work hard enough for them, and in 1959 good and great things did begin to happen in the Research Triangle Park. First, in May, the Chemstrand Corporation, leader in the chemical fiber industry, announced it would build a multi-million dollar research laboratory in the Research Triangle Park. Carl O. Hoyer, vice president and general manager of manufacturing, engineering, and development, came to Raleigh to announce with me his company's decision to locate its new research facility in the Research Triangle Park. He said the laboratory was expected to be in initial operation by late 1960 and by 1963 would employ over four hundred people, mostly scientists and technicians.

Dr. David W. Chaney, executive director of research for Chemstrand, in discussing the new laboratory location in the Research Triangle, emphasized the value of the academic environment to his company. He cited the availability to Chemstrand scientists of contacts with their professional counterparts and other attributes of the Triangle area, as compelling reasons for the selection of the Triangle as the location for the new Chemstrand research laboratory. He added that it was a pleasure to be able to locate the new laboratory in a controlled, planned development that actually had research as its reason for being. The pleasure was not all his.

This was indeed a wonderful announcement, especially right at graduation time. It held the promise for college graduates that we could offer them a better opportunity here at home than they could get out-of-state. A research laboratory of that size, with the type of employees it had to have, probably meant a payroll in excess of $2 million a year. There were many who deserved praise for helping to get the firm to locate its new laboratory in the Research Triangle. In addition to President Edens of Duke and President Friday of the University, Dr. Simpson and John F. Lee deserved special credit. Lee, head of the Department of Mechanical Engineering at North Carolina State, not only helped orient Chemstrand scientists in this area but had spent several days in Decatur, Alabama, discussing research with Chemstrand personnel.

The Chemstrand people got right to work. William R. Crabtree came up from Decatur to serve as office manager of Chemstrand Research Center, and to set up temporary offices in Durham pending the completion of the research laboratory in the park. Part of his job was to co-ordinate relocation activities in the Triangle area for some 175 families that were to move here from Alabama. In early October, Chemstrand acquired a deed for over one hundred acres in the park and construction began on their $4 million laboratory.

Later that October, I was able to disclose that the Camille and Henry Dreyfus Foundation of New York City had given a $2.5

million grant to the Research Triangle Institute to set up an international center for the study of polymer or synthetic fiber chemistry. The laboratory was to cost some $700,000 and was to be located in the park adjoining the site of the Robert M. Hanes Building, that was to house part of the Research Triangle Institute. The remainder of the $2.5 million was earmarked to support the synthetic fiber laboratory for ten years.

This was an exciting announcement. It was an illustration of the fact that North Carolina was extending its interests and its horizons far beyond the borders of the state or even of the nation. Director George Herbert was elated over this. He declared the laboratory would "draw attention of scientists from throughout the world. This is to be an international program and an international laboratory." He said at the time that an internationally recognized polymer scientist would be selected to head the operations at the laboratory.

The laboratory was to be built in honor of the late founder of the giant Celanese Corporation, and was to be named the Camille Dreyfus Laboratory. The Camille and Henry Dreyfus Foundation is a non-profit organization established as a memorial to Dr. Camille and Dr. Henry Dreyfus, Swiss-born scientists whose pioneer research contributed significantly to man-made fibers, plastics, and chemicals. The foundation was established to advance the science of chemistry, chemical engineering, and related sciences to improve human relations and conditions throughout the world.

The proposed fifty-member staff was to do basic research in the chemistry and physics of polymers (synthetic fiber research), including cellulose and its derivatives. It would in coming years provide for the employment from throughout the world of both internationally recognized scientists and promising young research men. Its head, who was not named until May of 1961, was Dr. Anton Peterlin, a Yugoslav scientist, who was then head of the Physics Institute at the Technische Hochschule in Munich, Germany. All of us acknowledge a lasting debt to Robert Armstrong, who was decisive in the conception and execution of the Dreyfus Laboratory idea.

It was great, and the best part of it was that it was really just beginning. The year 1960 showed a continuation of the progress of the Research Triangle, though not at as rapid a pace as I would have liked. In February, the Research Triangle Foundation approved bids totaling $321,815 for the construction of the Robert M. Hanes Building in the Research Park. In March, United States Senator B. Everett Jordan of North Carolina asked the Senate Appropriations Committee to provide funds for a soil and water conservation and research center in North Carolina. During the summer months another fund drive was conducted in the Research Triangle area to raise the balance of the initial cost of launching the Research Triangle, and it was successful. The Research Triangle Institute continued to get new research contracts.

December, 1960, was another gala month for the Research Triangle and for me, as I was nearing the end of my term as governor and was greatly pleased to see such progress being made. The United States Forest Service, on December 6, announced it would build a research laboratory in the Research Triangle Park. The laboratory, to be erected on a twenty-six-acre site donated by the Research Triangle Foundation, was expected to cost $250,000 for its initial unit and was for the study of the health and welfare of southern forests. It was scheduled to be completed in 1962.

The same day I announced that work would start immediately on a building in the Research Triangle Park for the use of research-oriented organizations. The building was to be erected by John B. Wilson, who had been in Durham until 1959 when he went to New York as assistant to the executive vice president of the Sperry Gyroscope Company. Wilson's action had double significance. It provided a facility for firms that wanted to lease suitable space for pilot operations and it demonstrated the faith that seasoned businessmen had in the future of the Research Triangle.

Friday, December 16, 1960, was a beautiful day for me. I do not recall the weather now, but regardless of weather that Friday was beautiful because it proved definitely that dreams do come true. That was the day that the $300,000 Hanes Building was formally dedicated in the Research Triangle Park. It was dedicated in the memory of Robert M. Hanes, who had spent his life using and developing the resources of North Carolina and who in the last months of his life had worked to develop the Research Triangle idea. The Hanes Building was also a monument to the North Carolinians who had given of their time, efforts, and money to change the dream of a few into the reality for many.

As I was driven through the Research Triangle Park, I could see how much work had been done. The main water line was in, the first roads were completed, and the feeder gas line was then being installed. Over the trees I could see the Chemstrand Research Center building with its great research program in full operation. Down the road construction was underway on the John Wilson rental building, and directly across the road from the Hanes Building was the location of the proposed Federal Forest Service Laboratory. The Camille Dreyfus Building was being erected only a few hundred feet from the Hanes Building.

In just five years the Research Triangle idea of using research facilities at universities in Chapel Hill, Durham, and Raleigh had developed into the Research Triangle Foundation, the Research Triangle Institute, and the Research Triangle Park. And they had developed into all of this. The future of the Research Triangle, with the continued support of North Carolinians, was and is unlimited. It will require more imagination, more dedication, more hard work, and more selling.

The result, however, will be worth it. It could mean, in twelve to fifteen years, a Research Triangle Institute with a staff of over a thousand. Many of these would probably come from out-of-state and would represent a payroll of several millions annually. They would buy homes and become an important part of our communities. But that would be but a small part if the Research Triangle

Park develops at the same rate. Then, within twelve to fifteen years, there could be twenty industrial and governmental activities, averaging three hundred employees each, for a total of six thousand. This could represent up to $30 million in new home construction, up to $25 million in new office, laboratory, and industrial construction, up to $100 million in new income revenue and proportionate increases in every phase of business activity.

Even that is a small part of the total benefit the Research Triangle could mean for North Carolina. Where there is research, there is industry. And if the Research Triangle develops as fast as I imagine it will, then more cities, towns, and communities across North Carolina will get their own industries, which in turn will supply more money locally. For the people of North Carolina, that means better education, better roads, better recreation, and, in general, a better and a more enjoyable life. The poet Emerson once wrote, "Progress is the activity of today and the assurance of tomorrow." The Research Triangle offers North Carolina an assurance of tomorrow, but only if we remember that "progress is the activity of today."

CHAPTER X

Labor and Management,
Law and Order

At the 3:00 p.m. shift change on November 15, 1958, some one thousand members of the Textile Workers Union of America walked out of the two Harriet-Henderson Cotton Mills at either end of the city of Henderson, and the long, bitter, violent "Henderson strike" was underway. From its beginning to its end, it was a blot on North Carolina. It was one strike in which just about everybody was at fault. Certainly both the management and the union were to blame for the things they did and said or failed to do and say. There were two remarkable features of the Henderson strike: during the long days of negotiating, not even an initial agreement that stood was reached, and during the months of violence, no one was killed.

My sworn duty to maintain law and order in North Carolina necessitated sending in up to 150 State Highway Patrolmen to the Henderson strike scene. Finally, when the patrolmen could not be spared from their normal duties any longer, another outbreak of violence brought an appeal from officials in Henderson and Vance County, and I ordered in units of the North Carolina National Guard to preserve the peace. Twice during the strike I tried to mediate between labor and management and twice my efforts were rebuffed, once even after an agreement had been announced. The strike was, as I told the Southern Governors' Conference meeting in Asheville in October of 1959, the most difficult single problem I faced as governor.

Considering its impact on my administration, the Henderson strike began rather inconspicuously as far as my office was concerned. The old contract between the mills and the union expired November 10, but had been extended on a day-to-day basis until November 15, when the walkout occurred. That was on a Saturday. Two days later, a Monday, the strike was underway. The mills shut down and the union started picketing the gates at the two plants. Representatives of management and labor continued to meet in attempts to work out some agreement. Several issues were discussed, including future wage cuts or raises and absenteeism, but the main point of contention was the arbitration clause of the contract.

The contract between the TWUA and the Harriet-Henderson Mills had been in force for fourteen years. In the contract was a clause which said that disagreements between management and labor would be arbitrated. The president of the mills, John D. Cooper, an interesting person, decided the union had taken advantage of the arbitration clause and had taken too many things to arbitration that should not have been arbitrated. His position was that arbitration had been very unsatisfactory to management. He proposed that arbitration be used only when both the union and the management agreed it should be used. The union would not agree to this. It proposed that no changes be made in the contract. The management insisted on the change in the arbitration clause, and the stalemate developed.

The negotiations continued, the pickets marched, and the mills remained closed. Christmas came and the economic effects of the shutdown were felt by some merchants in Vance County as well as by the strikers. Still there was hope that the issues would soon be resolved, the strikers would go back to the mills to work, and things would return to normal. The union representatives, however, came no closer to agreeing with those of management during January. Finally in February management proposed to the union that the mills be re-opened while negotiations continued. This the union representatives promptly rejected, and the mills announced they would re-open February 16. Union workers were invited to return to their jobs.

It was during this period that the Henderson strike was officially brought to my attention. As was customary in cases where violence threatened a community, officials in Vance County and Henderson had informally contacted the State Highway Patrol and had asked them to be alert to assist local authorities in curbing the violence expected if the mills did re-open with non-union labor. There was no request before me concerning the use of highway patrolmen to maintain order, but the informal request of local officials soon came to my attention in a roundabout way. It led to my first official look at the Henderson situation, which in the coming months was to take most of my time, despite the presence of the 1959 General Assembly in Raleigh.

On February 14, 1959, two days before the mills were scheduled to re-open, the sheriff of Vance County and the Henderson chief of police officially asked my office to provide highway patrol assistance to local law enforcement officers who were attempting to preserve law and order in and around the cotton mills. They told me that the strike at the mills was causing civil disorder and added that local law enforcement officers could not cope with the violence that could result from the opening of the mill gates on the following Monday. In view of this appeal, I immediately authorized the commissioner of motor vehicles to move sufficient State Highway Patrolmen into Henderson to assist local law enforcement officers in the maintenance of law and order. About fifty patrolmen were dispatched.

The two mills of the Harriet-Henderson Company opened on a one-shift basis February 16, 1959. Violence at the opening was kept at a minimum as non-union workers and a handful of union people went through the picket lines to work. Negotiation continued at its regular pace, the union maintaining it could not survive without the arbitration clause and the management contending it must be changed if agreement was to be reached. Federal and state mediators could not bring the two parties together.

Violence soon picked up considerably. Rocks were thrown at cars, causing minor damage. Windows were shot out at the mills, an explosion damaged the boiler room at one, and acid was thrown on forty-seven carding machines in another. Explosions caused serious damage to homes and cars of workers. Boyd Payton, Carolinas' Director of the TWUA, was found beaten and unconscious at a motel where he was staying. In mid-March a picket line incident flared, twenty-six were arrested in a ten-minute ruckus, and later fifty additional highway patrolmen were ordered in. Other near riots followed. Practically every day that the mills were opened, violence in some form was reported.

Despite every appeal to law and order, there were continued acts of violence. Between 100 and 150 patrolmen were sent to Henderson but the acts continued, though they were not as serious as they would have been had the patrol not been there. In the month following the re-opening of the mills there were reports of sixteen bombings. There were in the same period more than 150 arrests made, including thirty-nine charged with assault with a deadly weapon, forty-one charged with malicious damage of property, forty-nine charged with violating a restraining order which had been issued by Superior Court Judge William Y. Bickett, and twenty-seven charged with inciting a riot.

Throughout this time there had been a concerted effort to get me to enter the controversy in an attempt to mediate. All the while, of course, federal and state mediators had been working hard, if unsuccessfully, to get union and management to agree on a contract. As the violence increased it became evident that I would have to attempt to mediate. At the same time there was a strong probability that I could accomplish nothing. The union, on the one hand, had seen it was accomplishing nothing with normal collective bargaining and thus had nothing to lose and possibly something to gain by my efforts at mediation. The union was for it. On the other hand, it was evident to management then that it could operate the mills without the union and that it did not have to give in on the arbitration clause.

In short, to attempt to mediate would place me squarely in the middle of a problem which was not of my making and which could not be resolved within the proper limitations of my office. It was improbable, but still there was a possibility that, if I mediated, some agreement could be worked out that would settle the strike. I decided to try to mediate and on March 21 wired Mr. Cooper and Mr. Payton to meet with me at my office Monday, March 23, "to effect a settlement." Both the men, in statements to the press over the weekend, were hopeful but not optimistic that an agreement could be reached.

For the mediation sessions—and there was a series of long, long ones—the number of representatives from both management and labor was held to a minimum. John D. Cooper and William Camp, a company official, represented the Harriet-Henderson Cotton Mills; Boyd Payton and Julius Fry, of Greensboro, represented the union. The sessions were held at the Mansion, away from the press and curiosity-seekers. The purpose was, of course, to do our dead-level best to bring the two sides together.

I listened to long arguments from both management and labor. As a third party I was able to get agreement on several of the issues and was finally able to get both sides to agree to a modified version of the arbitration clause. It was not enough, however. There were statements and counterstatements, proposals and counterproposals made. At every turn there was a deadlock.

If the sessions had included only Mr. Payton, Mr. John D. Cooper, and myself, the strike could probably have been settled there in the Mansion. Mr. Cooper had come into the meetings with a desire to reach a settlement. The public spotlight had been turned directly on management as well as the union, and public senti- ment throughout North Carolina, as well as in the General Assem- bly, was that the strike should be settled. Mr. Payton was equally desirous that the strike end and at times appeared ready to agree. However, Payton had a very serious internal situation in that his assistant, Fry, was undercutting him all the time.

Mr. Fry was ambitious, sharp, insulting, kept the discussions at fever heat at times, and gave the impression to me that his prin- cipal polemic was: "All right, Boyd, if you agree to this, I will certainly see that the union membership knows who gave it away." Mr. Payton would have done his union and its membership great service if he had had the courage to override Fry's objections. The union would not have in the long run lost everything it had de- veloped in its long years there. There would have been a lot less grief, sorrow, and expense for all concerned.

Finally, it was evident that no agreement could be reached and, on April 2, I announced to the people that the negotiations were deadlocked and that I was withdrawing as a mediator. In a state- ment, I said, "The chief and major difference between the parties, when I intervened, was one of arbitration which the mill had, up until then, refused to grant. We were able to persuade the company to offer the union a new arbitration clause which was, admittedly, a limited one. The union finally accepted the rather extensive arbitration sections with the exception of two paragraphs.

"The negotiations finally broke down over the issue of job rights of the workers now in the mills compared with the strikers, also a question of check-off of union dues." In fact, as one reporter noted, about the only thing I could get complete agree- ment on from both union and management was that at the Mansion the coffee was good.

The situation in Henderson was then as it had been before I

had entered as a mediator. The strike scene had been reasonably calm, however, while we had been meeting. Now that the meetings had ended, I reaffirmed to the people that the textile company had the right to operate and continue operating its mills as long as it did so within the law. The union and the striking employees also had the right to strike and to continue striking as long as they did so within the law. Neither side, however, had any right whatsoever to resort to violence or to otherwise take the law into its own hands.

With union leaders Payton and Fry on my left and management representatives Cooper and Camp on my right, I told reporters at the end of the mediating sessions: "In North Carolina whoever seeks to win a strike by violence must be restrained. Whoever throws dynamite at Henderson, or elsewhere within our state, must be stopped and prosecuted. Peace and order must be maintained." That was and remained my number one concern throughout the long and bitter strike.

Immediately after the breakdown of our talks, the calm remained in Henderson. However, there was still much talk over Mr. Payton's claim that in late March a person in a passing car hurled rocks through the windshield of his car as he was driving toward Henderson. Attorney General Malcolm Seawell after some investigation branded the claim a "hoax" and said the windshield had been broken by some object like a hammer. This prompted Mr. Payton to announce that he would file suit against Seawell for libel and defamation of character. Seawell said he would welcome such a suit. It never came.

In efforts to keep down violence in Henderson, Mayor Carroll V. Singleton called upon citizens to observe a voluntary 10:00 P.M. curfew and about two hundred Henderson citizens began assisting law enforcement officers in patrolling the city. After another series of explosions, however, the State Bureau of Investigation set up a temporary office in a Henderson motel and delved into investigation. We called in city and county officials, including

Vance County Sheriff E. A. Cottrell, and emphasized their responsibility to maintain law and order at the local level. I was astonished to find an irresponsible timidity among some of the law enforcement people, especially in the sheriff's department.

The federal and state mediation people meanwhile were continuing their efforts to get the union and management to reach an agreement and had made some progress. Then in mid-April Mr. Cooper made a public statement that the mills could not survive on one shift and would have to go to three shifts or get out of Henderson. He announced that a second shift would begin April 20 and invited strikers to apply for jobs. An increase in violence was imminent unless something could be done to effect a settlement. The mediation people were hopeful that if I would try again a settlement could be reached. With some reluctance, I agreed to try.

With Robert Giles of my staff, I went to Henderson in the late afternoon of Friday, April 17, to meet again with representatives of the TWUA and the Harriet-Henderson Cotton Mills. It was three days before the second shift was scheduled to begin at the mills. We met in the company's office in Henderson and after a short while I felt that the general attitude exhibited, particularly on the part of Mr. Cooper, was surprisingly hopeful. He seemed to be willing to do more than just the minimum required by law for purposes of collective bargaining. As for the union officials, they appeared to be willing to accept almost any settlement that would get their members back on the job and keep the local union organization alive.

After several hours of negotiations an agreement was reached. My understanding was that union members then on strike would start coming in when the second shift started the following Monday. Many new workers had been hired for the first shift and Mr. Cooper had to protect their rights. This, however, did not mean that every job on the first shift was permanently filled, as some positions were still open and some people then on the first shift would probably want to move to one of the other shifts. It was clearly implied to me by the management that most of the jobs on the second and third shifts would be available for qualified union members who applied.

Before adjourning that session around 6:30 P.M., Mr. Cooper indicated that check-off of union dues was perfectly all right with him. The arbitration issue was simply to be left open for further discussion between the union and the company. Bob Giles and I then drove to a nearby restaurant for a sandwich, while Mr. Cooper presumably went to his house in town, and Mr. Payton met with the officials of the two local union chapters to discuss with them the terms of proposed agreement.

We reconvened at eight o'clock that Friday night. Even before we met, however, there was a general undercurrent of excitement in Henderson over the prospect that the strike at long last was going to be settled. The principal officers of the locals attended the meeting and I spoke with them briefly. They indicated their assent to Mr. Payton for him to go ahead and make an agreement in accordance with his discussion with them. An hour or so later, a brief statement had been typed and all parties had agreed to it. There was a great deal of handshaking plus an evident air of relief that the strike was finally settled.

As Bob Giles and I were leaving the company grounds, a large crowd of workers stood nearby. The word of settlement had already reached them and they cheered loudly as we drove by. I was the hero—momentarily. As we passed through the mill village the church bells began to ring out the cheerful news to all of Henderson that the long strike had been settled. It was a great relief although it took me almost the whole trip back to Raleigh to become accustomed to the fact that the parties had finally come to an agreement.

Two days later, the two locals approved the agreement. Mr. Payton sent a telegram to the company stating that "as collective

bargaining representative for your employees now engaged in concerted activity, the union hereby makes unconditional application
on their behalf for their former jobs, if available. If not available,
then any available jobs. The applicants will personally apply for
restoration through their respective foremen and will be ready,
willing and able to perform their duties as employees effective
Monday morning, April 20, 1959. The strike is terminated as of
this date."

What a good sound it had! "The strike is terminated as of this
date." No more picket lines, no more violence, no more discord.
Highway patrolmen not assigned to Vance County were sent
home; law enforcement was left to local agencies. Sunday night
Henderson was returning to normal for the first time in five
months. It seemed almost too good to be true.

The members of the Textile Workers Union of America turned
out in mass at the two Harriet-Henderson mills at the 7:00 A.M.
start of the first shift on April 20. They stood on what previously
had been the picket line, but that morning they did not carry any
signs and did not demonstrate. They gathered again for the 3:00
P.M. shift change and became unruly when they found to their
surprise and mine that there was only a handful of jobs open
for them in the mills. It had been assumed that nearly two-thirds
of the one thousand jobs would be open to the strikers and that
the others would be put back to work as other workers left in the
normal turnover at the mills. Needless to say, Mr. Payton that
afternoon declined to sign the earlier agreement and the strike
was on again.

That Monday night terror stalked anew in Henderson. The law
enforcement officers were unable to cope with the situation that
developed. Shots rang out, there were explosions, cars were
stoned, windows at the mills were broken out, there was a reported attempt at arson, power was disrupted at one of the mills,
and the majority of the working employees spent the night in the

mills. There was again no alternative but to send the State Highway Patrol back into Henderson in sufficient numbers to maintain
the peace. It was done, but not before that night of violence had
left its mark on North Carolina.

The management had failed to disclose to the union representatives or to me that they had very, very few jobs open that they
could fill with strikers. During our meetings the previous Friday
we had talked in terms of several hundred. Management had not
disabused our minds of that. Although they had been operating
only one shift, management at the Harriet-Henderson Mills explained later that they had hired a larger number of people than
was needed for one shift and had trained them to work on other
shifts. This should have been made perfectly clear in the meeting
with the union representatives and me, but it was not.

On April 22, I issued a statement reporting to the people that
the situation at Henderson remained critical and pointed out that
the union had refused to sign the contract agreed upon on Friday
because it felt it had been misled by the mills as to the number
of jobs open for strikers. The statement added:

When the mills started the second shift Monday afternoon,
April 20, only a dozen or so strikers had been given jobs with
the balance being workers hired on the first shift and, according
to the mill, before the agreement was concluded on Friday.

In a conference with the mill and the union held today [Wed-
nesday] in my office, the mill announced that of the 920 jobs
available in the two plants for three shifts each, they had filled
698 prior to the agreement on Friday, April 17, leaving 222 jobs
now available for old workers. Although the mills had not told
anyone how many people they had hired, the estimates from the
union and other sources never ran more than 450 to 500. The
revelation that they had hired 698 people was very surprising to
me and I think the mill should have been more frank in disclos-
ing the approximate figure.

I said that the management of the mills had "intentionally or otherwise" misled everyone as to the number of jobs available on the second and third shifts. However, I noted that "no numbers were mentioned" in the discussion, but management had given "the very clear impression" that "a substantial part of all the jobs on the second and third shift would be held for returning workers." I added, too, that "the union leaders in their enthusiasm probably oversold and misinterpreted the agreement."

Again I emphasized in my April 22 statement that some three weeks earlier I had stepped out of negotiations between union and management "because we had reached a deadlock, primarily because of the attitude of one of the union representatives. It is my earnest belief that, except for this situation we could have settled the contract at that time and saved 250 jobs for the strikers, plus a limited check-off of union dues. By the union's refusal to come to an agreement at that time, they have lost jobs and standing, all because of undue violence they have condoned or promoted."

Still I felt the failure to settle the strike in this last instance was the responsibility of management and on April 22 I wired Mr. John D. Cooper that I was disturbed about the developments and "the attitude on your part which has eliminated the signing of the contract on which agreement was made last Friday. Your failure to disclose the fact that you had hired around 700 people . . . has created an impossible situation and has embarrassed me and others. . . . I feel that you should hold off second and third shifts. Please wire."

Mr. Cooper wired back the next day, April 23, that the third shift starting time had not been announced but that "to shut down the second shift would, in my opinion, be an absolute surrender to force and violence. I do not believe that men will be denied the right to work and industry the right to operate by force and violence in North Carolina." With regard to my statement that

I had been misled as to the number of strikers to be taken back, Mr. Cooper said, "We made no statement as to the number of jobs filled or jobs available and are certainly not responsible for your conclusions." He said the shift had been announced the week before and the assumption from that would naturally be that enough people had been hired to start the shift.

I immediately wired back to Mr. Cooper that ". . . I presume your wire is refusal of my appeal. My request for you to defer operation of second and third shifts is not based on surrender to violence but on your personal responsibility for the present difficulty and your responsibility to the public." At the same time I wired union representatives concerning strike-connected violence. During the next two days a series of telegrams was traded by the Textile Workers Union of America and me. In the telegrams I sent I deplored any violence at the strike scene, and in return they denied any connection with it and offered assurance they would do all possible to prevent it.

The management began immediately to talk of starting up a third shift. The union, at a mass meeting, voted to recognize the management's actions as a lockout and began again their picketing activities. A delay was effected in the beginning of the third shift and I again urged both management and union to take every possible step to resolve their differences before the final shift was added. Violence continued. There were more rock throwings, more explosions, more rifle firings at the mills and the cars of the mill hands. There were several injuries, including gun shot wounds, but none was serious.

As the month of May began, however, the situation in Henderson calmed somewhat. The increase in vacation traveling on North Carolina highways also necessitated moving the extra highway patrolmen out of Henderson and back to their regular posts. There were some fifty-five local law enforcement officers at Henderson and I felt they were enough to maintain order. But if they were not, I emphasized I would send in units of the North

Carolina National Guard. I stressed, however, that "the full responsibility for whether or not the state has to use National Guard troops will rest with those people in Vance County who choose to break the law and cause violence."

Just in case it was necessary, however, the General Assembly then in session passed a bill giving National Guardsmen power to make arrests if called out by the governor in an emergency, such as maintaining order at a strike. Under the old law the guardsmen would not have been able to arrest violators of the law unless they had been individually deputized by the county sheriff. Even with the change in the law, I hoped the guard would not have to be sent to Henderson and stated publicly that I would not send it unless I received a written request to do so.

During the weekend of May 9 and 10, I directed that practically all the highway patrolmen from the Henderson area, other than those permanently assigned there, be removed. I announced in advance that this was being done. I added that I hoped it would not be necessary for the state to have to intervene in the Henderson strike situation again and that local law enforcement agencies could take care of any problems that might arise. However, I made it perfectly plain that if further state assistance was required to curb violence, I would have to call out National Guard troops and assign them to Henderson for such time as would be necessary to prevent a breakdown of law and order in that community.

Violence erupted again Monday night, May 11. It was almost as if the perpetrators were intent on having the National Guard called in. As the shift changed at the two mills, workers' cars were hit by rocks and fired upon. Early Tuesday morning a dynamite blast wrecked a small, unoccupied nursery building at the North Henderson plant. The local authorities were unable to cope with the situation and again requested state aid, which this time meant the National Guard.

"I said PEACE, DAMIT!*"*

Tuesday morning I gave instructions to Adjutant General Capus Waynick to call out the guard. General Waynick was and had been known for years to be very friendly to labor. In the weeks preceding the calling out of the National Guard, I had used him to counsel with me and to talk to the union people to see if we could not get some settlement and to see further if we could not discourage some of the lawlessness. When the order was handed to mobilize units of the National Guard, however, there was no hesitation on his part and he carried through magnificently.

By early afternoon National Guard units from several towns in northeastern North Carolina and Greensboro were rolling toward Henderson. Colonel B. A. "Pete" Peterson of Ahoskie was designated to command the guard in Henderson and came to Raleigh for final orders. He was instructed to preserve the peace and to

enforce Superior Court Judge William Y. Bickett's order to re-
strain violence and mass picketing. The first unit to arrive, a
military police platoon from Greensboro, got there in the late
afternoon. Other units, all of the 2nd Battle Group of the 119th
Infantry of the 30th Infantry Division, began arriving soon
afterward.

The units arrived none too soon. Violence had flared again at
the 3:00 P.M. shift change. As workers were leaving the North
Henderson mill, shots rang out across the gates and a large crowd
of strikers gathered. There were only six Vance County deputy
sheriffs in the area and some two hundred workers decided to
wait inside the gates. Later about twenty Henderson police
arrived, but again it was decided to wait until the guard arrived.
The police left. After 5:00 P.M. some of the crowd outside the
gates began to disperse and it was decided that an attempt should
then be made to get the workers out. They drove out and their
cars were blasted with bricks and rocks. Windows were reported
broken in a dozen or so of these cars.

Colonel Peterson, who was in complete charge of the guard at
Henderson, ordered approximately 150 National Guardsmen to
each mill before the 11:00 P.M. shift change. At each mill the
guardsmen formed a line of bayoneted rifles in front of the mill
gates. At each mill they were greeted by a jeering mob and rifles
being fired at the mills. There was, however, less violence Tuesday night than there had been the night before the guard units
arrived. This was the beginning of the end of violence at the
Henderson strike scene.

In the days that followed, incidents of violence steadily dimin-
ished. The National Guard, which at one time had a strength of
slightly over six hundred men there, kept the situation under
control. Its patrols located troublemakers, made arrests, and at
all times behaved well. A rotation system was set up in the coming
weeks to keep from having some units activated for too long a
period. The guardsmen, including some members of the Air Na-

tional Guard, served throughout the summer maintaining law and order. They allowed union members to walk the picket lines in a court-approved number and prevented any interference with the rights of the owners to operate the mills and the rights of non-union workers to go to and from their jobs in those mills.

The management of the Harriet-Henderson Mills announced on May 20 that the third shift would begin at both mills on May 25. This was greeted by some violence despite the presence of the National Guardsmen, but there were no incidents of violence reported on the Monday night that the third shift began. The strike, for all intents and purposes, was then broken. Of the total of more than one thousand TWUA members who had gone on strike in November, 1959, fewer than a hundred went back while their fellow-union-members continued to picket outside the mills.

Meanwhile, the state was spending considerable money to keep the National Guard in Henderson. It was costing North Carolina several thousands of dollars a day. The General Assembly in late May tacked on sufficient funds to the state's 1959-61 budget proposals to maintain the National Guard troops at Henderson beyond June 30, the end of the fiscal year. A total of $750,000 was added to the contingency and emergency fund for the next biennium for use if needed to cover expenses of the guardsmen.

Soon after that I called on Vance County and Henderson officials to provide funds to employ between one hundred and fifty and two hundred law enforcement officers and thus permit a reduction in National Guard troops there. The appeal, however, came to naught. The National Guard, in steadily diminishing numbers, stayed in Henderson as long as it was needed there and the state paid the bill.

All the while, the State Bureau of Investigation had been at work looking into incidents of dynamiting and other forms of disorder and lawlessness in the Henderson area. On June 17, eight members of the Textile Workers Union of America, including

Carolinas' Director Boyd Payton, were arrested and were arraigned in Vance County Superior Court on charges of conspiring to dynamite the boiler room at the Harriet Cotton Mill, the mill office, and the Carolina Power and Light Company's substation that served not only the mills but the community. Bond for each of the eight was set at $15,000.

In addition to Mr. Payton, those charged included Lawrence Gore of Greensboro, who had assisted Mr. Payton during the strike; Charles Auslander, a TWUA official in the Reidsville area; Johnny Martin, vice president of the Harriet local of the TWUA; and union members Warren Walker, Calvin Ray Pegram, Robert Edward Abbott, and Malcom Jarrell.

A special two-week term of Vance Superior Court was scheduled for mid-July to try the eight men. Judge Raymond Mallard of Tabor City, who had presided over earlier sessions dealing with cases arising from the strike, was to preside. The special session opened July 13 and the courtroom was packed, as it was throughout the trial. Jurors came from neighboring Franklin County and were selected from a special venire of 250 men.

The state's case was based mainly on the testimony of Harold Aaron of Leaksville, who testified that he had talked either in person or over the telephone with the eight defendants while appearing to be a part of the conspiracy and while informing the State Bureau of Investigation. A number of witnesses, including several SBI agents, supported Aaron's testimony of incidents that allegedly occurred from Leaksville to a motel in Roanoke Rapids. The defense rested its case without calling a witness, except character witnesses, to the stand. The defense, however, launched a heavy attack at Aaron and his testimony, calling him a "Judas" and accusing him of "enticing" others into the plot.

After dismissing a host of motions, including ones for mistrial and to quash, Judge Mallard charged the jury and sent it out to reach a verdict. It stayed out for three and one-half hours and then returned a verdict of guilty on each of the three charges for each of the eight defendants. Judge Mallard sentenced Payton, Gore, and Auslander to not less than six and not more than ten years in prison. Four others—Martin, Walker, Pegram, and Abbott —were each given five to seven years at hard labor. The eighth defendant, Jarrell, was given from two to three years because of what the judge called his "lesser activities."

Judge Mallard emphasized several times as he sentenced the eight men, "I hope all of you gentlemen will come to understand that the law is bigger than you, bigger than the union, bigger than any organization, bigger than anything up to the whole of the people.... The good people of North Carolina will not tolerate anyone holding himself above the law ... be he you or be he me."

The sentences were appealed immediately. Bonds totaling $167,400 were set by the court and soon afterward were posted for the eight men. Payton, Gore, and Auslander were each placed under $300 appeal bonds and $25,000 appearance bonds. Martin, Walker, Pegram, and Abbott were placed under the $300 appeal bonds and $20,000 appearance bonds. Jarrell's bonds were set at $200 for the appeal and $10,000 for the appearance.

While waiting for the North Carolina Supreme Court to rule on the appeals, the strike gradually wore down. The National Guard was withdrawn August 10. Violence flared briefly three days later but local enforcement officers moved in quickly to put it down. After that they kept order. About the same time the National Labor Relations Board ruled that there was insufficient evidence to warrant further proceedings in the Textile Workers Union of America's charges of unfair labor practices against the Harriet-Henderson Cotton Mills.

The first anniversary of the strike, however, was celebrated in a big rally by the two locals in Henderson. There were speeches, gifts from various labor organizations, and a "Payton for governor" parade. I was criticized for doing my sworn duty in maintaining law and order at the strike scene. They pledged to continue the strike, and the pickets continued to march at all shift changes. But, with the exception of a dynamite blast at the Harriet Cotton mill that slightly injured eleven people early in December, the year 1959 ended with peace in Henderson.

In mid-January, 1960, the North Carolina Supreme Court handed down a decision upholding the convictions of the eight union men charged with conspiring to damage the cotton mills. Justice William D. Rodman, Jr., handing down the decision of the court, said that rulings by Superior Court Judge Mallard were "not prejudicial but favorable to the defendants" and concluded, ". . . we find nothing from our examination of the record which leaves the impression that the defendants were not afforded a fair and impartial trial. . . . We find nothing which in our opinion would justify another trial as to any defendant."

Justice William H. Bobbitt, however, dissented as to the conviction of Mr. Payton. He maintained that the evidence was "insufficient to show that defendant Payton was a party to the conspiracies charged in the bills of indictment." Justice Rodman, in the decision of the court, said, "The evidence is, we think, sufficient to show Payton's participation in the proposed plan to dynamite the properties of the cotton mill and the power company, conceived for the purpose of promoting Payton's job of keeping the mills from operating and is sufficient, if accepted by a jury as true, to establish the guilt of all of the defendants."

Immediately the eight filed appeals to the United States Supreme Court. In the late summer of 1960, the United States Supreme Court refused to hear the appeal, and the eight men had no legal recourse left.

The trial and conviction of Boyd Payton and the seven other members of the Textile Workers Union of America in July of 1959, plus the Henderson strike in the light of the convictions, was with me for the rest of my term as governor. My duty had been fulfilled when law and order had been restored at Henderson, and, of course, I had no more than a citizen's interest in the conspiracy trial and the appeals which followed. There was, however, tremendous pressure on me as governor not to let them go to prison or to let them out quickly as soon as they got there. Letters and telephone calls flooded my office and demands in behalf of the men came from local, state, and national levels.

As the time approached for their prison sentences to begin, the North Carolina Supreme Court reaffirmed its decision upholding the conviction. Finally, attorneys for the defendants appealed directly to me in a petition to extend executive clemency to Mr. Payton and the seven other TWUA members. I replied several days later with the following telegram:

I have given careful consideration to the petition for executive clemency in the Vance County conspiracy case. I have personally read the briefs and record of this case as submitted to the North Carolina Supreme Court.

Under the laws of North Carolina a conspiracy to commit a crime is in and of itself a criminal offense. This is not a new law. The extent to which the criminal laws of this state were violated in this case and by whom was a matter appropriately decided by the trial jury in Vance County Superior Court in July, 1959.

In accordance with the rights available to all persons, the defendants in this case have, since the trial fifteen months ago, availed themselves of appeal to the North Carolina Supreme Court and then to the United States Supreme Court. The decisions of the appellate courts are to the effect that the defendants have had a fair and impartial trial free of prejudicial error.

The petition for executive clemency does not present any new evidence or information which was not available at the time of the trial. Rather the petition for executive clemency seems to me to be based on the premise that I should substitute my judgment for that of a twelve-man jury, and that I should reach the conclusion that the court processes in this case have somehow failed to do justice. If information had been placed before me showing that the defendants had not received a fair and impartial trial or showing that the defendants had been wrongfully convicted, I would have had some basis for exercise of executive clemency.

In addition to my own study and following the usual custom, I have had the State Board of Paroles make an independent and thorough review of this case. In its report to me, the board said, "There seems to be no doubt of guilt and had arrests not been made by the State Bureau of Investigation, there is every reason to believe that the dynamiting which was planned would have taken place.... After a close study of these cases the recommendation of the Board of Paroles to the Governor is that no executive clemency be granted. We are further of the opinion that parole should be considered as in other cases when a sufficient amount of time has been served to make the defendants eligible for parole consideration."

I have earnestly endeavored to give this matter a completely conscientious and prayerful review. I regret that I must inform you that I cannot act favorably on the petition for executive clemency.

Mr. Payton and the seven other union men convicted of the conspiracy charges turned themselves over to Henry W. Hight, Vance County Clerk of Superior Court, on Thursday, November 3, 1960. Before doing so, however, they held a press conference in the Vance Hotel in Henderson. William Pollock, general president of the Textile Workers Union of America, was present and falsely accused my administration of throwing "its influence" behind management in the strike and also falsely attacked North Carolina's system of justice by stating that the conspiracy convictions "were obviously pressed to justify that course of action."

The eight men were sent immediately to Central Prison in Raleigh to begin their terms ranging from two to ten years. Payton, Gore, and Auslander, who had received the stiffest sentences of six to ten years, would under the state's requirements for parole have to serve only one-fourth of the minimum time, provided a good prison conduct record was maintained. For these three parole eligibility would come after eighteen months in prison. For the other five it would be even less. (Actually my successor as governor was to commute their sentences and all were to be released in 1961.) Later they were sent to camps about the state. Payton was sent first to the camp in Union County but later was returned to Central Prison.

The second anniversary of the strike, November 17, 1960, came and passed with little notice in Henderson. There was peace and quiet there. Pickets continued their protest marching but an official of the TWUA said the strikers were "too busy with other things" to hold another anniversary rally. At that time the national TWUA officials said the strike would go on as long as the locals wanted it to. (It officially ended the middle of 1961.) The Harriet-Henderson Mills continued to run on a three-shift basis five days a week. Violence had completely died out. Henderson, except for some deep scars, was back to normal and was growing.

In prison, Payton continued to contend he was completely innocent of the charges on which he was convicted. In December, Jim Carey of the AFL-CIO and Arthur Goldberg, then general counsel of the Steel Workers Union and now secretary of labor in the Kennedy administration, came to Raleigh. I was not in the capital at the time but the two men talked with Robert Giles of my staff at some length about the case. Giles told them that under North Carolina procedure there was simply no basis for the governor to take the extraordinary action of signing a document that would permit Mr. Payton to be released from prison under parole. He noted, too, that no new evidence had been produced.

During the course of their conversation, Giles suggested that, since Payton continued to protest his complete innocence, it might be that a lie detector test would, if it showed that he was telling the truth in his denial of guilt, afford some justification for the governor of the state to grant executive clemency. Mr. Goldberg's immediate reaction, as Giles told me later, was this should be very carefully considered and might very well be a reasonable approach.

At the time of their visit with Giles there had already been some speculation that I would be named Secretary of Commerce in the cabinet of then President-elect John Kennedy. This was brought up and Carey in effect implied that if I did not turn Payton loose organized labor would look with great disfavor upon my nomination for any public office on the national level. His implications, according to Giles, were that organized labor's opposition would be sufficient to keep me from being named to any position in the cabinet. Mr. Goldberg tried to keep Carey toned down, Giles said, but did not enjoy too much success in this.

It was understood between Giles, Carey, and Goldberg that their visit to Raleigh and the discussion of the Payton case was to be strictly a private visit. They told Giles they did not desire to have any publicity whatever on it. However, that afternoon Mr. Goldberg left on an airplane, but Mr. Carey stayed over and obviously went straight to the offices of the Raleigh *News and Observer*. Despite his earlier insistence that the story not be given out, he related it in full. The next day's paper carried the story with implications to the effect that Payton had been mistreated and that there was a responsibility on me to see that justice was done.

Early in December, Johnson Matthews, chairman of the State Paroles Board, visited Payton in Central Prison and offered him the opportunity to take a lie detector test to support his contention he was innocent of charges of conspiring to dynamite the facilities at the mills. Payton declined. Then several days later Payton announced through the newspapers that he would take a polygraph examination. On December 15, Payton, against the wishes of his attorneys, was given a lie detector test by Cleve Backster, director of the National Training Center of Lie Detection located in New York City. (It set no precedent; every year some prisoners in the state system are given such a test.)

According to Backster, the very latest and most refined polygraph (lie detection) equipment was brought to North Carolina from New York City and used during the examination of Payton. It "indicated and recorded relative changes in blood pressure, rate and strength of pulse, breathing pattern, and galvanic skin response" during the test while Payton was answering the questions. Backster said that "as an additional assurance of accuracy three completely independent polygraph techniques were utilized, each acting as a cross-verification of the other two." The examiner stated that "each of these questions were agreed upon as being completely fair and unbiased by Payton, who was allowed to make suggestions, help formulate, and give his approval of the final version of the question concerned."

Backster's conclusions of the test included:

In the opinion of the examiner, after careful analysis of all charts, Boyd E. Payton was attempting deception when he gave each of the answers indicated next to the pertinent questions.... Based on the restricted scope of the pertinent questions asked, in regard to the specific conspiracy in question, it is the further opinion of this examiner that Payton had definite knowledge of, and did directly or indirectly authorize the specific acts outlined in the conspiracy charge against him.

It is also the opinion of this examiner that Boyd E. Payton deliberately attempted to distort his polygraph charts by movement and other concentrated efforts to produce extraneous responses.

The report of the examiner was included in a letter to me from Paroles Board Chairman Johnson Matthews. The letter was concluded by the statement: "The Board of Paroles does not recommend executive clemency for Boyd E. Payton."

Despite the continued pleas of his innocence, the "not surprised" attitude of one of his lawyers who had opposed the test, and the charge by a national TWUA official that the test was forced upon him, there was no serious support left for the suggestion by some that a grave miscarriage of justice had been done in the Payton case. There could be no responsible question about the lawfulness of his trial and conviction and the fact that after his conviction every opportunity had been afforded to him, and then some, to establish his innocence of the charges. This Mr. Payton had failed to do.

The matter did not end there, however. After it was announced by President-elect Kennedy that I was his choice for Secretary of Commerce, Jim Carey of the CIO came out and publicly stated that I should not be confirmed to the cabinet position because of my actions regarding the Henderson strike and Payton. The opposition did not have any effect on my appointment by President Kennedy and approval of the appointment by the United States Senate.

Looking back now, I consider the Henderson strike and its aftermath the most tragic single matter to confront me during my administration as governor. The violence there was terrible and out of context for a developing industrial state like North Carolina. It cast a pall over practically the entire 1959 General Assembly and necessitated my sending in first the highway patrol and then the National Guard to preserve the peace. It was my responsibility as governor to maintain law and order and to have no favorites. That rule I followed during the Henderson strike and its aftermath.

North Carolina and its citizens, as well as other states and their citizens, should have learned much from the Henderson strike. First and foremost, the strike emphasized that local authorities must accept their specific responsibility for law and order. Failure to do this—and the failure on the part of the Vance County sheriff's department was marked—can bring on trouble of the worst sort. In addition to the probability of loss of life and property, such failure could bring on a breakdown of law-enforcing authority. This would be a fatal weakness in government. County and city governments have the power, the opportunity, and, above all, the responsibility to maintain law and order.

If the city or county or any one layer of our government is weakened or fails for other reasons to do its duty, then it passes the buck and the responsibility to the next higher echelon. In the case of the Henderson strike, Vance County shamefully passed the buck to the State of North Carolina. Had we failed, the next step would have been for the federal government to step in. Carried to an extreme, the failure of popular democratic government to function properly at each level creates great risks of ultimate dictatorship. Naturally, the antidote to such a development lies in an informed and interested citizenship and electorate, plus elected and appointed officials who put duty above popularity or personal gain.

CHAPTER XI

Foreign Lands and
Foreign Visitors

IN the summer of 1959, I took a three and a half weeks'
tour of the Soviet Union. I talked with Russian workers as well
as with Russian officials and tried to learn as much about that
country and its people as I could. At the same time, I told
Russians whenever I could about the United States and North
Carolina and our people. I passed out countless good North
Carolina cigarettes and colorful post cards showing scenes in
the Tar Heel state. I talked about our state, what it was doing
in industry, in agriculture, in education, and how we were preparing for an ever better future. It was an opportunity to learn
a lot about their country and, I think, helped in some small
way to create a better understanding of the United States among
many of the Russian people I met and talked with.

I was one of nine members of the executive committee of the
National Governors' Conference that made the trip.* The venture was sponsored by the Institute of International Education
with funds from the Alfred P. Sloan Foundation and the Rocke-

* The others were Governor LeRoy Collins of Florida, who was then chair-
man of the executive committee, and Governors Robert Meyner of New
Jersey, William G. Stratton of Illinois, George D. Clyde of Utah, Cecil H.
Underwood of West Virginia, Stephen L. R. McNichols of Colorado, John E.
Davis of North Dakota, and Robert E. Smylie of Idaho.

feller Brothers Fund. There was no public money involved in the trip.

Before leaving for the Soviet Union, we met with President Eisenhower and other federal officials in Washington. The President was keenly interested in what we might accomplish or learn and requested that some of us come back through Washington on our return trip. After these interviews we flew from Washington to New York to Paris to Moscow. There, at the Vnukovo Airport, we were met by Alexander Kuznetsov, vice chairman of the Soviet Committee on Cultural Relations and others and were whisked off in a fleet of limousines to the Sovietskaya Hotel on the other side of town. Soon after began talks with many Russian officials who talked about Soviet advances and Communist values.

On our last day in Moscow before leaving for a tour of some of the Soviet republics, we went to the Industrial and Agricultural Exposition. By this time everyone in the delegation and most of the Soviet officials knew that I wanted to see Russian tobacco. I had made it quite plain that I wanted to see tobacco plants or leaves and a tobacco factory where cigarettes were made. At this exposition they took us to the Armenian building where I had the opportunity to look at leaves of tobacco that had been grown in Armenia. I could not resist the temptation of taking out a pack of North Carolina cigarettes and comparing it with the Soviet tobacco.

I was still interested in getting to see a tobacco factory, but I had to wait until our group went to Leningrad to see one. The Minister of Economics there personally arranged for me to see the factory and I spent an hour or more looking around. They showed me everything and gave me samples of all their cigarette products. This factory produced "paperos" or the short cigarettes attached to long cardboard holders. The cigarette boxes were done up in fancy style. They had automation, but their machinery was old and far behind ours. Their costs, however, and the selling prices were not too far off ours. The plant manager told me with some pride that the factory produced ninety million cigarettes a day. He was somewhat amazed when I told him that North Carolina produces several hundred *billion* cigarettes a year.

Later, in Tbellissi, I was able to visit a textile mill, see cotton yarn being made, and see some full-fashioned hosiery being made. There were about three thousand workers in the mill, and they worked eight hours a day for five days and six hours on Saturday. The machinery in the plant was quite old, although it had some modern attachments. The markings on the machines indicated that they were made in the Soviet Union, although some of the carding machines came from East Germany. I was able to see the housekeeping and sanitary conditions of the mill, the various educational rooms, and the recreation grounds. Many more people were employed there than were needed for an efficiently operated mill. Later I saw a more efficient and modern mill at Tashkent.

Because of all the effort I had been giving to the industry program, I had been kidded a little before leaving North Carolina about the possibility of my trying to get a Soviet industry to open up a plant in our state. In Leningrad, while talking with the Minister of Economics, I thought of this and decided to see what would happen. I told the minister that I had seen or heard of some unique hospital equipment that the Soviets had invented that would cost only a fraction of what it would cost elsewhere, including the United States. And then I asked if he would consider putting a plant to produce such equipment in North Carolina, since we were always looking for new industry. I pointed out to him that the question was one of policy as well as economics and that I would like to get his answer.

While I was only half serious, I was curious to know his reaction. My question created amusement among most of the Russians as well as among our own party. The minister, however, took it quite seriously and said after a moment that their officials would have to think that over. He added that I would have to go through channels to present the matter. The next night at a party, he came up to me and, through an interpreter, told me they had been thinking over what I had said and that it created a most interesting situation. He stated, however, that the officials he had talked with about it thought such a relationship would be quite excellent. I told him something could probably be done, but for the present we should think more seriously in terms of better understanding and improved relations between our two countries.

All across the Soviet Union, our delegation talked with Russians. Although Russians in the cities of Moscow and Leningrad took our visit rather matter-of-factly, we were greeted very warmly in places like Kiev, Tiflis, Tashkent, Samarcand, and Alma Ata. Near Kiev, for instance, a Russian housewife brought out a cake. There was not enough to go around but I got a piece of it. It was good, and she was all smiles when we complimented her. Later I gave a man a cigarette lighter and then had a rough time keeping him from giving me a watch in return. And after we had been shown around a collective farm, a milkmaid invited us to "come back to visit us next year and see our progress."

Twice during the trip I had cause to take exception to things that local Soviet officials said. Once it was after an official in the Republic of Georgia gave a toast calling for peace and left the direct impression that only Russia was interested in peace and peaceful uses of atomic energy. This bothered me and I took issue with it. I told him that I thought the "man on the street" that I had met in Russia was just as interested in peace as we in the United States were. I added, however, that the "man on the street" in Russia had not been told by his leaders that the Soviets were not the only ones interested in peace.

I explained that at our own North Carolina State College experts were doing work on the peaceful use of atoms on peanuts. I related the experience I had had some years before when I was

"It was his brainwashing, I just got carried away!"

an observer at the United Nations and the then Ambassador Gromyko refused the United States' offer to stop making atom bombs for destructive purposes and to use atomic energy for peaceful purposes. Then I said that Russia had no monopoly on peace. We in the United States wanted it and prayed for it. The message was as direct as I could make it and was well received. The deputy minister of the republic later referred to it in one of his toasts.

The other time I took exception to something a Soviet official said came at fabled Samarcand. A local representative of the Russian Intourist Service launched into a brief tirade about churches and said that they were absolutely no good. He contended that churches meant nothing to people and that atheism was the only sensible answer. It had been a hot and tiring day and this was simply too much for me. I asked Governor Collins, the chairman of our group, if I could reply and he promptly agreed.

I told the Soviet official there that we appreciated the hospitality of our hosts and that we were happy to share in their toast to peace and friendship between nations, but that I thought that since we were in Samarcand as tourists and friends some respect would be shown for our own feelings and beliefs. Continuing, I said that we had listened patiently and politely to all their propaganda about Soviet progress but that we did not have to listen to their propaganda about atheism. We Americans believe in God and in our own religious faiths, whether Christian or Jewish, and I concluded: "I am weary of hearing you berate the church and God."

There was a deadly silence for a whole minute. We adjourned that meeting quickly and returned to our hotel. Many people in our group expressed approval of what I had said, and later one of our guides who was connected with the Security Department of the Soviet government commended me for my action. The fact that he took me behind a tree to pay his compliment was rather significant.

We governors had our summit meeting with Premier Nikita Khrushchev on Tuesday, July 7, 1959. It lasted three hours and forty minutes. It was a great experience, yet it was filled with concern, mainly because of the capability and dedication of the man Khrushchev. He was the shortest man in the room in height, but he made up for that in many ways. He was a man of many moods. He was as smart a man as I have ever met anywhere. He could be suave, ruthless, full of humor, or show a clinched fist. He not only gave his side of the story with details and dates, but took on each of the seven governors who attended the session on any point, and out-maneuvered each person who really argued with him.

After we were seated in his office, Mr. Khrushchev extended his greetings, and, although he did not smoke, he offered Russian cigarettes to us, saying cigarette smoking will give you cancer. Of course, I took occasion to place a pack of North Carolina cigarettes on the table with the ones he furnished and said to him, "Our North Carolina cigarettes won't give you cancer." He was most cordial and made us feel at ease. In his welcoming speech, Mr. Khrushchev said, "We are glad to see you folks from America, a country that is rich and strong. We want to be like you." He reiterated the idea of wanting to be like America time after time during the next three hours.

Naturally, Mr. Khrushchev did most of the talking. On any question, whatever it was, he did not hesitate to answer. Some of our questions and some of the comments from our side were searching and somewhat bitter and at times displeased him. Most of the time, however, was spent in exploring vital issues and trying to develop better relations. He was fairly placid during most of the interview, except when he became aroused while talking about the German situation, war, and the suspicion he had toward the United States. Throughout our talk, he had a colorful small knife in his hands which he fingered with his short stubby fingers.

After the opening remarks by Governor Collins, Mr. Khrushchev said that he was glad that we had come to his country and that it would make for better friendship. I later took up this point and said that our visit with the people in the various republics had been helpful. I noted that we had found the Russian people friendly to Americans as individuals and that I thought a further exchange not only of tourists but of officials would be most helpful. I suggested that he spend at least $10 million during the next year in sending Russians, particularly students, to the United States on an exchange basis. In turn, I told him that we would try to persuade President Eisenhower to do the same thing. He agreed but stated, "We can't forge the dollars, so how are we going to pay for it?"

I countered this by pointing out he could reduce Soviet spending for bombs and other things designed for destruction and use that money for an exchange program. He dismissed this immediately with a tirade about trade, and that was one of his main subjects from then on. He contended that Russia was being discriminated against because United States laws were bad for trade along certain lines. In the midst of this tirade, he suddenly stopped and asked, "Shall we speak frankly on all matters, or, shall we hedge and try to be nice to each other?" We all immediately urged him to speak as frankly as he wished.

Then Mr. Khrushchev said, in part: "What is it that you want? I think I can tell you what you want, or at least what we think you want, and you will never achieve it. You can't achieve what you want by the exchanging of people or sending the American papers in, because you want to turn our people away from the Communist way of life they have adopted. You may try to do it but you will never succeed. We have made tremendous progress [under communism]."

Finally, he made an indictment we ought to consider seriously. He said, "I know your great country. I know its history from the time it was founded, your breaking away from colonialist England and the marvelous progress you have made since that time, which we want to emulate. But have you grown fat and smug, and are you looking down your noses at the other people in the world? Have you forgotten to think realistically? Pardon me if I am rude." It was a very sobering and effective speech.

Our discussion finally got around to Berlin. It had been agreed beforehand that I, because of my experience in Germany and having been in Berlin during the 1948 blockade, would defend the American position. However, one of the other governors raised the question of Berlin and another, in the heat of the discussion, impatiently took up the argument and there was a very heated

exchange with some fire between the questioner and Mr. Khrushchev. My only comment was that "there are Democrats and
Republicans sitting around the table, but we are American citizens over here and we stand as one as far as our country's policies
are concerned." Mr. Khrushchev said he understood that and respected it. He continued to talk about the German situation.

Toward the end of our conference, Governor Collins thanked
Mr. Khrushchev and asked him what message we could take home
from him to President Eisenhower and the American people that
would help to lessen the tensions between our countries and help
to achieve an enduring peace. Mr. Khrushchev apparently took
this request quite seriously. He dropped his head slightly, folded
his hands, and began his answer in a very low voice.

"What do we want?" he asked as he answered the question. "We
want peace and friendship. We want peace with all nations, especially the United States of America. If the U.S.S.R. and the United
States have friendship, there can never be a world war, and if
another nation starts a world war we together can stop it. A conflict between us would be terrible. Your country and mine have
a greater responsibility than do smaller nations. Let us work together." On lessening tensions, he suggested agreement on ban-
ning atomic tests and suggested that we had a good chance of
agreeing. He also mentioned solutions to the differences over Germany and disarmament agreements as ways to easing tensions.

On insuring peace, Mr. Khrushchev declared, "We want peace
with you. The United States is rich but we are not envious. We
want to be like you. We would like to co-operate and expand our
economic ties.... We do not want war. War between us would
be calamity. We have no desire for expansion. We would like to
co-operate with the United States of America in aid to undevel-
oped countries, and leave off spending as much money as each
of us is spending in the armament race."

If we can believe what he said toward the end of the conference, and I am an optimist and feel that we can believe some of

it, then there is always hope for a peaceful future. At least in the
desire for peace the average American and the average Russian
have hope in common.

In mid-1959, Sekou Touré, president of the new African republic of Guinea, was planning for a sixteen-day tour of the United
States. As part of this good-will trip, he insisted that he be allowed to visit the South. It was said by some that he wanted to
visit the South because he felt he would not get good treatment
and that would give him ammunition against the United States
and the West. The State Department was worried somewhat over
this, I understood, because President Touré was a smart African
leader and the timing was critical in our relations with his country. One southern state, I understood, was called first to see if
Touré could visit there, but for political reasons that state's officials declined to extend an invitation.

When Director of U.S. Information Agency George Allen called
me about the possibility of President Touré's coming to North
Carolina for a brief visit, I told him, "I don't know what it entails
or where we will come out, but if it will help the United States,
the answer is 'yes.' " It was decided that he would come to North
Carolina in late October after seeing President Eisenhower in
Washington. His visit to our state was to be the first by a head of
state since President Celal Bayar of Turkey came in 1954. We
made elaborate plans to entertain Touré, although his visit was to
last only twenty-four hours and during that time he would tour
institutions and businesses in Chapel Hill and Durham.

Before President Touré's arrival at the Raleigh-Durham Airport
in mid-afternoon on Wednesday, October 28, I held a conference
to brief representatives of the news media on our program and to
let them ask questions. We had a good meeting and toward the
end of it Bill Armstrong of WRAL-TV in Raleigh said he would
like to say a few words. He told us he had been called by a representative of a national network and asked to furnish about two

hundred feet of film on the visit of President Touré to North Carolina. Bill said he told the man he would be glad to do it and asked him what part of the visit he would like to have.

Bill said the network representative said he wanted film on the "riots in the streets" that would greet President Touré when he arrived in North Carolina. Bill said he told the man, "You don't understand North Carolina and Governor Hodges. There will be no riots and no trouble." The network had no further interest in the film, Bill added, and the representative hung up the phone.

A crowd of two hundred people, predominantly Negro, greeted President Touré when he arrived at the airport. I welcomed him to North Carolina and he was welcomed to the area by Chancellor William B. Aycock of the University of North Carolina, Chapel Hill's vice mayor Gene Strowd, and North Carolina College President Alfonso Elder from Durham. Included in the President's party were other officials of Guinea, members of the United States State Department, and American Ambassador to the Republic of Guinea John H. Morrow, a former professor at North Carolina College in Durham.

The group then went to Chapel Hill for a tour of the University of North Carolina, a press conference by President Touré, and a private dinner party that evening. At the dinner, I again welcomed him and said, "We hope that in the short time you are in the State of North Carolina you will obtain a greater understanding of our people. We hope that we will impress you as good neighbors, because four and one half million North Carolinians join with the President of the United States and all other Americans in extending to the Republic of Guinea our expressions of friendship and good will."

The next day, Thursday, the red carpet was rolled out in Durham for President Touré. At North Carolina College President Alfonso Elder conferred on him the honorary doctor of laws degree. It was the first such presentation in that school's history. In downtown Durham, President Touré and his party toured the North

Carolina Mutual Life Insurance Company and the Mechanics and Farmers Bank, both Negro owned and operated. Durham Mayor E. J. Evans presented President Touré with the key to the city. At Duke University, he was greeted by President Hollis Edens and later was the guest of that university at a luncheon.

I rejoined the group later that afternoon as President Touré was leaving North Carolina for Chicago. As he boarded the plane, he told reporters, "I am very, very happy with my visit to this state." When he was asked if the visit had changed any of his conception of southern racial relations, he answered, "No ... it reinforced my previous conceptions. If my ideas had not been favorable before leaving Guinea I should not have come here." Of the Negroes he had seen in North Carolina, President Touré said, "I saw in their eyes the joy and confidence they had in their own activities and I was struck by the size and amplitude of their organizations ... especially in the insurance company ... and by the results of their common activities" as at North Carolina College.

Ambassador Morrow said that President Touré and his party had been "very much touched and moved" by the reception they received in North Carolina. He was given a good impression of North Carolina and its people. We were trying to co-operate with President Eisenhower and the rest of the country in entertaining President Touré and I believe that this helped maintain good relations between the two countries.

I received only two letters of complaint against my inviting President Touré and his party to visit North Carolina. Only one of these letters was from North Carolina. On the other hand, we received scores of approving messages from all parts of the world. Later George V. Allen, then director of the United States Information Agency, told the *Durham Morning Herald* that North Carolina's reception for President Touré had paid international dividends for the United States. Allen added that the relations between Guinea and the United States had been "altered very materially in our favor primarily from the reception received in North Carolina" by President Touré.

In the late fall of 1961 I was asked by President Kennedy to represent him at the Independence Day celebration of the newly formed nation of Upper Volta in former French West Africa. This trip to Africa gave me an opportunity to repay the Touré visit to North Carolina so I arranged to take my party from Ouagadougou, the capital of Upper Volta, to Freetown, Sierra Leone, a former British colony, and from there to Guinea.

President Touré was exceedingly cordial. His ambassador and other officials met us at the airport, provided us a private villa with an honor guard and President Touré paid us an official visit at which we discussed some matters of mutual interest to the United States and Guinea. The President spoke in most friendly terms of his North Carolina visit.

After the 1960 elections were over and my administration in North Carolina was drawing to a close, I joined a number of other governors for a two-weeks tour of Argentina and Brazil. This trip was to allow our group to meet with our counterparts and other officials in these South American countries and to discuss state-craft and problems affecting these officials and their jobs. The trip was arranged by the National Governor's Conference partly because of the success of the trip that nine of us took to the Soviet Union in 1959. These two South American countries were selected for the tour because of the sesquicentennial of the first attempted liberation in Argentina and because of the founding of the new capital, Brazilia, in Brazil.

About thirty governors and their wives, plus a couple dozen paying guests, made the trip. As on our trip to Russia, there were no public monies used. After much negotiation with foundations, a program was worked out under which the Argentine and Bra-zilian governments invited the U. S. governors and their wives to come as their guests. Their purpose in this was to make what they called "propaganda" and what we called "public relations." In my group on the trip, other than Mrs. Hodges and I, we had Mr. and Mrs. Thomas J. Pearsall of Rocky Mount, Mrs. Mary Laurens Richardson of Raleigh, and Mrs. Mildred Andrews of Vienna, Virginia. They paid their own expenses.

Our group met at the airport in New York about noon on Saturday, November 12. After the other governors and other similar groups had gathered, we attended a briefing by a representative of the State Department and then boarded an Argentine airliner for the flight south. We stopped at Trinidad for refueling about midnight and arrived at Rio de Janeiro early Sunday morning and at Buenos Aires about noon Sunday. There they really rolled out the red carpet. A large number of Argentine officials greeted us and there was quite a welcoming speech ceremony. They had even built an arch with the flags of all the countries of the Organization of American States.

All of the governors on the tour were assigned automobiles for the entire visit, with the name of each governor on the license plate of "his" car. We went from the airport to the hotel. Activities began almost immediately. However, Mrs. Hodges and I were a little tired so we stayed at the hotel and rested. Later we took a tour around the harbor and visited friends.

Monday started a busy schedule for us all. We first went to the United States Information Agency for a briefing by the new Ambassador from the United States to Argentina, Mr. Roy R. Rubottom. We later went to the monument of General San Martín, who led the fight for the liberation of Argentina. There four governors placed a big wreath in a most impressive ceremony. After that, there began a series of meetings with the various governmental officials at which we talked over a number of subjects and asked questions of one another. Similar sessions were held practically everywhere we went and were most informative.

Before noon, we gathered in the White Room of the Government House where we were greeted by the various members of the President's cabinet. Soon after the President of the Republic, Mr. Arturo Frondizi, came in and shook hands with all the governors. He then gave a speech, describing the relationship between his country and ours. He told us of some of the ideals and ambitions of Argentina as it faced the future following the Perón dictatorship. He spoke feelingly of how his country, with such a promising future, had lost ground in the Perón era. President Frondizi struck all of us as being a dedicated man working under great difficulties. Governor Mennen Williams of Michigan responded to President Frondizi's speech in Spanish. He did very well indeed, as I was told, and his speaking their language certainly made a hit with the President and others present.

A luncheon followed attended by a number of Argentine and American businessmen. The speech of welcome and a discussion of Argentina was given by an Argentine businessman. Governor Steve McNichols of Colorado, then chairman of the National Governors' Conference, asked that I respond. In the conversation at my table, I gathered that there was some concern among businessmen about the election of John Kennedy. In my response, I stressed that the new administration would certainly be sound, financially and otherwise, and would work to improve trade relations, as well as friendly relations generally, with Argentina. My talk was well received.

Incidentally, since we had arrived in South America there had been a great deal of speculation about my being selected by Mr. Kennedy to be Secretary of Commerce in his administration. I knew nothing about it except what I had read in the papers, but people kept coming up to me and talking about it. Even when Governor McNichols introduced me at the luncheon, he referred to the rumored cabinet position and presented me as the next Secretary of the Interior. His mix-up of cabinet positions brought plenty of laughter and jokes.

Mar del Plata, the province (state) that we visited Tuesday, was a most attractive place and the visit was a lot like going to a beach in North Carolina in early May. We were welcomed at the airport by a fine crowd, including the well-known mayor, Mr. Teodoro Bronzini, and by Governor Oscar Alende. After getting settled in our hotels, we boarded cars for the trip to the estancia or ranch owned by Señor and Señora José Martinez de Hoz. It was a wonderful place. Following lunch, we visited the stables where we saw the famous stud horses that this man had for his racing stables and later saw a game called "pato"—something like a basketball game on horses.

We were interested in seeing an industry, so they took us to Cordova, where we saw the big Kaiser automobile plant. We found it very efficient and the people most friendly. A couple of days of comparatively relaxed activity followed—and we needed it. We visited the resort town of Bariloche in the Patagonia section of Argentina. The program called for a visit to Victoria Island, but Governor Williams and I decided that we would rather fish. The guide we found was quite a person. He had come to Argentina from Texas some fifty years before. He told us his father had felt that Texas was closing in on him and he just wanted to get to an open spot. He certainly found it in southern Argentina. His name was Sam Wagner.

Sam told us of having fished with President Eisenhower. President Eisenhower did not get many fish, Sam said, but quickly added that he was there in an off-season. Sam also mentioned, as former fishing partners, King George of England, the Prince of Wales, General Pershing, and many others. He knew his fishing, too. I hooked and lost two salmon—big ones, of course—and then brought in a twenty-seven inch, seven pound brown trout that was a beauty. I also landed a small salmon of "eating size," as Sam called it. Soapy Williams landed three salmon and they were good ones. The next day Soapy and I went fishing again. I let another big one get away, and Soapy got one fairly sizable fish.

Back in Buenos Aires, we had another full day to round out our full week in Argentina. We saw horse racing, went to a sesquicentennial celebration of Argentina's May, 1810, Revolution, held a press conference, and attended a black tie dinner given by the minister of the interior. This dinner, like all the others, went on into the night and was a gala affair. We left Buenos Aires the next morning after a happy week in Argentina.

We arrived in Rio de Janeiro a little after lunch time and in fog and rain. After getting settled at the hotel, we met with the governor of the new State of Guanabara. This state had been created since the federal capitol had been moved inland to the new city of Brazilia. Later we went up to the United States Embassy and heard the ambassador, Mr. John Cabot, and some of his staff talk of our relations with Brazil. That night we attended a brilliant reception at the beautiful mansion of Foreign Minister and Mrs. Horacio Lafer. It was quite an affair.

Our second day in Brazil, a Tuesday, a press conference was held by several of our group. During this conference I was asked if I thought it was proper for Mr. Kennedy to meet with Mr. Khrushchev at a summit meeting. It is always good for heads of nations to meet together as a principle, I said, but there was much that needed to be discussed at lower levels before these two men met. I also noted the difficulty our government had had in the past with Mr. Khrushchev at such meetings.

We were given a luncheon that day by the American Society in Brazil and by the American Chamber of Commerce of Rio. One of my Rotary friends told me that the Botofoga Rotary Club was meeting in an adjoining room and asked me to come over and say a few words. I went over and told them about my having been in Rio in 1948 as chairman of the International Rotary Convention. That evening we were entertained by Ambassador Cabot at his home in Rio.

Later during the week, I went for a walk on the beach and stepped on a rusty nail. It was a small one and did not go too far into my heel. A native woman saw me pull out the nail and rushed over to where I was. She made all kinds of gesticulations and talk that I did not understand. She finally took the shoe I was wearing and beat the dickens out of my heel. I presume that was her idea of curing it. It sounds ridiculous, but it might have helped. Soon after that, I went to see a Brazilian doctor. He checked the heel, said there was no danger of serious infection, but gave me some pills. The heel soon got well, but it was sore for a while, either from stepping on the nail or from the beating that woman gave it.

We flew from Rio to the new capital, Brasilia, about six hundred miles inland, on Thursday, November 24. It was Thanksgiving Day in the United States and I suggested that we have a Thanksgiving service. Governor McNichols, the chairman of the National Governors' Conference, asked me to prepare a program. Governor Wesley Powell of New Hampshire led in singing "God Bless America." Governor Hugo Aronson of Montana, a Swede who came to the United States when he was eleven and who never ceased telling of his pride in our country, gave a five-minute talk. Prayer was offered by Governor Pat Brown of California. It was quite impressive to hold a Thanksgiving service high in the air while traveling at better than five hundred miles an hour.

The usual reception greeted us at the airport at Brasilia. As we drove through the new city, I was impressed by the daring and the imagination of moving the capital from Rio. It was something like moving the capital of the United States from Washington to, say, the open plains of Kansas or Oklahoma, far from any town. Brasilia had been cut out of the wilderness and when we arrived the capital had been under construction for only three years. There was much talk about how much the new capital would cost. The government had mentioned $100 million, but some people thought it was as much as $1 billion and more.

In my opinion, President Kubitschek showed great courage in moving the capital into the interior. It should help to open up the country and should lead to the exploiting of Brazil's natural resources. Nobody really knows how much wealth they have out in all that vast territory. A sidelight on the move, we understood, was the reduction in the number of federal employees who, like ours, can hardly be removed from the payroll. One of my friends said there were many thousands on the payroll in Rio but that a much smaller number would be needed at Brazilia. The move, he said, would eliminate the surplus because any number of people did not want to go to what they called "this God-forsaken place out in the wilderness."

The hotel was the first building we entered at Brazilia. It was modern in every respect, but its floors—like those in all the other buildings we entered—were covered with red clay, such as we find in sections of North Carolina. The streets there were still being built, and from the red clay it was evident that they had a long way to go to achieve what they wanted in the way of beauty not marred by clay. The hotel was unique. There did not seem to be a window in it and from the outside it looked like one giant rectangular honeycomb.

Later "governors only" were invited to visit the president of the Senate and the speaker of the House of Deputies. From the outside, the Congress buildings looked like two thin slabs running up twenty to thirty stories. On either side and almost flat with the ground were the chambers of the Senate and the House. One was designed to look something like a giant bowl turned upside down and the other was designed to look something like a giant bowl turned right-side up. Both chambers are beautifully decorated. We met in the Senate president's office for a brief ceremony and then briefly visited the two chambers.

After the visit to the House of Congress, we were driven to a beautifully laid-out street where trees from the fifty states of the United States of America had been planted. North Carolina had sent down its pine tree, and, with it, we had sent two plaques just in case one was lost. The Brazilians had proceeded to plant two trees and to erect two plaques for North Carolina. I recognized our pine tree without any trouble, but for the life of me I could not figure out the strange tree that had been put beside our second plaque. This did not bother the Brazilians in the least, however. They had received two plaques from North Carolina and had to use them both.

The presidential palace is really something. It is the first building furnished in Brazilia and it is just as modern as the rest. It is surrounded by a wall, there are reflection pools out front, and the building appears to be made almost entirely of glass. Inside there are mirrors everywhere. Instead of stairs, there is a long walkway, covered in red carpet. The President and his family greeted us in the big reception room and then he proceeded to make a long speech of welcome. After this ceremony was ended, the President led the way to the dining room for refreshments. Not wanting refreshments, I continued to look about the presidential palace, and the more I looked, the more I was impressed.

The State of São Paulo, in southeast Brazil, was our next stop after Brazilia. This was the home of Quadros, who succeeded Kubitschek as president of Brazil. Several times during our stay in São Paulo, Communists demonstrated in front of our hotel or the places in which we were meeting. On the night before we left there, we had arranged to have a series of cars drive us out into the country to a dinner. We were to have a police escort, but the Communists, according to our host, actually persuaded the police to leave.

During the stay in São Paulo, I attended the governor's reception at his official palace and it was a brilliant affair. Later we went to an automobile exhibition, the first public exhibition of its kind held in Brazil. At the invitation of officials of the Champion Paper and Fibre Company, who have a plant at Canton, North Carolina, I toured their facility near São Paulo. Later I talked with the manager of the Pan American Investment Company and other businessmen. That evening I attended another reception, this one given by the American Consul General at São Paulo.

On our last day in Brazil, we took a trip up into the coffee and sugar country.

The tour had been fabulous, but we were all glad to be on our way home again. Mrs. Hodges and I slept through the stop at Trinidad but were awakened as we approached New Orleans early the next morning. There, more than half the governors transferred to other planes, and we came on to New York. In New Orleans and New York, representatives of the news media asked my reaction to the trip. I told them that, of course, we felt it had had a good effect. It had been on a more person-to-person basis than would be possible with the protocol of the federal government or the State Department.

I felt, too, that we had acquired a better understanding of the problems that Argentina and Brazil face. And we got the impression that they were looking for something in the way of a "miracle" from the Kennedy administration. I told the U.S. press on arrival that I had told the people in South America that they could not expect such "miracles" to happen. However, I felt that they would get good attention from the Kennedy administration and that certainly they would not "just drift" as the United States had allowed them to in the several preceding years.

CHAPTER XII

Many Mansions

THE Governor's Mansion in Raleigh serves many functions. First of all, it is the personal home of the governor and his family. The downstairs part of the Mansion is for official entertaining and for the public to see. The upstairs belongs to the family. With seven bedrooms and seven baths, there is plenty of room for guests. There is also a third floor that includes a tremendous attic and what we called a plunder room. In this room I kept trophies and mementoes of various kinds, including sixty or seventy cartoons that were done from time to time as take-offs on me when I was governor.

We did quite a bit of personal entertaining while at the Mansion. Mrs. Hodges used to say that when I was in town, I had someone there as personal guests on the average for at least two meals a day. The family was pretty well scattered here and abroad, although Luther, Jr., was at Chapel Hill for a good part of the time we were in the Mansion. He would come over infrequently and would have his friends for dinner on a Sunday night now and then.

At Christmas times, we tried to have the two girls of our family come to the Mansion with their families. Betsey, who lived out in the state of Washington, came with her husband and three children, and on occasion we had Nancy come from Rangoon, Burma, with her British husband and three children. This was great fun. We always observed the ritual of the Christmas tree and the hanging of stockings. While in the Mansion, we continued a Christmas morning practice started at our home in Leaksville in 1922. The whole family would get together at the head of the stairs, march down to the Christmas tree, and open the presents from the stockings only. After breakfast, we came back to the tree and opened the gifts under it. We had a wonderful time.

During the time we were in the Mansion, we had another ceremony every Christmas Eve night. At this one we would get together all of the servants in the Mansion, including the full-time employees and the prisoners on duty at the Mansion during the day. This ceremony with the present and former prisoners was a tree ceremony and occasionally we would bring in a preacher who would talk for a few minutes and lead us in prayer. At other times we would do it ourselves. There would be singing on the part of the prisoners, and then gifts would be exchanged. Each servant usually received from six to ten gifts. The most precious gift was the one I presented them as governor. This was a commutation of one to five years of their prison sentence, if they were still in prison.

There was one violation I allowed of the so-called personal life of the governor at the Mansion, and that was to read my mail and do dictation in the sitting room upstairs next to my bedroom. I had a desk there and each night Sergeant Harold Minges, the highway patrolman assigned as my driver and aide, or one of the servants would put a large brass-handled box at the desk. It contained all the mail to be signed and all the mail to be read and answered. I would attend to this in the evening, if I did not have company and if I were at home. I dictated replies to letters the next morning when I felt fresh. I was usually at the desk by 7:00 A.M., after getting to bed by 10:00 or 10:30 the night before. The mail was taken back to the office at the Capitol for handling.

During my six years in the Mansion, I allowed myself one great luxury. I had breakfast served in bed the whole time I was there, unless there were guests in the Mansion. Mrs. Hodges did the same thing. This was the one rest period we had.

The Mansion is the official as well as the personal home of the governor, and it was this combination of official and personal that brought the first criticism down on me when I became governor. Many visitors to Raleigh, including bus loads of touring school children, want to "take in" the Mansion along with other "public" buildings. They came at all times of the day, trooping down the wide halls, looking in all the rooms on the first floor. Miss Laura Reilley, the hostess-housekeeper, never knew when to expect anyone, the servants were often disturbed in their cleaning chores, and no one could ever tell when some group would be on the front porch trying to get in.

I simply announced publicly that such touring groups of school children or other groups who just wanted to see the Mansion should come in the mornings only between certain hours, and that if any group wanted to have a tea or otherwise use the Mansion, they would have to make arrangements through Miss Evelyn Clement, the Capitol receptionist who also served as Mrs. Hodges' social secretary.

There was some criticism of this action, but it was not general and not important. I recall one of the cartoons in the *Greensboro Daily News* that showed me more or less circumspectly in the bathtub scrubbing my back with a brush and a school teacher with children peering behind her, looking into the bathroom and saying, "You mean these aren't visiting hours?"

It may be hard for the average citizen to believe, but up until the time we made this little announcement, a representative of any organization could come to Raleigh, go in a public telephone booth, call directly to the Mansion and say, "I want to have a meeting or a tea next Tuesday or next month. I am going to have forty or four hundred people and I would like to have you take care of it." It had become so customary that neither the governor nor his wife wanted to say no.

"You mean these aren't visiting hours?"

Our new announcement did not mean that we would refuse people permission to come and have tea or a visit. But it did make the visits more orderly. We were somewhat more circumspect and had a chance to know when someone was coming. The household and the servants could at least get organized. The groups of people who came to see the Mansion or those who were entertained semi-officially or officially totaled between five and six thousand persons annually. An event of some kind, large or small, occurred on the average of about once every two weeks. And in between, probably every day or so, one or more people came for a luncheon or a dinner. There were also a tremendous number of breakfasts, especially during the time the General Assembly was in session.

The beautiful old Mansion has had many important people come through its doors for a visit. These include the last three Democratic Presidents of the United States—Franklin D. Roosevelt, Harry Truman, and John Kennedy. It was equally a home to society leaders, businessmen, and governmental officials on the state, national, and international level.

One of the most interesting visitors Mrs. Hodges and I had at the Mansion was Lady Astor. She almost broke up a dinner with her salty talk and repertoire directed primarily at Archibald Henderson of Chapel Hill. Both were near octogenarians and both enjoyed taking each other apart and saying things about each other that were pretty risqué. It was all in fun and the twenty guests were highly amused. Lady Astor started before I had even finished saying grace at the beginning of the meal. She interrupted me and stated, "Governor Hodges, you and I were born in the same county [Pittsylvania County, Virginia]. We had a home in Danville. My father, when he would say a blessing, would drop his head and say 'Lord, bless this food to . . . shut the damn door.'"

Lord Caccia and Lady Caccia from Great Britain visited us at the Mansion. Lord Caccia was at the time ambassador from Great Britain to the United States. John Motley Morehead, who has done so much for the University of North Carolina, visited us several times. Various governors honored us with their presence. These included Governors Collins of Florida, Clement of Tennessee, Williams of Michigan, Stanley of Virginia, and Zimmerman and Hollings of South Carolina. General Carlos Romulo, ambassador from the Philippines to the United States, was with us on several occasions, and Paulo Lang of Italy, then president of Rotary International, stopped in. David Rockefeller of Chase Manhattan Bank and Crawford Greenwalt, president of the DuPont Corporation, were overnight visitors at the Mansion. Senator John Kennedy came when he was a presidential candidate.

Sir Leslie Munroe, then president of the General Assembly of the United Nations, stopped by the Mansion for a visit one afternoon. It was hot and Mrs. Hodges asked him if she could fix him something cool to drink. He answered, "Yes, I will take Scotch and soda." Mrs. Hodges very diplomatically explained that she could serve him Coca Cola or orange juice or water. No hard drinks were served at public functions in the public area of the Mansion.

Many business groups visited the Mansion, and I found these visits could be most fruitful. We did not have them for that reason, however. The business groups were there as guests. I suppose we had as many as forty or fifty meals for one or more industrialists. The gift by the Dreyfus Foundation for its wonderful laboratory in the Research Triangle Park started with a discussion over lunch at the Governor's Mansion. There were several members of the Dreyfus Foundation present, along with people from the Research Triangle Institute.

The many North Carolina groups which had receptions and teas at the Mansion included cultural groups, music clubs, the Sir Walter Cabinet, debutantes, the Farm and Home Women, members of the Council of State and the Supreme Court, the entire legislature, and many others.

For all of the guests and events, as well as for everyday use, there were always flowers to fix at the Mansion. The flowers were grown in the prison hot houses and delivered to the Mansion early every morning. If they were just for the family or for small groups of guests, Mrs. Hodges took great pleasure in arranging the flowers and spent a great deal of time doing this, and she did it well. She might not like to have it told, but she broke her arm arranging flowers. She had fixed a vase of flowers and had a sheet spread on the rug. When she stepped back to look at her arrangement, she tripped on the sheet and broke a small bone in her arm.

One of the things that Mrs. Hodges and I take pride in having done at the Mansion was completing the group of portraits of the governors who have served North Carolina since the beginning of the century. After a portrait of Governor Morrison was presented to the Mansion by his family, Mrs. Hodges and I decided to try to get all of the other portraits hung before we left. The portraits of Governors Gardner, Ehringhaus, Hoey, Cherry, Broughton, Scott, and Umstead were all put in the Mansion with the family and friends of these governors paying for their portraits.

We were able to get the General Assembly to authorize the payment of $4,000 for the painting of governors' portraits in the future. I asked that they exempt me, but the legislature disregarded my request and made an appropriation to have my portrait painted. It was painted by Albert Murray of New York. It was placed in the Mansion on the left side of the door as you enter, the theory being that the picture will be moved one place back as portraits of future governors are introduced.

In connection with the presentation of each of the governors' portraits, with the exception of one family that declined, Mrs. Hodges and I always gave a dinner for the widow and family of the governor. Following the dinner, there was a very dignified and impressive ceremony of portrait presentation and acceptance in the hall of the House of Representatives at the Capitol.

The legislative breakfasts were a delightful practice that I continued. Early in every session of the General Assembly, I would invite all 170 members of the two houses, plus the lieutenant governor, chief clerks, and the press to the Mansion for a breakfast. The table, which could be extended for the full length of the large dining room, would hold about twenty-eight people comfortably. We would have from six to eight breakfasts for the legislators over a period of three weeks on Tuesdays, Wednesdays, and Thursdays. At the first of these breakfasts, we always had the lieutenant governor occupying the position on my right and the speaker of the House of Representatives at the position on my left. Members of the House and Senate were invited from an alphabetical list, some from the top and some from the bottom.

No business was discussed at these breakfasts. They were held for us to get better acquainted and were usually a lot of fun. One of these breakfasts during the 1959 General Assembly provided more fun than was usual, and certainly more than had been expected. Before the session, there had been a lot of talk about the race for speaker of the House. It was rumored that I was for Representative Carl Venters of Onslow County and opposed to Representative Addison Hewlett of New Hanover County. The truth of the matter was I never made a move in favor of either one, but the talk could not be stopped.

Representative Hewlett won the speakership, so there was more than just a passing interest in that first legislative breakfast of the 1959 session. He would be seated on my left, and since he was speaker and I had my legislative program ahead of me, it was natural that I take pains to be extremely nice to him. I liked Add very much personally and thought he did a great job in the House. There was certainly nothing I could do at the breakfast but see that he was served like everybody else. However, I wondered if a bigger breakfast might not help my legislative program.

A day or so before this breakfast, I asked Mrs. Hodges what she was going to serve. Her answer was, "Bacon and eggs." I told her I wanted country ham served, but she countered, "Luther, it is too expensive. We have to pay the bills ourselves." I told her that I knew it was expensive, but the tradition was to serve country ham, and I added, "I think we ought to serve good North Carolina country ham." I knew she would serve the ham since I had requested it, but I was certainly not prepared for what happened at the breakfast.

The lieutenant governor was on my right and Speaker Hewlett was on my left when they brought the ham into the dining room. As was the custom at the Mansion, I was served first and the platter was carried to my right around the table. It took a long time to get around the table. The country ham looked good, smelled good, and as Clarence, the waiter, passed the ham to the twenty-seventh person, or the one just before the Speaker, I saw with horror that the plate was empty. I said, "Clarence, bring Mr. Hewlett some ham right quick." And, after a pause, Clarence answered, "Governor, there ain't no more."

In a short while, I found that Mrs. Hodges had told the cook that I had insisted on serving country ham but had added that she wanted only twenty-eight pieces cooked. She did not want any of the expensive ham wasted. She did not count on a certain representative taking two pieces of ham as the platter was passed to him. That is what happened, and Speaker Hewlett did not get any ham. I was embarrassed, but the rest of the guests were amused. The story got around the legislature pretty fast.

At our breakfast the following morning, we had ham again. This time there were six or eight pieces of ham left over; Mrs. Hodges had determined there would be enough this time. At that breakfast freshman Representative Sam Burrow of Randolph County asked me if he could go back into the kitchen. When I asked why, he told me that he wanted to get some ham for Add Hewlett. Everybody laughed, but later Sam did get some pieces of the ham. When the House convened at noon, Sam had a paper platter of some kind, and he put the ham on it and called for a page to come to his desk. With great flourishes, he made a speech and sent the ham toward the Speaker's desk. Yes, the page stumbled and fell and the ham ended up on the floor.

I was surprised that my administration got as much legislation approved by the House that session as it did.

Although I did my dictation and read my mail and other things there, the Mansion and its organizational set-up gave me little reprieve from the rather tight, efficient work that we tried to do at the office in the Capitol. At the office, I used practically all my time talking with people. I normally set aside an hour a day for four staff members—fifteen minutes each—and then I had engagements with people from the various governmental departments or from outside right through the day. I tried to limit each interview to about fifteen minutes, and since I had a good staff, we were able to handle just about all callers on time.

When Harold Makepeace served as my private secretary, he would sometimes spend an hour or more with somebody who ought to have had five minutes or nothing. He marveled at my ability to get an important visitor out of the office at the end of his fifteen minutes. All I did, however, was to stand up and courteously thank the caller for coming by to see me. That is, unless he was in the middle of something very important and had not really given me the subject of what he came in for. I would have much preferred sitting down at great leisure with a few people and talking at length, but I wanted to get lots of things done because the state and its needs challenged me almost every minute of my waking time.

We early established the practice of having a press conference on a regular basis—every Thursday. One week we would hold it in the afternoon for the morning papers and the next week we would hold it in the morning for the afternoon papers. It was also well attended by radio and television newsmen. I recall being asked after my first press conference, which was pretty fast and interesting, "How long have you been holding these conferences?" I replied that that was the first one and someone said,

"Well, you seem to answer the questions pretty directly." I replied that I had been told by someone that if I told the truth and answered the questions, I would not have to remember what I had said and I could answer quickly and directly. That suggestion I followed throughout my administration.

The hundred-and-twenty-five-year-old Capitol in which I had my office has been called a "gem of a Capitol" by no less a person than Gutzon Borglum, the late sculptor of note, who is supposed to have thus described it when he visited Raleigh back in the 1920's. He declared it one of the most beautiful buildings he had ever seen. Mr. Borglum emphasized that it should not be disturbed. If more room were needed—for legislative chambers, for example—he suggested that we should dig under the Capitol and have two floors under the square. Mr. Borglum was looking far into the future and planning ahead, and state officials should have been doing the same.

Capus Waynick told me some years ago that he urged the late Governor J. C. B. Ehringhaus in the early 1930's to buy up two or three blocks on each of the four sides of the Capitol to make it more beautiful and at the same time provide room for future expansion. Of course, as Mr. Waynick told me, Governor Ehringhaus could not do as he suggested at the time. It was in the middle of the depression and he was unable to raise money for teachers' salaries and other necessities and did not dare to ask for money to buy property. It was a pity. During Governor Ehringhaus' administration the state could have purchased all of this property for what the state during my administration had to pay for several lots that it bought.

The lack of planning for the growth of the Capitol, for the state building complex around Capitol Square, or for state government in general was one of the first things that caused me concern when I became governor. I talked about this with the members of the Council of State, but, with the exception of one or two, I found no great interest and enthusiasm on the part of that body. I finally appointed a long-range planning committee from the Board of Public Buildings and Grounds, which at that time was a subdivision of the Council of State. This committee did very little. Its members looked at specific current problems, but they never came in with a long-range plan.

Sometime later the Board of Public Buildings and Grounds was abolished and its functions were absorbed by the new Department of Administration. This department, under Paul Johnston's fine leadership, did some informal planning and purchased some property with some idea of the future in mind. This included the old YMCA building, immediately across the street from the Capitol Square. The idea at the time was to pick up most of the buildings on that block in order to put a Capitol annex or legislative building across from the old Capitol.

It was evident to anyone attending a session of either the Senate or the House of Representatives that something would have to be done soon to provide the General Assembly with the additional room it needed. The Senate and the House chambers are on either side of the second floor of the Capitol, and are much, much too small for the work that goes on in them. The legislators did not have enough room for all of the material they needed and they had to stack their books and papers on their small desks. These stacks always seemed to be falling off the desks onto the floor. The galleries for visitors were far too small, the press facilities were entirely inadequate, and the legislature's staff was scattered in other buildings.

The need for a new legislative building was again emphasized as the 1959 General Assembly approached. Lynn Nisbet, dean of the Raleigh press corps, renewed his plea for more adequate work space for newsmen covering the legislature. Ed Rankin, my secretary, came up with the suggestion that a temporary structure be erected on the East Portico of the Capitol to serve this purpose.

I thought the suggestion had merit, and had it checked out with the Department of Administration engineers and architects, who designed a neat, prefabricated structure that could be placed in the East Portico floor space and be removed promptly after the close of the General Assembly. The Council of State approved the project, with the full understanding that the structure was temporary, and the announcement was made of these plans to help newspapers, radio, and television do a better job of covering the General Assembly.

The Raleigh *News and Observer,* which always values its opinions above the judgment of governors and state officials, immediately attacked the project as a "desecration" of our beloved State Capitol. It hinted darkly that the governor would never remove the structure after the General Assembly went home. Dean Henry L. Kamphoefner of the School of Design at North Carolina State College was quoted as being greatly distressed by such an architectural affront.

Our long-time Secretary of State Thad Eure, who had attended the Council of State meeting that approved the project, was quoted by the *News and Observer* as saying that the structure, if erected on the East Portico, would look like "the nose on a buffalo."

We decided not to take Mr. Eure's comment or the *News and Observer* too seriously and to give a light touch to the matter. So we established the "Order of the Buffalo" and had certificates, complete with a sketch of a buffalo, made up. It read, in part:

To all to whom these presents shall come—greeting:
This is to certify that the Order of the Buffalo has been organized for the solemn and special purpose of supervising closely and carefully the installation of a temporary and detachable nose on our Ancient Buffalo. This is to certify further that we share a common affection for the Buffalo and will unite our efforts to guarantee the complete removal of said nose from our Buffalo immediately after it has served its ex-press purposes.

Press room trophy

At the bottom of the certificate were the names of Thad Eure, "founder and president"; Henry Bridges, "secretary and auditor"; *News and Observer* Editor Jonathan Daniels; and Dean Kamphoefner. My name was signed as "keeper of the nose."

Certificates were presented to Mr. Eure and other signers, as well as to the Raleigh press corps. They made a great hit with the newsmen, who promptly named their new temporary legislative home: THE BUFFALO'S NOSE. The "Nose" was fully utilized by press, radio, and TV representatives during the 1959 General Assembly and then taken down at the close of the legislature to be stored. It was used again during the 1961 General Assembly.

I went before the 1957 and 1959 General Assemblies and declared that the Capitol was indeed an architectural gem which should never be changed. However, and this was emphasized by the crowded condition of the House in its joint session, the Capitol could not take care of the needs of the state. I told them that "we need a modern structure, ample room, including press galleries, and all that the present day demands." Our beautiful old Capitol could not take care of the needs of an up-surging state.

We presented a recommendation of $7.5 million for a Capitol annex or a legislative building. This was a reasonable figure. Governor Buford Ellington of Tennessee showed me around their remodeled Capitol in Nashville for which they had spent $8 million just on repairs, changes, and decorations. Other southern states had new or at least adequate capitol buildings. Yet our $7.5 million request was cut down by the Advisory Budget Commission and the legislature to $4.5 million. And, even then, it was included in the bond issue authorized by the General Assembly. Otherwise, the funds for a legislative building might not have been approved.

The 1959 General Assembly also authorized a Legislative Building Committee. Representative Thomas White of Kinston was selected to chair the committee.* This committee went to work in earnest.

Holloway and Reeves, a Raleigh architectural firm, was engaged by the committee. As consulting architect, it hired Edward Stone, an internationally known architect who designed the United States pavilion at the World's Fair in Brussels and the famous United States Embassy building at New Delhi, India. Then the committee traveled to several states to study the capitol buildings there and to get ideas for our own legislative building. After much discussion, the commission decided on a location north of the Capitol. It was decided that it should be erected across Halifax Street looking south to the Capitol. A mall was to connect the two. This was the first real planning and the most imaginative thing done in state building since the Capitol had been built in the 1830's.

The Legislative Building Committee realized before too long that the building it wanted could not be built for just $4.5 million. In 1960, its members went before the Advisory Budget Commission and were successful in getting the commission to recommend additional funds. These were later approved by the 1961 General Assembly. I was at the Budget Commission meeting and urged that the building committee include a modern voting system that would take care of the voting of the legislators on an automatic basis.

Construction work on the new legislative building began early in 1961, and it will be completed and ready for occupancy by the 1963 General Assembly. It will be quite a change from the historic old Capitol chambers, which will remain as they are for future generations to see. There will be adequate House and Senate chambers, adequate committee rooms, an office for each member

* Members were Representative Byrd I. Satterfield of Person County, Senator Archie Davis of Winston-Salem, Senator Robert F. Morgan of Cleveland County, A. E. Finley of Raleigh, Oliver Rowe of Charlotte, and State Treasurer Edwin Gill of Raleigh.

of the legislature, offices for various key employees of the House and the Senate, adequate galleries and work space for the news media, and quarters for the secretary of state. This new legislative building will be beautiful beyond anything we have seen in the state in many years. It is a radical departure from the conservative building trends of the past.

I traveled chiefly for two purposes while I was governor. One was to make official and, I hope, helpful visits to organizations and groups around the state, and the other was to cover a variety of engagements outside the state. In this latter area were the industry-hunting trips we took to several cities in the United States and to Europe, as well as my trip to Russia with other governors. Governors' conferences, on both the national and regional levels, were always highlights and interesting meetings to attend. The National Governors' Conferences were held at places like Chicago, Atlantic City, Miami, and Williamsburg, Virginia. The Southern Governors' Conferences were held from Asheville to Hot Springs, Arkansas.

After the first couple of years of these governors' conferences, I was usually either on the resolutions committee or the nominating committee and never had much time for the social part of the conferences. Still, it was good to meet and exchange ideas with fellow governors, either on the regional or national level. I learned a lot and found that generally speaking North Carolina's governmental set-up is pretty good. However, we did not show up too well in comparative rank with other states on economic and educational ratings.

Some people thought that I traveled too much. But I had to get out of Raleigh to really learn what was going on and what was in people's minds. My program had to be sold and to do that I had to take it to the people concerned, whether they were in Charlotte or Ahoskie, New York or Munich. My speeches ran from one hundred to one hundred and fifty a year and most were written.

There were no actual duplications. Miles traveled averaged around sixty thousand a year. I traveled every way possible, usually flying in any kind of plane I could find, including helicopters and jets. Once during a hurricane, I even traveled by road scraper.

There were times when I had some difficulty in getting planes. Theoretically, the National Guard planes were at the bid of the governor if he were on official business. Neither of the two guard planes available were very modern or fast. Later the Highway Department bought a plane for highway photography use and I used this several times. Generous owners of private aircraft made their planes available from time to time. Although we had to use these planes on several occasions, it was not good to borrow planes from private people. I always made it clear that we did not want to use a private plane if its owners expected anything from us in return. I had one or two personal friends whose planes I could use without worry.

The people at the air base at Goldsboro once arranged for me to ride in a jet airplane with a good pilot. We broke the sound barrier. It was extremely interesting to fly from Goldsboro out over the Atlantic, then up as far as Manteo and then back to Goldsboro, all in just a little more than thirty minutes. I always wanted to parachute from a plane when I saw the people jumping at Fort Bragg, but my better judgment prevailed. And luckily I never had cause to do so.

Actually, the first ride I took in a jet came back in 1955. I was in Chicago attending my first National Governors' Conference. When I got off the National Guard plane at O'Hare Field in North Chicago, a man came up to me who said he was a Captain Ellis from Johnston County, North Carolina. He told me that if I needed anything while in Chicago to call him. During the first night there, we heard radio reports of a hurricane approaching the North Carolina coast. I told Ed Rankin to get hold of Captain Ellis and to see if he would fly me home. Captain Ellis agreed to fly me in a jet.

It was not too long before I was on my way. We were out a little way from Chicago, when I looked at the instruments there in the rear seat and saw the speed indicator point to only 335 miles per hour. I asked the pilot if we were not going pretty slow, and he explained that we were still climbing and were actually going much faster than the instrument registered. When we got up further, I asked him how fast we were really going, and he answered that he did not know. "You don't know," I exclaimed. He said wait a minute, and called Wright Field in Ohio, I believe. Then he said, "I am so-and-so with such-and-such plane out of Chicago. Would you mind telling me where I am and how fast I am going?"

Right then, I said to myself, "What in the tarnation are you doing up here if you don't know where you are?" He found out that we were less than an hour from Chicago and were then over Greensboro on our way to Charlotte. Because of the radio beams, I was told, we had to make a dog-leg to get from Chicago to Charlotte. I had another plane waiting for me in Charlotte and I flew in it to the Raleigh-Durham Airport. At Raleigh, I counseled with General Edward Griffin, the state civil defense director, and others, and then made my way down to the coast.

There were a few people who criticized me for going into the eye of the hurricanes that hit North Carolina and for always visiting the various parts of the state where the hurricanes did damage. This criticism never bothered me, because I felt in my own heart that I should be where the people of the state were in difficulty. There may have been danger with debris flying about or with flooding, but the people remained and I was interested in their welfare. As long as I live, I will never lose my interest in the Outer Banks and what nature has done to them mainly because of mistakes made by human beings.

My personal interest in the damage caused by hurricanes helped to create an interest on the part of civil defense and other people in Washington—including Republicans. They found out what was going on, and North Carolina was able to get federal money for rehabilitation that we might not otherwise have received had we not given personal attention to hurricane damage.

A few said I was quick to rush to the coast after a hurricane because I was trying to get votes. This was not true, of course, but, recalling an experience Ed Pate told me about, I expect it would have been a good way to get some votes. Ed told me that he was going from his cottage at Atlantic Beach to Salter Path right after the primary in 1956. He stopped to talk with a native, and commented, "I notice you voted for my friend, Luther Hodges, down here about two hundred and some to two." All the native said was, "Yep. He rid out the hurricanes with us."

I took a great interest in the 1960 national campaign, and I felt my party had a good chance for the presidency. I believed our opposition could be Governor Nelson Rockefeller of New York, who early appeared to be a strong candidate because he had a popular following, but I said then that I did not think the Republicans would be wise enough to nominate him. Everyone knew that the old-time Republican pros were for Vice President Richard Nixon and I believed almost any good Democratic candidate could beat Nixon. I said scores of times, both before and during the campaign, that Senator John Kennedy could beat Nixon by five million votes if it were not for the religious issue. I have never changed from that view.

Like most of the North Carolina delegation to the Democratic National Convention in Los Angeles and most of the delegations of the southern states, I was for Senator Lyndon Johnson of Texas for the Democratic nomination. I never criticized anyone who was for Senator John Kennedy. However, I felt and said many times that many other sections of the country, especially the North, were prejudiced toward a southern candidate and that such an idea was not only unfair but bad for the country. Although some

southern leaders had given the nation a wrong image of the South,
I felt this could be changed. If Senator Johnson received the
party's nomination for president, I said he would win the election
and would make a good president. This would help restore the
South to a position of greater influence in national leadership,
which would be good for the country and for the South.

Senator Kennedy knew how I felt and respected my point of
view. I told him early that if he won the nomination, I would
work night and day anywhere in the United States for his election.
Again I felt keenly all of us should combat the prejudice of the
religious issue against Kennedy. I did work hard for his election,
and not only in North Carolina. I delivered speeches and held
press conferences from Pennsylvania to Texas and spent most of
my energy on two issues: Kennedy's attitude toward business and
the religious issue. I was asked by Kennedy and Johnson to head
a national committee of business and professional men. I accepted
and the committee was moderately successful in its undertaking.

The day before the November election we were having a morning meeting of the executive committee of the University of North
Carolina trustees in my office at the Capitol when I received a
telephone call from Robert Kennedy. I excused myself from the
meeting and went to talk with him. "Governor," Robert said in his
usual calm and casual voice, "would you mind monitoring Mr.
Nixon's all-afternoon talkathon today. He is talking from Detroit
for several hours and we would like to have you answer it on a
statewide broadcast." I told him I would enjoy doing it and, as
soon as he hung up, I gave instructions to set up arrangements
for monitoring and to see what arrangements could be made for
a broadcast. Then I went back to the trustees meeting.

In about an hour—around noon—Mrs. Rachael Havnaer buzzed
me again and said "Mr. Kennedy must talk to you again." I took
the call and Robert said, "Governor, Jack said he sure would like
to have you appear with him on his television program tonight at
Manchester, New Hampshire. It's at 6 o'clock." I reminded him

he had just asked me to monitor the Nixon talkathon. "Well," he
replied, "Jack said he would sort of like to have you do this, and
I believe it will be more important for you to do. There will be
two programs, one with you and Jack and one with you and him
and his sisters. I don't know what the programs are going to be
about, but he would like to have you here."

I told him all right, I would be there. He had offered transportation from Washington, but I told him I would get there on
my own. Then began one of the wildest scrambles I have been
through, as we tried to find a plane and a pilot for the trip.
George Watts Hill, Sr., of Durham, who was at the trustees meeting, immediately scouted about to see if he could get a plane,
and I had my office try to find Mr. Omar Dodson, pilot for Mr. Ed
Richards of Raleigh, who had a fast plane. It was his day off and
he could not be found. Finally Watts, after several more phone
calls, said the plane he secured would be standing by as quickly
as I could get to the airport. Dodson had, in the meanwhile,
called his office for some casual reason, had been asked about the
trip, and said he would be glad to fly me up to Manchester.

Patrolman Lloyd Burchette rushed me to the airport and the
Richards plane was waiting. We got preference in leaving the field,
and then we beat it toward Manchester. When we got up around
Atlantic City, instead of following the airlane, the pilot struck out
across the corner of the ocean and came in up toward Manchester
more quickly. We were met at the airport there and were driven
straight to the television station. I got there at one minute of six,
just as the presidential nominee, Mr. Kennedy, walked up the
steps to the front door. My host, a New Hampshire politician
who had driven me from the plane, told me to put my hat and
coat in a room where he would wait to take me back to the plane.
I never saw this friend or the hat again.

No arrangements whatsoever had been made as to what kind
of program would be used. We had only ten minutes of conference with Press Secretary Pierre Salinger and others as to the

program. I saw then, as I have seen since, that Mr. Kennedy pretty much calls the shots. He knew what he wanted in the way of lights and spots and where the emphasis ought to be. When I found he planned to talk on broad subjects, I suggested that I be given the chance to ask some questions about unemployment and the fact that some people were working less than forty hours a week and still had to pay high prices for groceries. He agreed with my suggestion to talk down-to-earth to the people of the country.

We had an effective telecast I think. Governors from several other states called me later and said it had had a good effect in some of the southern states and I had messages from over the country commending us on the realistic and down-to-earth program. The other telecast was with the candidate's three sisters. The sisters would ask Mr. Kennedy questions and he would answer them and I would chime in from time to time.

When these telecasts were completed, Mr. Kennedy still had a closing speech to give in Boston. We were rushed to the airport. He headed for Boston, and I headed for North Carolina. The next day was election day.

Soon after the election, I went, as I have recounted, with about thirty other American governors to Argentina and Brazil. When our plane touched down at Rio on a Sunday morning, there were newspaper men there who quoted to me a statement in the *New York Times* by Bill Lawrence. It stated that President-elect Kennedy had selected me as his Secretary of Commerce. The reporters asked for comments. I told them I knew nothing about it, and I did not. In all my meetings with President Kennedy as a candidate, we had never discussed anything from the standpoint of "Governor Hodges' interest in anything in the future." After telling the reporters all I knew about the matter—which was nothing—I continued on the two weeks' tour with the governors.

Sometime after returning to North Carolina, I was in Chapel

"Goodness! What an odd looking frog!"

Hill presiding over an intergovernmental relations meeting when a telephone call came from President-elect Kennedy in Palm Beach. He wanted to know if I could be down there the next morning. He did not say what for but just asked that I be there at 10:00 A.M. I told him I would.

Although I prefer to fly, I wanted to make sure that I was not delayed somewhere by bad weather so I decided to take the train. I thought it would get me there without fail at 9:00 A.M., in plenty of time for the engagement with the man who was soon to be the President of the United States. However, the Seaboard had a wreck on its main line, probably the first one in many years, and the passenger train I was on was held up for an hour or more. I could get no co-operation from the train crew or the conductor and could not get a message to the President-elect that I was going to be a little late. I did not tell them who I was or what I was going for, but even that may not have made any difference.

I am always on time, but that time I was an hour late for one of the most important events of my life. I finally arrived at the Kennedy home at Palm Beach, got through the secret service men, and found to my surprise that nobody was in the living room. Finally in the dining room I found Steve Smith and his wife, one of Mr. Kennedy's sisters, having coffee. They invited me in to have a cup and I accepted.

About a quarter of an hour later, Jack Kennedy stuck his head in the door from another room and said, "Hey, Governor, I didn't know you were here." I probably showed surprise because I thought they were as concerned about my being late as I was concerned about not being there on time. But I found out the Kennedys are very casual. Nothing seems to disturb them and they readily adapt themselves to any situation. It was a good thing to learn.

Soon after that, President-elect Kennedy and I spent about ten minutes together in conference. He then asked me if I would serve in his Cabinet as Secretary of Commerce. I discussed certain parts of the offered job with him and then accepted. In a few minutes, he made the announcement to the press that I would become Secretary of Commerce in his administration. Later that day I returned home to get ready for my new job and to put the finishing touches on my six-year administration in North Carolina.

CHAPTER XIII

Looking Ahead

SERVING as governor of North Carolina is a job for three men. One man is needed to answer the mail and to carry on the detailed work of the office. A second one is needed to get out, make speeches, and travel around the state. The third man is needed for work with special projects, such as the Research Triangle, and to plan many things necessary to insure a good future for our state. During my six years and two months as governor of North Carolina, I gave as much time to all three of these major jobs as was humanly possible. In looking back over my administration and ahead to the future, there are a number of ideas that I think people in North Carolina today should consider for their state and its government tomorrow.

I have a strong feeling regarding the term a governor ought to be allowed to serve North Carolina. Under our state constitution, a governor can serve a four-year term and cannot succeed himself. He can serve four years, then stay out four years, then try getting elected again. Tradition is against this, however. We had good reason at the time for putting this limitation of one four-year term in our constitution, but times have greatly changed since that was written nearly a hundred years ago, and today a governor should be allowed to succeed himself.

The governor usually comes into office after a hard campaign with its necessary compromises and a resulting need to proceed slowly. He simply does not have time in a single four-year period to get a full-fledged program more than just started. Seldom does he have the opportunity to complete his program or even a major part of it. When he comes into office, he has a legislature on his hands immediately, and he has numerous appointments to make as soon as his first legislature goes home. By that time, a new governor is completely embroiled in the day-to-day activities of the job, which is in itself too big for one man.

For these reasons, I suggest that the citizens of North Carolina allow their governors two successive terms of four years each. They do not have to elect him to the second term if he has not done well the first four years. But a governor ought to be given the privilege of running the second time and completing the program he has started. The people would back a governor if they believed in his program and felt he was doing an honest job. If they did not, then they would vote in a new man. An alternative consideration would be one six-year term, but this is a little out of line with what other states are doing. The two successive terms of four years each would be better.

The veto power should be given to North Carolina's governors. At present, our governor is the only one in the fifty states who does not have the veto power and the privilege and the responsibility of signing a bill into law. Under our present system, of course, we have generally had the kind of governors who by their influence have gotten a fairly good legislative program through the General Assembly. And, since our governors do not have the veto, we theoretically have had more responsible legislators in that they cannot pass the buck or the responsibility to the governor. I believe, however, it is getting more important day by day for the governor of North Carolina to have the authority to veto legislation he thinks bad or unnecessary.

The governor should also be given decent office quarters. I have

visited many governors' offices and they are generally commodi-
ous, dignified, beautiful, and comfortable. The office of the governor of North Carolina is crowded, unattractive, and undignified.
It does not even have a private wash room. If the office of our
governor is to stay in the present beautiful old Capitol, then he
ought to be given more room and great improvements ought to
be made. I am very happy to see that the legislators have at last
been given decent and dignified quarters. The new statehouse
will be a magnificent edifice in keeping with North Carolina and
her needs. Now something must be done for the governor's
quarters.

The North Carolina General Assembly should, in a short time,
consider meeting once a year instead of biennially. When I was
sitting behind the governor's desk, I did not relish the idea of
having to confront a legislature annually, but I realize that by
doing so the legislators could tend to the state's business more
efficiently and, over-all, perhaps spend less time away from their
homes and positions. One year, the legislature should meet to
consider the budget and financial matters, and the next year it
should consider other state business.

In the year of the biennium that the General Assembly would
consider the matter of revenues and appropriations, there would
not be a tendency to deal with other legislative matters that could
lead to trading back and forth between legislators and even sections of the state. This, I believe, would in some cases insure that
a far better revenue and appropriation measure would come out
of the General Assembly. I would limit each of these annual
sessions by law to from sixty to seventy-five days. In that length
of time, the legislators could finish up their business without any
trouble. Other states already do it.

Legislators should also be paid an annual salary that would be
dignified and decent. The way that the pay for legislators is now
handled in North Carolina is undignified and not conducive to

"The governor isn't looking too well."

good relations with the public. They presently get so much a day for seven days a week even though working sessions are only held on the average of about four days a week. But the legislators' total pay is not enough. They have to supplement the low salaries by putting in bills for their own expenses and their travel to and from their homes. Many of them would prefer not having their money coming in this way, but at the present time it is the only way they have of getting reasonable compensation.

The General Assembly ought to have a continuing legislative committee to operate with specified authority during the period when the legislature is not in session. It could be called the Legislative Liaison or Legislative Reference Committee. Such a committee, appointed by the lieutenant governor and the speaker of the House and approved by the two houses, could be made up of some of the best minds in the General Assembly. It would be of great help to the governor and the Advisory Budget Commission during the recess period and could come in with recommendations to the General Assembly when it convenes. I suggest that we do not hurry into this but recommend we send a committee around the country to check the procedures and the effectiveness of such legislative committees used in other states.

The importance of the office of lieutenant governor should be emphasized more. When I ran for lieutenant governor, I found that too few citizens were interested in this number two office in the state. I am not sure to this day how much attention people paid to my suggestion that the governor might die in office sometime and that they ought to be very careful when selecting a lieutenant governor because he might suddenly be governor. The office of lieutenant governor is important in its own right. The lieutenant governor presides over the State Senate when it is in session and appoints the many important committees of the Senate. The lieutenant governor, with the speaker of the House, signs all the bills passed by the General Assembly. In addition, he is on many boards and commissions and represents the state at many functions, and in the absence of the governor he acts as governor.

A governor of North Carolina has tremendous responsibilities. And the job is getting more difficult all the time. He has large budgets to struggle with. He has a growing school system. He has the college situation to handle. He has a tremendous task in highways, mental institutions, prisons, and many other things. And all of these things are becoming more complex and more difficult year after year. For this reason, a governor of North Carolina should have a team of his own that would carry out his program. We ought to have, in other words, a short ballot in North Carolina and let the governor appoint many of the officials now elected. We should not elect so many constitutional officers independent of the governor.

This is in no way a reflection upon the dedicated men who occupied the offices of secretary of state, commissioner of labor, commissioner of insurance, commissioner of agriculture, and superintendent of public instruction during my administration. These members of the present Council of State ought to be appointed by the governor and should serve as his "cabinet." Their appointments ought to be subject to the approval of the State Senate, or, if necessary, the Senate and the House of Representatives. This would hold the governor accountable and, at the same time, keep him from appointing people without anyone else's approving them.

I would recommend that the people continue to elect the attorney general, an auditor or controller, and a treasurer. The state treasurer, the attorney general, and the state auditor are now members of the Council of State and should so continue. These men should not be subject to the will of the governor but should act as checks upon the governor.

One of the many evidences of need to make some of the now elected state officers appointive was referred to in a report to the 1959 General Assembly from the Committee on the State Constitution. This committee, among other things, pointed out a serious discrepancy or conflict in the constitution affecting the authority of the superintendent of public instruction, as an elected officer, and the State Board of Education, appointed by the governor and confirmed by the Senate. It pointed out that even though the State Board of Education has the policy-making power of the constitution, the constitution on the other hand designates the state superintendent as the chief officer.

This, in effect, allows the state superintendent to refuse to obey the board. In other words, regardless of the ideas of the board or the governor, the state superintendent—or the other elected Council of State members—can do or not do just about what he wants. The committee's recommendations regarding the state superintendent were not accepted by the legislature because again there was great hesitation on the part of the people who ought to have been helping do something about this problem. But it did trouble the legislators and it troubled the public to such an extent that I am sure it will not be too long before the conflict will be corrected. A governor should at least have the right to implement his program—be it industry, education, or agriculture—without having these independent officers who can oppose or ignore him. I never had any insuperable difficulty with the present set-up but the system is not a sound one.

North Carolina also needs to continue its present system of reorganizing certain agencies or departments, as has been recommended by the various commissions on reorganization of state government. The commissions on reorganization work, with the Institute of Government in Chapel Hill, make studies of existing departments and agencies to see where consolidation or change could be effected, where overlapping could be reduced, where economy can be achieved, and where greater service can be rendered. The separation of the Prisons Department from the Highway Department is a prime example of the good that can come from the reorganization of state agencies and departments.

North Carolina is basically conservative, particularly in fiscal matters. Still, I believe, a good deal of money could be saved if department and agency heads would take the interest and the time to make a real effort to cut down their part of the cost of government. I do not like cuts, horizontal or across the board cuts, but I am inclined to think that that is about the only way we can ever really save money in either the state or the federal government. It might hurt in a few places, but I dare say that there is hardly any department or agency that is not doing some duplicate and unnecessary work. This is not a reflection on the workers, but it is a reflection on the leadership, the organization, and our system of government.

There is a great need for planning on the part of the state. I said publicly on many occasions that North Carolina was far too conservative in its plans, especially for the comfort and convenience of its officials and its employees. Few people realized the inconveniences the members of past General Assemblies put up with in the crowded Senate and House chambers of the old Capitol. This will be different starting with the 1963 session, which meets in the new and modern State House. Perhaps that will be an inspiration for the legislators and the state to start now planning for future development and growth of state departments and agencies.

Politicians generally have been too scared to ask for public funds for anything unless it was for teachers' salaries or welfare or something of that character. Only when we have had dedicated, hard-working politicians like John Umstead of Chapel Hill, who has done a wonderful job for the state's mentally ill and retarded, have we been able to get other things of importance accomplished. Tom White and others who worked on the commission for the new State House are other examples. It is high time the state authorize a long-range planning commission, including legislators, to plan for the future. Constitutional officers and other elected state officials simply do not have the courage or the time to do much about long-range planning.

In this area, we recommended to the state and the General Assembly that the state plan now for a "cultural center" on the block facing Blount Street across from the Governor's Mansion. And we also felt that the Highway Commission should sell its present building across from the Capitol to the general fund of the state and move out from the middle of Raleigh. These ideas are still being considered and in time may be adopted. The General Assembly, I found, is very conservative but will face up to an issue when it is presented to them honestly and vigorously. A planning commission would be a major asset.

North Carolina has shown the way to many states in its industrialization program. In numbers of firms and employees engaged, as well as in the variety and diversification of the plants that have been brought in, North Carolina has set the pace. The state has carried on some unusual experiments in approaching industrial prospects both here in the United States and abroad. Now and in the future, however, we cannot live on past momentum and we cannot take things for granted. North Carolina ought to continue aiming for national excellence by aggressive, but dignified, action. It should take part in trade fairs, not only its own but those in other parts of the country and other parts of the world. These trade fairs provide double-barreled action. They influence people from other states and they influence people inside our state.

We in North Carolina ought to take a long hard look at where our state is likely to be going in the next decade or so. We should decide now what industries North Carolina will need in the future to be a better balanced state as against the present predominance of textiles and furniture. We ought to decide soon whether or not we need steel mills, metal working, further development of electronics, or whether we should go in for some of the missiles and some of the components of satellite communications systems. The future will present many opportunities and many problems. North Carolina ought to plan ahead now to seek the opportunities it wants and to solve the problems that concern it most.

The battle to raise the average per capita income of North Carolinians to or above the average per capita income of the nation is just beginning. I believe we made a successful start during my administration and that it is continuing. Before the goals can be accomplished many years will pass. More industry will have to develop here or move here. Agriculture must play an even larger part in the future. There, too, we must do forward planning and develop a long-range planning committee of leaders to project a program of agriculture for North Carolina.

North Carolina still has a percentage of people living on its farms that is more than twice as high as the national percentage of people on farms. This fact compounds our farm problems. And coupled with it we have the problem of too great a dependence on one particular crop. That is, of course, bright leaf tobacco, which brings in over half of North Carolina's annual farm income, or something over $500 million yearly. This is of greater value than all the wheat in Kansas or all the hogs in Iowa. North Carolina manufactures more than half of the tobacco products of the United States and raises about two-thirds of the flue-cured tobacco used in cigarettes.

Our farmers produce about a billion pounds of tobacco a year and get about a half billion dollars for it. It is a tremendous sum. But it is deceptive money, and because it is so big it lulls us to sleep. Tobacco is an expensive crop to raise. Because of this few farmers, and fewer still of the small ones, ever get rich from raising tobacco. But the fact that the farmer can get cash for his crop and get it immediately does something to him psychologically. It makes him want to keep raising it, which is fine, but it discourages him from raising other crops. It discourages diversification, and this is holding back our progress in North Carolina.

There are exceptions, of course, and farmers are slowly getting into the production of greater quantities of chickens, hogs, and cattle. And many still produce the older standard crops such as cotton, peanuts, and corn. But tobacco is still king, and our agricultural dependence is on that one crop. If we should ever lose our tobacco price-support program we would be in real trouble in North Carolina. With no acreage controls, the price might fall to the ruinous levels of the depression. Even if the price supports continue, which is probable, decreasing acreage allotments will tend over the long term to produce smaller tobacco farms which in time will give us greater difficulty.

A great deal is right about our agricultural system in North Carolina, but some of it is not for the good of the state, and too many of us politicians have been afraid to speak out about this. I spoke out on our farm problems throughout my administration, and I was not the only one. People at the State College School of Agriculture and some of the people connected with the Extension Service did too. We preached diversification, food processing, and industrialization, and pointed out that if we were not blessed with price controls, the North Carolina farmer would be in a desperate economic situation. I was criticized for my stand, particularly by the people in the eastern section. Landlords, who benefited greatly from the tenant tobacco system, were extremely critical and said I was interested only in industry. They were so wrong.

I organized a very strong Governor's Agriculture Committee and requested that its members go into every phase of our agriculture program and come up with suggestions. This committee was headed by State College Dean of Agriculture D. W. Colvard and included among its membership Commissioner of Agriculture Stag Ballentine and many farm leaders. This committee discussed many times the suggestions of raising more chickens, more cattle, more food and vegetables, more hogs, and of processing more agricultural products. In turn, I took the committee's findings and suggestions to the people in many speeches.

Across North Carolina I found too many farmers like the sweet potato grower I met outside my office in the Capitol one day. He had come to Raleigh to complain about how little the farmer got. I said, "Since you are in the sweet potato business, may I ask if you followed the suggestions of your county farm agent or the Extension Department as to the quality and type of sweet potato you ought to raise? Do you get them to a market where they can be properly graded and checked for quality?" He answered, "I've been growing 'taters a long time. I know what kind I like to grow, and I ain't changing from what I'm doing." He will change, of course, but it may be awfully late.

The agriculture people have done a wonderful job with the crops we raise. Farmers are now producing more on less acreage, and they are beginning to diversify and find profits in other crops, but the process is not fast enough. What happens to our farmers if the farmers of Rhodesia and other places take a greater part of our market for tobacco? It could be bad, unless we have other crops to fall back on or to step up to. In addition, I hope that the people at State College continue their research to find uses for tobacco other than smoking and chewing. It might be found that tobacco can cure certain diseases.

Let me make my position on agriculture abundantly clear. I do not want to see our tobacco economy lost or cut, but I do want to see us improve our methods of producing and curing and distributing. I hope we can keep our price protection, but I do not want to see us get caught short on the national or international markets. I wish our tobacco research people would give greater attention to research on other uses for tobacco. We possibly could achieve a break-through in tobacco as we have, for example, done in coal, which today has many uses.

North Carolina must have farms that operate the year around

and farmers who work the year around, and not farmers who work extraordinarily hard at times but have little or nothing to do the rest of the time. To accomplish this, North Carolina must continue to do the things we have started in our research and in our diversification. In addition, there must be more forward planning, an active committee of agricultural leaders, and more emphasis on the state's agriculture program.

We have a great state with a wonderful climate and a fertile soil for agriculture, and we have abundant resources and sites for industry. We have fine people on the farms and in the factories. With proper guidance and planning ahead, these farmers and industry workers can bring a greater prosperity to North Carolina and a higher standard of living to all its citizens.

Our schools in North Carolina probably give a better average or minimum instruction to our children than do the schools of most other states. But in our state the education is on the minimum side rather than the quality side. The system we have of letting the state pay practically all of the teachers' salaries and substantial parts of operating costs other than school buildings does guarantee a necessary minimum support for education, but it also tends to keep over-all support close to that minimum.

The fact that we have followed the philosophy of protecting the local communities and the counties from paying more of the school expenses, particularly teachers' salaries, has hurt our school system a very great deal. It has given us what I would call a "minimum point of view." We think in terms of the over-all state system rather than in terms of quality education. There is no need in my recounting here the figures that show North Carolina is trailing badly below the average among the fifty states in the number of its students who go through high school and the number of those who finish college. It is pretty sad in comparison with other states.

We must now, before the situation gets worse, encourage every one of the 174 school districts in North Carolina to add substantially to its local support. Even if we do start now, it will take years to get it done. It will take years to get the best teachers that can be found. But it must be done. Professional teachers, starting with the superintendent of public instruction, must determine that we will have quality education, as must the legislators and the taxpayers. The teachers we secure must be equal to or better than those in the rest of the country. We can do this. It will cost us more than we can afford, but we cannot afford not to do it.

It may mean that we will have to take a look at our college graduates, particularly our teachers, to see where the deficiencies are. Maybe we will have to work back to the requirements for the high schools and even the grade schools. And we should, as soon as possible, plan to use all our schools on a twelve-month basis. It makes sense, and it will certainly save us money in the long run. For the many boys and girls who do not want to or cannot finish liberal arts colleges, we should have industrial schools, vocational schools, and specialized schools. It is a big job, but the sooner we get started on it, the better off North Carolina will be.

I would like to see our boards of education sponsor a study that would produce specific recommendations for our entire school system from the university level down to the first grade. I would like to see this study projected over a twenty-five-year period and include estimates of the cost of buildings, the cost of operation, the cost of teachers, the number of pupils, the kind of courses that may be coming or may be needed, and the goals we should seek. Such a commission, composed of our best people with maybe a few consultants from the outside, could take a long hard look at our school system and get information and suggestions, not only from people in the United States, but from other parts of the world.

As we are looking ahead in North Carolina, we must also think in terms of our total population and its needs. More economic opportunities are needed for Negroes. Right now North Carolina is spending millions of dollars on our schools and colleges to train our Negro youth. When they get trained in the various professions, including engineering, for the most part they have to go out of the state and out of the South to find a job in keeping with their training and ability. This procedure ought to be changed. Perhaps the state in its various governmental agencies such as the Highway Department should set the example of furnishing employment to qualified Negroes. This would do much for the spirit of the state and for the economy and is the natural and correct thing to do. We will find that our Negro graduates as well as Negroes not so fortunate as to have college educations will do a better job if challenged and if given more equal opportunity for employment.

North Carolina can be proud of its labor force, of its workers generally. They have a good attitude toward work, believe in giving an honest day's work for a proper day's pay. They are honest, dedicated, and patriotic. They are productive people, far better than workers in many states, and our state and our industries and our citizens ought to appreciate this. We ought to see that we maintain high standards of wages and working conditions for our laborers of every age, sex, and race.

Our welfare agencies should be checked carefully to see and to insure that the deserving people are getting enough funds to take care of their basic needs. North Carolina should also continue the great strides it has been making in its health work. Further study should be made to see that there is proper correlation between the activities of the State Health Department and the work done by the mental hospitals and other groups in the state. The great work to provide cure, where possible, and comfort for the mentally ill and retarded should be continued. More should be done in the area of correction for our young people.

Turning to our cities and counties, I think it would be wise for the League of Municipalities in North Carolina and the state organization of county commissioners either jointly or separately to make a study of their revenue needs and their projected expenditures over the next ten or twenty years. There should in the near future be some agreement with the state on the kinds of taxes that will be reserved to the cities and counties. North Carolina has been more forward looking than many of the other states in that it does not use the property tax for any of its revenues but leaves that to the cities and counties. There are other taxes that the municipalities and the county governments will need if they are going to build for a growing future and this ought to be considered soon.

There needs to be a better public relations campaign put on by the cities and the counties to inform the people of the services they are performing—at lower rates than those in other parts of the country. They should compile typical city and county rates from all over the United States in an attractive and readable pamphlet to be distributed to organizations and individuals across the state. Our citizens would get a better appreciation of what their local governments are doing now. They would also realize that they have a long way to go if our cities and counties are going to increase their services to the point where they will keep up with a state that is moving forward along many lines.

North Carolina has been very fortunate in its highway system and its highway building program. Going back to the early 1920's, North Carolina was in the forefront of those states that looked ahead and saw the need for good roads to take care of a growing state. We were the first state in the nation to take over all of the roads on a state level, and since then we have improved far beyond what would have been done under the old system of one hundred different county road systems. We have made great progress, but now we again need to take a long look at where we are going and what our highway program is going to cost us. We should think in terms of a statewide system of roads, both primary and secondary, built entirely according to need and merit, and without any reference to political influence.

Much needs to be done in the way of planning. Road building is expensive. The process of getting rights of way is almost primitive. We ought to be thinking in terms of purchasing rights of way as far as ten years ahead of the time we might be using them. Even if we fail to use some of the land, it would be worth more than what we paid for it, if the present trend continues. Tens of millions of dollars could be saved by North Carolina if it pursued such a policy. We must also link our roads directly with our safety program and be sure of design and construction. We must do research of all necessary kinds to insure that we build better roads as economically as possible.

North Carolina has boasted that it has no toll roads or toll bridges. That was very good in the days when our roads and bridges cost little and I would like to see us keep the highway and bridge system relatively toll-free. But I would recommend that tolls be put on roads and bridges in those places where greater service is needed and where we have a tremendous amount of out-of-state traffic. We should give this careful attention.

Under our present policy, we delay construction of necessary bridges and operation of adequate ferries because we do not want to place tolls on them. Somewhere in the not too distant future this problem must be faced realistically. We simply do not have enough money in this state to afford the luxury of toll-free roads or the delay that would come if we waited until we had the money to pay for these improvements. Other states, including some of our neighbors, are not trying to do it all on a toll-free basis. People, especially inter-state travelers, are willing to pay a moderate sum in the way of tolls and fees if they can get better and shorter roads, better bridges and quicker ferries.

One of the highway problems we have had in North Carolina resulted from the diversion of millions of dollars of our limited highway revenues for prisons, paroles, and probations. Part of this has been corrected in the last few years; but the separation of the prison system from the highway operation should be completed, fiscally as well as administratively, so that North Carolina can spend for highways all of the money that comes in from highway taxes.

Speaking of prisons, I hope that as we look ahead to the future we can continue our programs of development work for prisoners, particularly in agriculture and in certain classes of industry. We have, in the last few years, developed prison industries from almost nothing to between $7 million and $8 million a year, and it could easily be several times that without hurting anyone. Of course, one of the greatest benefits of a program like this is not the money but the value of furnishing constructive work for the prisoners. Since many of our prisoners are in prison for only a short time, we ought to make a special study to see what kind of work would be most adaptable to these short termers.

Thus far, the state has done little in rehabilitation and in the education of its prisoners. We have lost twenty years at least by not having a truly constructive educational program for our prisoners, and we must make up for lost time. We are beginning to do this. I strongly recommend that North Carolina give ever greater emphasis to prisoner education and rehabilitation.

Turning again to the highway program, there is another idea which has merit. Where building roads requires heavy fills in areas where there is water, the highway people should consider making the fills stronger and impounding the water rather than carrying it away by large culverts. This water could be impounded on the state's right of way or on private land under agreement with its owners. In this way water could be stored for later use for irrigation, for industrial purposes, or for human use. And while we are impounding this water along the highways and harnessing our rivers and streams, we ought to be making lakes and reservoirs. Our waterways and streams should be thought of in the same way we think of highways.

North Carolina, through its Water Resources Board, has made progress in its planning for water conservation and development. Still we have hardly scratched the surface of the program, although the board has a good deal down on paper. This program is going to take vision and imagination—and a lot of money. We need to build multi-purpose dams on several of our wonderful streams coursing through the state. A large-scale, comprehensive program of water conservation and construction of large and small dams must be adopted. As we intensify our agriculture and bring in more and more industry, we will need more and more water. A long-range study on what we will need in the way of water conservation and water development in the next twenty to twenty-five years would be most helpful.

One of the things that concerned me greatly during my service as governor was the destruction of the Outer Banks. Our people have too often been careless with this area. Cattle and horses have been allowed until quite recently to practically denude the entire area of its protective grasses. The state, taking a leaf from the book of the federal government, has made some starts in buying up some of the land along the Atlantic Ocean. The federal government, for instance, has the responsibility in its National Seashore Park of maintaining and developing about seventy-five miles of ocean front from south of Nags Head to the southern end of Ocracoke.

If we cannot get the federal government to take the state's mileage over for the Seashore National Park, then the state should develop it and protect it against the ravishing storms and hurricanes and start rebuilding it by planting grass and establishing dunes. This is a job that must be done. The state must not falter or the beautiful Outer Banks might end up like the first English colony in the "new world"—lost.

We must also think more about the leisure hours of the people of North Carolina. The state has already done much in this field, but there is a need to revitalize our state parks system because it will have to accommodate increasingly large numbers of Tar Heels. We must also encourage cities and counties to do more along this line. We should set aside on a dedicated basis plots of ground in our communities, roadside parks throughout the state, and recreational centers in all the counties. This would not only take care of our own people, especially our young people who need attention, but it will take care of the tourists who are coming in by the hundreds of thousands. The tourist industry is one of North Carolina's largest.

Irvin S. Cobb wrote in the late 1920's that all North Carolina needed was a good press agent. He was everlastingly right. We needed a press agent then and we need one now, although we are a whole lot better off now than we were then. I remember traveling as a young man through the western part of North Carolina where I did some hiking and camping. Not too far off a state highway there was a beautiful waterfall. It was wide and high and in an exquisite setting. A native told me it was called "Onion Skin."

I said then, and I still feel the same way, that if this wonderful waterfall had been in New York, California, or Virginia, it would have been given an attractive name and have been surrounded by a beautiful fence. There would have been a road built to it and a charge made for a visit to the falls. Then the tourists would have come by the thousands to see and admire it. Tourists are always looking for somewhere to go and something to see. North Carolina is just beginning to learn this. The state now operates many natural attractions and many historic sites. The program should be expanded even more.

North Carolina has shown its heels to her sister states in the development and perpetuation of folk dramas. The most famous is, of course, *The Lost Colony* which has been presented every summer for twenty-five years on Roanoke Island in coastal Dare County. It is the dramatic presentation of the attempts to colonize

the area by Sir Walter Raleigh and his followers. Then at Boone
we have *Horn in the West,* the story of Daniel Boone and the
westward movement, and at Cherokee there is the famous *Unto
These Hills,* a story of the Cherokee Indians. All of these attractions are an expression of North Carolina's feeling for history, and
all Tar Heels should take pride in them.

North Carolina has also shown progress, though belatedly, in
historic building restoration. Fine progress is now being made in
the restoration of Old Salem, and the state has a real gem in the
recently restored and very beautiful Tryon Palace in New Bern.
Mrs. Maude Moore Latham, the wife of the late James E. Latham
of Greensboro, was a native of New Bern and dreamed that the
colonial Governor's Palace should be restored. She made her
dream come true through her own generosity and poured millions
of dollars into the work. Her daughter, Mrs. May Gordon Kellenberger, and her husband, John Kellenberger, saw that the restoration was made. It is a wonderful example of what can be done
with generosity and dedication and purpose.

North Carolina has done much in cultivating the arts and it
should do more. Our state is the only one in the nation that has
a state-supported symphony. This symphony, under the patient
and loving care of Dr. and Mrs. Benjamin Swalin, has for many
years challenged the state and entertained countless adults and
children in every area of North Carolina. It has played good music
and it has interested others in good music. It is partially supported
from state funds, which have been very meager. They should be
increased. The North Carolina Symphony is a credit to the state.

We also have a wonderful North Carolina Art Museum in Raleigh, which though young has already acquired many beautiful
works of art, including a number of masterpieces. It was started in
the late 1940's when the General Assembly approved an appropriation of $1 million to match a gift of $1 million in works of art
from the S. H. Kress Foundation. Both the appropriation and the
gift were largely the result of the patient and devoted effort of

Senator Robert Lee Humber of Greenville, with the help of Edwin Gill and others. During my administration, the Art Museum moved into the old highway office building, and since then it has continued to be developed. I had the pleasure of helping the museum get extra appropriations to make the interior of the building beautiful and serviceable. The state has continued to make small appropriations to the Art Museum, and corporations and individuals have made gifts of many beautiful paintings and other works of art.

By the end of my administration, there were representative special collections of the American, Dutch, English, Flemish, French, German, Italian, and Spanish schools. The Art Museum is a wonderful thing for the state and its people, and during my years as governor I took many visitors over from the Capitol to see it. They, too, were very favorably impressed. Even though the Art Museum is beautifully located at the present time and will be there for some years, we should be thinking about another permanent home for it, perhaps on the block facing the Governor's Mansion.

In thinking of the Art Museum, the North Carolina Symphony, and the many other cultural, historical, and recreational features that North Carolina has provided for its people, I recall a thought I read somewhere and have remembered: "If I had but two loaves of bread, I would sell one loaf and buy white hyacinths to feed my soul." The "I" in that thought reminds me much of North Carolina. As poor as it is and plagued with a low per capita income, North Carolina has indeed sold a loaf of bread to buy white hyacinths to feed its soul.

I felt a touch of sadness that January day in 1961 when I took the white carnation off my lapel for the last time. For eight years —twenty-two months as lieutenant governor and six years and two months as governor—I had never been without a carnation on my lapel, unless it was brushed off. Only on one or two occasions, when I was riding in an airplane or helicopter, had I lost the carnation and then people whom I met would ask where the flower was.

After my trip to the Soviet Union in 1959, I received letters from various parts of the world asking where I got the white carnation in Russia. Even the other governors on the tour wanted to know how I kept a carnation in Russia. Well, in the Soviet Union I used an artificial one, as I did on other rare occasions. But, with these few exceptions, there was the fresh white carnation on my lapel daily. It was either grown in the prison hot house in Raleigh and sent to the Mansion or I purchased it wherever I was.

After turning over the keys to the Mansion and the Great Seal of the State of North Carolina to my successor, I took off the white carnation, never to wear one again. As it had become to many Tar Heels the symbol of my administration, so too had the white carnation become a symbol to me of the faith in the future and service to the present that North Carolinians everywhere were willing to give their state.

Index of Names

321